SCHOOL PHOBIA AND ITS TREATMENT

SCHOOL PHOBIA
AND ITS TREATMENT

NIGEL BLAGG

CROOM HELM
London • New York • Sydney

© 1987 Nigel Blagg
Croom Helm Ltd, Provident House, Burrell Row,
Beckenham, Kent BR3 1AT
Croom Helm Australia, 44–50 Waterloo Road,
North Ryde, 2113, New South Wales

Published in the USA by
Croom Helm
in association with Methuen, Inc.
29 West 35th Street
New York, NY 10001

British Library Cataloguing in Publication Data

Blagg, Nigel
    School phobia and its treatment.
    1. School phobia—Treatment
    I. Title
    371.2′95   RJ506.S33

    ISBN 0-7099-3938-8
    ISBN 0-7099-5050-0 Pbk

Library of Congress Cataloging-in-Publication Data

Blagg, Nigel.
    School phobia and its treatment.

    Bibliography: p.
    Includes index.
    1. School phobia—Treatment. I. Title.
RJ506.S33B58   1987   618.92′85′225   87-13444
ISBN 0-7099-3938-8
ISBN 0-7099-5050-0 (pbk.)

Phototypeset by Sunrise Setting, Torquay, Devon
Printed and bound in Great Britain
by Billing & Sons Limited, Worcester.

Contents

Acknowledgements
Foreword *William Yule*
Preface

*Part One: The Nature and Treatment of School
Phobia. A Critical Review of the Literature*   1

1. The Nature of School Phobia   3

2. Psychodynamic Approaches to the Treatment
   of School Phobia   36

3. Behavioural Approaches to the Treatment of
   School Phobia   61

4. A Comparison of Behavioural and Psychodynamic Approaches   93

5. Treatment Approaches — Summary and Conclusions   109

Part Two: The Rapid Treatment Approach to School Phobia   115

6. Diagnostic Considerations   117

7. Treatment and Resistance to Treatment   141

8. Case Studies   162

Appendix: School Phobia Record Form   194
Bibliography   213
Index   223

Acknowledgements

The ideas contained in this book stem from an extensive research study carried out in Somerset between 1974 and 1978 written up as a doctoral thesis in 1979. I am especially grateful to Dr William Yule, Professor of Applied Child Psychology, Institute of Psychiatry, University of London. Dr Yule not only gave invaluable guidance with research but also provided immense support with timely injections of enthusiasm throughout the period of the study.

I should also like to thank Dr Denis Lawrence, former Principal Educational Psychologist, for stimulating my interest in the treatment of school phobia and for his consistent encouragement throughout the period of the study. I am also grateful to Mr Barry Taylor, Chief Education Officer; Mr Dereck Esp, former Deputy Chief Education Officer (Administration); and Mr Roy Jones, former Education Officer (Schools) who gave their official backing to the research.

In addition I am grateful to my educational psychologist, psychiatric and social work colleagues who supplied detailed information about individual cases and allowed free access to their files. In particular I should like to thank: Mr John Cole, Principal Educational Psychologist; Mr David Knapman, Senior Educational Psychologist and Mr Les Jordan and Mr John Woodhouse former Senior Educational Psychologists; Dr A. Bakker, Dr S. Bailey and Dr E. Ostler, Consultant Pychiatrists; Mr D. Mackey, Principal Nursing Officer; Miss J. Foley, Mr A. Powell, Mr R. Stevens, Mr R. Wade, Miss M. Wilson, Social Workers; Mr S. Cosgrove and Mr M. Furlong, Area Social Services Officers.

I am also most appreciative of the time and consideration shown towards the children involved in the study by the many teachers (too numerous to mention) who helped in the treatments. The sensitivity, understanding and flexibility of individual teachers played a crucial role in the effective treatment of many of the school phobics.

Finally, I wish to express my thanks to Mr Richard Gardner for drawing the cartoon in Chapter 6 and to Mrs Linda Morely and Miss Colette Smith for typing the script and remaining cheerful in spite of the many revisions.

Foreword

School phobia or school refusal is a puzzling condition, or rather set of conditions, which is still insufficiently understood. Fifty years after Broadwin's (1932) classic description of it as being 'incomprehensible to the parents and the school', and twenty-five years after Hersov's (1961) classic studies which demonstrated that school refusal differs considerably from truancy, being part of a neurotic or anxiety-based disorder, *The Times Educational Supplement* opens 1987 by publishing a muddled piece on the educational needs of children who find ordinary secondary schooling difficult. In it, Meigham (1987) states: 'I have begun to harbour serious reservations about those educational psychologists who invented and sustain the dubious condition they call 'school phobia' since it has caused so much distress and misery as well as absolving schools from blame.'

The present book should go a long way to reassuring Meigham, and, more importantly, to bringing to the attention of teachers, psychologists, education welfare officers, social workers, child psychiatrists and parents not only up to date thinking on the nature of school phobia but also practical ways of treating the problem. Children who suffer school phobia are not solely suffering from separation anxiety, as early psychodynamic authors believed, they also have real and imaginary fears about aspects of school life. Schools cannot be absolved from some responsibility for causing some of the difficulties; schools can be helped to reintegrate the children quickly.

In this volume, Blagg reviews what is known about school phobia and its treatment, drawing on two complementary studies undertaken as part of his doctoral studies. In the first study, school phobics are compared to truants on a variety of personal, home and school factors and, replicating Hersov's earlier studies, they are again shown to be two distinct groups. School phobics are not simply refusing to attend school. They are not naughty children. They do have real difficulties which require sympathetic understanding for their resolution.

In part, that understanding comes from detailed enquiries into the circumstances surrounding the non-attendance at school. Blagg argues convincingly that attention to detail at an early stage is one of the main ingredients for successful outcome of treatment. From a careful evaluation of the therapy literature, he concludes that a quick return to school is the lynch-pin of most successful interventions. He describes his rapid treatment approach based on behavioural principles and provides sufficient detail to permit other therapists to follow his approach.

Some readers will be concerned that a rapid return to school may be counterproductive. When the details of treatment are written down, they may seem over-prescriptive. Anyone who feels this need only read the fascinating case reports to see how these principles can be implemented both sensitively and imaginatively. The ultimate proof of their value is that not only did the study children return to school very quickly, but a year later they were happily attending over 85% of possible attendances — a major achievement in the treatment of secondary school children presenting with school refusal.

For me, the mid-1970s were very much enlivened by Nigel Blagg's regular visits to London to discuss his study. His capacity for clear thinking and hard work and his ability to understand the children and their predicaments paid handsome dividends. All this was done as part of his duties as an educational psychologist. If ever evidence were needed that good studies can be undertaken in real-life settings, then this book provides it.

William Yule
Professor of Applied Child Psychology
University of London

REFERENCES

Broadwin, I.T. (1932) 'A contribution to the study of truancy.' *Orthopsychiatry*, 2, 253–9.
Hersov, L. (1961) 'Persistent non-attendance at school.' *Journal of Child Psychology and Psychiatry*, 1, 130–6.
Meigham, R. (1987) 'Education otherwise: the family way.' *Times Educational Supplement*, No. 3679, 2 January, p. 16.

Preface

The origins of this book lie in a comparative treatment study carried out in Somerset between 1974 and 1978. Prior to the study there was considerable debate within the county as to how school phobics were best treated. At the time it was commonplace to provide children with home tuition and psychotherapy at the various child guidance clinics. Unfortunately, many of the cases failed to return to school and presented month after month for therapy. Educational psychologists were largely involved in the planning of educational programmes. Treatment was carried out by psychiatrists, psychotherapists and psychiatric social workers.

In 1974 the author started experimenting with a rapid behavioural treatment approach as an alternative to the traditional means of handling the cases. The treatment was community based actively involving the parents and teachers with support from the educational psychologist. The approach proved to be remarkably successful and in view of this, colleagues in the psychiatric, psychological and social work services co-operated in a comparative treatment study over three years. The treatment findings were eventually published in Blagg and Yule (1984).

This book falls into two parts: Part One provides a comprehensive literature review on the nature, aetiology and treatment of school phobia. The syndrome is clearly delineated from truancy before considering various attempts at developing typologies of school phobics. Important elements in the more successful treatment approaches are highlighted and Chapter 5 provides a brief résumé of the main conclusions. Part Two provides a detailed step-wise account of the rapid behavioural treatment approach utilised in the Somerset study. Chapter 8 illustrates the approach with a series of case studies.

Part One

The Nature and Treatment of School Phobia. A Critical Review of the Literature

1

The Nature of School Phobia

INTRODUCTION

Persistent non-attendance at school has been the subject of considerable concern amongst educationalists for well over a century. In recent years many local education authorities have started to carry out annual attendance surveys and there have been a number of large-scale national surveys. Estimates of the extent of the problem have varied. For instance, a one-day Department of Education and Science national survey in Britain carried out in January 1974 revealed that approximately 10 per cent of all pupils twelve years or older are absent from school with 2 per cent absent without legitimate reasons. Amongst children aged fifteen years on 31 August 1974 absenteeism reached 14 per cent and unjustified absenteeism 5 per cent. However the National Association of Chief Education Welfare Officers (NACEWO, 1975), reporting on their own survey of 27,000 pupils from sixteen local education authorities, note that 24 per cent of secondary pupils are absent with an estimated 3.5–7 per cent absent without a good reason.

However, survey data can be misleading for reasons well explained by Williams (1974) and Macmillan (1977). In most cases, percentage attendance figures do not indicate whether a large number of children are absent a small amount of the time, or a few children are absent most of the time. Furthermore most percentage figures for individuals reveal nothing about the pattern of attendances so that two individuals with the same percentage figure could have very different sorts of problems, with the one child having regular weekly absences of one day and the other child showing one large continuous period of absence.

3

Commonly, attendance figures refer to an average for a school and this obscures any variation in attendance that might occur with differences in sex, age and ability. It is well known that attendance rates rise in the final two years of schooling particularly amongst low achieving children (Galloway, 1980, 1985).

The reasons for persistent absence from school have been well explored in Galloway (1985). The majority of absences are due to physical illness or some other legitimate cause. However, some children are unlawfully withheld or else actively or passively encouraged to remain at home. A few are absent because of economic reasons like inadequate clothing. Nevertheless it is two other groups of persistent non-attenders that have attracted particular interest in the literature: school phobics and truants. Furthermore, it is school phobia (commonly referred to as school refusal) that has been the subject of most research.

The special clinical significance of school phobia has been highlighted by Miller, Barrett and Hampe (1974). These authors point out that school phobia is more prevalent than any other childhood phobia. Whilst the problem accounts for less than 1 per cent of the school population, the ratio of papers on the topic to that of other phobias is at least 25:1. Graziano, DeGiovanni and Garcia (1979) suggest that the higher referral rate of school phobia may be due to the high cultural value and legal requirements placed on school attendance. Fears of the dark and birds, etc. are socially and legally more acceptable than avoidance of school. Certainly school phobia generates massive anxiety in both parents and teachers. From a developmental point of view, the condition is interesting in that it can be a precursor to major psychiatric problems in adulthood (Berg, Marks, McGuire and Lipsedge, 1974; Tyrer and Tyrer, 1974).

In spite of the plethora of research articles on both school phobia and truancy, our knowledge and understanding of these syndromes has been hampered by: (a) inconsistent and vague use of terminology; (b) a failure on the part of some researchers to define their groups adequately; (c) a tendency to make statements about the conditions based on small-scale studies that suffer from sample bias; and (d) a general lack of controlled statistical studies.

The majority of school phobics have been selected from middle-class families and truants are generally reported as coming from the lower socio-economic groups. Thus it might be argued that school phobia and truancy are clinical artifacts being merely correlates of the social class differences which tend to exist between treatment samples. Indeed some educational psychologists and sociologists have doubted the relevance of distinguishing between different types of non-attenders (Reynolds and Murgatroyd, 1977; Kavanagh and Carroll, 1977).

This chapter will examine the available research in the area with a view to clarifying important issues. The clinical presentation of school phobia will be described and the condition delineated from truancy. Attempts to classify school phobia will be reviewed and the implications for treatment considered. Finally, the aetiology of the syndrome will be discussed.

HISTORICAL BACKGROUND

Early investigations of persistent non-attendance talked only in terms of truancy. Somewhat curiously, Kline (1897) likened truancy to a migratory instinct similar to that found in birds and animals. This simple view failed to explain the condition. Early pioneer studies by Healy (1915) and Burt (1925) produced evidence that firmly linked truancy with delinquency. Poor parental control, mental dullness, temperamental instabilities and broken homes were cited as important factors contributing to truancy.

Broadwin (1932) was the first to describe a form of truancy that was later most commonly referred to as school phobia or school refusal.

> The child is absent from school for periods varying from several months to a year. The absence is consistent. At all times the parents know where the child is. It is near the mother or near the home. The reason for the truancy is incomprehensible to the parents and the school. The child may say that it is afraid to go school, afraid of the teacher or say that it does not know why it will not go to school.

This classic description has become a standard quote in the many subsequent papers on the condition (Frick, 1964; Hersov, 1977). Partridge (1939) in a review of truancy noted a group of children that he labelled 'psychoneurotic'. They appeared to differ from other truants in that they were obedient, reasonably well-adjusted and liked school. He regarded them as victims of 'an emotional bond between parent and child, the basis of which lies in undue attachment and overprotection'. Johnson, Falstein, Szurek and Svendsen (1941) further delineated this special form of truancy and coined the term 'school phobia' emphasising the role the school played in the condition.

> When the teacher as a more consistent disciplinarian frustrates the child, she roused his rage. Being less dependent on the teacher, who is a diluted form of the mother, the child's rage, inhibited toward the mother, can now find expression through displacement and the teacher in her milieu becomes the phobic object. To avoid the teacher and school is now the defence against being placed in the situation in which the overwhelming anxiety is roused.

Johnson *et al.* (1941) felt that the basis of the problem was separation anxiety with the mother exploiting the situation.

Following Johnson's example a number of other American workers adopted the term 'school phobia' (Goldberg, 1953; Suttenfield, 1954; Talbot, 1957; Coolidge, Hahn and Peck, 1957). However, these authors did not regard the condition as a specific entity but rather a loose description of any school attendance problem based on emotional disturbance with phobic, hysterical and obsessional tendencies often overlapping. Eisenberg (1958) and Rodriguez, Rodriguez and Eisenberg (1959) regard school phobia as a variant of separation anxiety but recognise that the symptoms may also be indicative of schizophrenia or other disorders.

In Britain the term school phobia has been favoured by Davidson (1960–61), Chazan (1962), Berg, Nichols and Pritchard (1969) and Blagg (1977); but regarded as too specific by Hersov (1960–61a), Kahn and Nursten (1962), and Smith (1970), who have preferred to use 'school refusal'. Eysenck and Rachman (1965) feel the term school phobia should be retained where the child is truly phobic about something in school, but distinguished from 'separation anxiety in a school situation'. Somewhat confusedly Bakwin (1965) has used the term school phobia to refer to cases of general non-attendance at school including those refusing without anxiety whilst Cooper (1966a) uses school refusal as an umbrella term to include school phobics and typical truants.

THE CLINICAL PRESENTATION OF SCHOOL PHOBIA

The clinical presentation of school phobia has been particularly well described by Hersov (1977);

> The problem often starts with vague complains of school or reluctance to attend progressing to total refusal to go to school or to remain in school in the face of persuasion, entreaty, recrimination and punishment by parents and pressures from teachers, family doctors and education welfare officers. The behaviour may be accompanied by overt signs of anxiety or even panic when the time comes to go to school and most children cannot even leave home to set out for school. Many who do, return home half way there and some children, once at school rush home in a state of anxiety. Many children insist they want to go to school and are prepared to do so but cannot manage it when the time comes.

Anxiety symptoms often manifest themselves in a variety of somatic forms including headache, stomach pains, nausea, dizziness, fevers and so on. Sometimes the child protests with tears or temper tantrums leading to destructive or aggressive behaviour. Some children become lethargic and depressed and a few threaten suicide. Usually, once the pressure to attend school has been removed, the symptoms accompanying the school avoidance dissipate.

Although these descriptions paint a fairly vivid picture of the nature of school phobia, the majority of authors fail to state explicit behavioural criteria for diagnosing the condition. Berg *et al*. (1969) are unusual in this respect in providing a very clear definition. Among the cases that he and his co-workers selected for treatment, their studies focused on those who show good evidence of:

1. *Severe difficulties in attending school*, often amounting to prolonged absence.
2. *Severe emotional upset* — shown by such symptoms as excessive fearfulness, undue tempers, misery or complaints of feeling ill without obvious organic cause on being faced with the prospect of going to school.
3. *Staying at home with the knowledge of the parents* when

7

they should be at school at some stage of the course of the disorder.

4. *Absence of significant anti-social disorders* such as stealing, lying, wandering, destructiveness and sexual misbehaviour.

Children suffering from psychosis, gross physical illness, bronchial asthma, truancy and neurotic disturbances other than school phobia, are excluded from their investigations. A number of other workers have adopted Berg *et al.*'s (1969) formulation, including Baker and Wills (1979) and Blagg and Yule (1984).

DISTINGUISHING SCHOOL PHOBICS FROM TRUANTS — THE RESEARCH STUDIES

The case for building typologies of persistent absentees rests largely on information coming from descriptive studies of school phobics, truants and persistent absentees, together with comparative studies of truants, phobics and control groups. Whilst there is quite a lot of agreement between these studies, the data need to be interpreted cautiously because of the methodological weaknesses inherent in many of the investigations.

A large number of the workers dealing with school phobics are based in specialist clinics (Goldberg, 1953; Waldfogel, Coolidge and Hahn, 1957; Davidson, 1960–61 and Chazan, 1962) or hospitals (Hersov, 1960–61a, b; Berg *et al.* 1969; Nichols and Berg, 1970; Smith, 1970). Inevitably, child-guidance clinics and hospitals receive rather skewed referral samples. There is the additional problem that many authors do not state whether they are reporting on a treatment series or selected cases. Finally, the majority of authors do not state explicit behavioural criteria for diagnosing school phobia in the first place. One of the problems in this area is highlighted by a remark in Smith (1970). He says that some of his 63 hospital cases were only minimally anxious in their refusal to attend school. This raises the question of just how anxious the child should be before being included in the school phobic group and the associated problem of how one should assess levels of anxiety. It is well known that fear-ratings based on physiological measures, subjective self reports and observed behaviour do not necessarily correlate (Lang, 1970). Researchers are obliged to opt for one or more of these measures.

However investigators frequently fail to state which of the measures they are using.

Descriptive studies of truants suffer from similar limitations. The majority of these enquiries have been based on samples involving hospital referrals or children who have appeared before the court for non-school attendance (Tyerman, 1958). Two studies are worthy of particular mention. Tennent (1971) compared 65 truants on remand for non-attendance at school with a stratified random sample of 166 property offenders also on remand. A major study by Tyerman (1958) looked at 137 truants who had been prosecuted for regular non-attendance between 1941 and 1952. Children who had been withheld from school were excluded from this study. Tentative conclusions about this group were tested by a more detailed investigation of a further 40 truants who were compared with 40 non-truant child-guidance cases. At the very beginning of his article Tyerman (1958) states that 'Truants are children who absent themselves from school without lawful cause and without permission of the parents.' However, later in the study he points out that 5 of his 40 representative truants were absent despite parents' knowledge; two of these being school phobics as defined by Broadwin (1932) and subsequent workers.

A number of review articles have highlighted differences between school phobia and truancy by comparing the findings of independent studies on the different syndromes. For instance, Frick (1964) compares a study of 32 school phobics by Thompson (1948) with a similarly designed study by Mohr (1948) on 40 truants. However, to date there have been few truly comparative studies. Warren's (1948) study is probably the earliest. He compared 8 special cases of truancy with 12 typical truants. All cases considered were hospital referrals and no specific criteria were stated for allocating the children to the different groups. Cooper (1966b) investigating the part played by home and school in truancy and school phobia compared 40 cases of non-attendance from education department welfare files. Cooper makes the assertion that previous research has indicated that children persistently refusing school fall mainly into two groups:

(a) those where refusal to attend school was thought to be a manifestation of a wider psychoneurotic syndrome associated with the parent/child relationship, having been referred to the school psychological service as school phobics;

9

(b) those, where refusal took the form of persistent absence without lawful reason who were not attending the school psychological service, but were the concern of the school welfare department as truants.

However, there is some doubt that Cooper's assertion is correct (Galloway, 1976b). Furthermore, it is by no means certain that children referred to by education welfare officers as truants would be regarded as such if they were to undergo a full psychological assessment. Cooper does not state specific behavioural criteria for diagnosing school phobics and truants and one wonders whether his comparative study has been blurred by an overlap in the two groups being studied.

In a classic study by Hersov (1960–61a, b) three groups of children were compared: (i) 50 school phobics, (ii) 50 truants and (iii) 50 normal controls. All of the phobics and truants had been absent from school for at least two months in spite of pressure from school and parents. The phobics showed a preference to remain at home whereas the truants wandered alone or in the company of other truants when off school. The whereabouts of the truants was unknown to the parents. The control group consisted of a random selection of 10 per cent of a sample of 1,000 first attenders of school age during 1955–56. Cases of 'epilepsy, brain damage, mental defect, psychosis, truancy or school refusal' were excluded.

A similar study was conducted by Blagg (1979) reported in Blagg and Yule (1987). Seventy school phobics were compared with 57 truants and 18 other poor attenders. The school phobics were selected on Berg, Nichols and Pritchard's (1969) criteria. The truants were defined as: 1. absent from school without good reason on at least five occasions in one term; 2. the child shows no evidence of a marked emotional upset accompanying the non-attendance at school; 3. the child is absent without the parents' permission or approval. The majority of the time off school being spent away from home. Sometimes the parents were aware of the absence from school but unable to exert any influence over the child. Finally the other poor attenders were described as: 1. absent from school without good reason on at least five occasions in one term; 2. showing no evidence of a marked emotional upset accompanying the non-attendance at school; 3. remaining at home with knowledge and permission of the parents. The reliability of these behavioural criteria was tested very early on in the study by an independent judge. On a sample of 10 cases, there was 100 per cent agreement between the classifications of the experimental and the independent judge.

Very few studies have examined unselected samples of persistent absentees. Galloway (1976a) has looked at the schools and social backgrounds of all children who were absent 50 per cent or more of the time over a seven week period in the autumn term, 1973. The Sheffield study covered 30 comprehensive schools and their feeder primary schools. Cases where absence was due solely to physical illness were excluded from the investigation. Galloway categorised the cases according to their reasons for the unjustified absences as assessed by the education welfare officers. The seven categories used were:

1. absent with parents' knowledge, consent and approval
2. socio-medical reasons (e.g. no shoes)
3. school phobia
4. parents unable or unwilling to insist on return
5. truancy
6. psychosomatic illness
7. mixed reasons but including some illness.

As Galloway (1980) points out the categories 'were intended to be meaningful to the officers concerned rather than to follow traditional diagnostic categories'. Unfortunately, however, as the categories overlap and are open to subjective interpretation it is difficult to place much reliance on them for research purposes. It was not possible to produce evidence of the reliability or validity of the categorisation of each pupil as each family was usually known to only one officer. Categories 1 and 4 do not appear to be reasons for absence at all, although they may well be factors associated with reasons for absence. Furthermore, psychosomatic illness (6) may be evidence of a masked school phobia (3). Finally it was difficult to rule out physical illness as a partial explanation for absence over a seven week period. Not surprisingly 48.3 per cent of primary and 26.7 per cent of secondary children were not specifically classified in the 1974 survey, i.e. they were placed in category 7.

Kavanagh and Carroll (1977) have compared good, moderate and poor attenders at three comprehensive schools. Poor attenders were made up of those children who attended less than

85 per cent of the time during the first half of their fourth year. No attempt was made in this study to classify the persistent non-attenders into various groups. Reynolds and Murgatroyd (1977) report on a sociological study into the relationships between factors within schools and rates of absenteeism in a Welsh valley community. Along with Kavanagh and Carroll (1977), Reynolds and Murgatroyd (1977) do not believe in the development of typologies of persistent absentees. They argue that it is more useful to look for causes within the school. These workers may be quite correct in emphasising the importance of researching into the relationship between school factors and non-school attendance. However, they seem guilty of 'throwing the psychological baby out with the bathwater'. The two approaches of: focusing on problems faced by the individual and investigating school factors are not mutually exclusive. An interactionist position would accept that children with certain vulnerabilities are more likely to breakdown in school attendance in some sorts of school than others. To ignore individual differences in children is as short sighted as to ignore differences between schools.

DISTINGUISHING SCHOOL PHOBICS FROM TRUANTS — THE FINDINGS

Prevalence

There is very little reliable evidence about the prevalence of truancy although, as Tyerman (1972) states, truancy is certainly more common than school phobia. Tennent (1971) analysing Bransby's (1951) studies, concludes that truancy accounts for between 0.74 per cent and 3.3 per cent of school non-attendance. The NACEWO (1975) study estimates that school phobia and truancy combined accounts for less than 1 in 20 absences. Furthermore, the figures quoted for this study suggest that there are three times as many truants as phobics. All of these figures can only be regarded as speculative, bearing in mind the terminological confusion surrounding truancy and the problems associated with large-scale surveys.

Estimates of the prevalence of school phobia have varied according to the sample studied. Kennedy (1965) reports 17 cases per 1,000 school-age children per year in the United States. Chazan (1962) estimates that school phobia accounts for 1 per cent of a complete sample of attenders over ten years in the United Kingdom. A study of the total population of ten and eleven-year-olds on the Isle of Wight revealed less than 3 per cent of all children with psychiatric disorders were diagnosed as school phobic (Rutter, Tizard and Whitmore, 1970). However, there is some evidence that many cases of school phobia go undetected. Waldfogel, Coolidge and Hahn (1957) reported an upsurge in referrals following the establishment of a special clinic for these cases suggesting that increased awareness and understanding of the condition led to higher referral rates.

Age of onset

Hersov (1960–61a,b) noted that the mean age of his truant group was significantly higher than the phobic and control groups with 62 per cent being 13 years or older. The age range of the truant group was 8–15 years. Blagg (1979) and Blagg and Yule (1986) report similar findings. The mean age of the truant group at the time of treatment was slightly higher than the phobic group with the age range of the phobics being 9–16 years, in contrast to the truants who were in the 11–16 year age range. None of the truants in Blagg's (1979) sample showed problems below the age of 11 years and the mean age of onset was 13.27 years.

The majority of American writers have suggested that the age of onset for school phobia occurs mainly between 5 and 10 years of age (Thompson, 1948; Goldberg, 1953; Rodriguez, Rodriguez and Eisenberg, 1959). Hersov (1960–61a,b), Davidson (1961) and Smith (1970) report that in Britain, onset occurs mostly at 11 years or thereafter with smaller peaks between 5–7 years and 11–14 years. Blagg (1979) and Blagg and Yule (1986) note that school phobia occurs throughout the entire age range but agree that major peaks occur at 5–6 years, 11–12 years and 13–14 years. The mean age of onset for the phobic group in Blagg's (1979) study was 10.29 years.

Sex distribution

The DES (1974) survey failed to reveal any significant differences between the numbers of boys and girls absent from school without good reason. Fogelman and Richardson (1974) found

13

that at the primary level, teachers suspected a greater number of boys truanted than girls. Hersov's (1960–61a,b) comparative study noted no significant difference in the sex distribution between his truants, phobics and controls. There were more boys than girls in each of his phobic groups. These findings were also repeated in Blagg's (1979) study.

Leventhal and Sills (1964) and Frick (1964) have reviewed the literature and made tallies of the reported numbers of cases of school phobia amongst boys and girls. They conclude that the syndrome is fairly evenly distributed between the sexes. This was confirmed by Blagg (1979) who noted 37 boys and 33 girls in his school phobic sample.

Birth order

Chazan (1962) reports that 21 out of 33 cases were extreme in birth order with a further six cases of only children. Warnecke (1964) also reports that oldest, youngest and only children account for the majority of school phobics; 90 per cent of his sample of 47 school phobics fell into these categories. These findings are not surprising given that average family sizes in the United Kingdom are quite small.

However, Hersov (1960–61a,b), Blagg (1979) and Blagg and Yule (1986) note significantly more only and youngest children amongst phobic as against truant groups. Blagg (1979) noted that there were more children in his phobic group occupying the youngest position than any other family position lending support to Talbot's (1958) and Smith's (1970) views.

Pattern of associated symptoms

A number of studies have stressed the similarity of the characteristics of truants and delinquents (Young, 1947; Murphy, 1958; Tennent, 1970). Hersov (1960–61a,b) found that truants were significantly more likely than phobics and controls to show evidence of: enuresis, juvenile court appearance, persistent lying, wandering from home, stealing, destructiveness and disapproved-of sexual activity. These findings agreed with Warren's (1948) study and were broadly confirmed by Blagg's (1979) study although no difference was noted between phobic and truant

14

groups with respect to incidence of enuresis. Davidson (1961) emphasised depression as being a marked feature in 23 out of her 30 phobic cases. However this was not confirmed in Blagg's (1979) study in which only 17 cases out of 70 showed evidence of depression. Nevertheless, there was a difference between the phobic and truant groups on this factor in Blagg's (1979) study with none of the truant sample showing evidence of depression. Chazan (1962) and Goldberg (1953) note that a high proportion of school phobics show eating and sleeping problems. Hersov (1960–61a,b) found a higher incidence of eating disturbance and somatic anxiety symptoms in the phobics as compared with the truants. These findings were further substantiated by Blagg (1979). Blagg and Yule (1986) note that on Rutter and Yule (1968) Behaviour Rating Scales completed by both parents and teachers, the majority of school phobics exhibit a neurotic disorder (as described by Pacella, 1948 and Cameron, 1955) whereas most truants evidence a conduct disorder (as referred to by Van Ophuijsen, 1946; Cameron, 1955).

Family size and social class

Hersov (1960–61a,b) and Cooper (1966a,b), report that truants more often come from larger families of lower socio-economic status than phobics. Blagg (1979) and Blagg and Yule (1986) confirm these findings with respect to family size but found no significant difference between their phobic and truant groups in relation to social class. It seems likely that the social class differences in Hersov (1960–61a,b) and Cooper (1966a,b) were a function of sample bias with middle-class cases being taken on for treatment. In contrast, Blagg and Yule's (1986) study involved all cases of school phobia occurring in a given geographical area over a specified period of time.

Nevertheless, Blagg (1979) and Blagg and Yule (1986) do comment on highly significant differences between phobics and truants in connection with levels of unemployment amongst the fathers and mothers. Unemployment was rare in the phobic group with only 1.8 per cent unemployed in comparison to 26.7 per cent unemployed amongst the truant group. A similar trend was also noticed in the number of working mothers. More of the phobics (67.2 per cent) as against 47.3 per cent of the truants, had mothers with full or part-time jobs.

Factors relating to the home and family

Mohr (1948), Warren (1948), Hersov (1960–61a,b), Blagg (1979) and Blagg and Yule (1986) note that truants have experienced far more upheaval and disturbance at home than phobics. Blagg (1979) noted that 74 per cent of the truants in his study came from disturbed or broken homes. Hodges (1968) notes that in a sample of 110 truants nearly half had fathers who were either dead, separated or away from home a good deal. Blagg (1979) and Blagg and Yule (1986) note that amongst the truant group, out of 26 homes that were broken through death or a marital break-up there were 11 subsequent re-marriages or common law relationships. Amongst the larger phobic group there were no re-marriages out of a possible 15 and only one case where there was a common law relationship.

These findings confirm earlier comments by Thompson (1948) and Waldfogel *et al.* (1957) who point out that the homes of school phobic children are rarely broken. Hersov (1960–61a,b), Chazan (1962), Cooper (1966a,b), Blagg (1979) and Blagg and Yule (1986) indicate that school phobics tend to come from small, united, cohesive families. Only Goldberg's (1953) clinic-based study of 17 Jewish children runs counter to this finding.

Material standards of homes amongst truants are often reported to be poor (Tyerman, 1968). Home discipline is said to be inconsistent (Hersov, 1960–61a,b) and excessive, with particular use of corporal punishment (Tyerman, 1968). Parents of truants are also supposed to be lacking in concern about school attendance (Cooper, 1966a,b; Tyerman, 1968).

There is good evidence to suggest that phobics and truants differ in relation to their pattern of home-related anxieties. A number of studies emphasise the frequent occurrence of separation anxiety in school phobics (Estes, Haylett and Johnson, 1956; Waldfogel, *et al.*, 1957; Johnson, 1957; Davidson, 1960–61; Hersov, 1960–61a,b; Blagg, 1979). Smith (1970) and Yule, Hersov and Treseder (1980) note that separation anxiety tends to occur in cases where difficulties have arisen at a very early age. Davidson (1960–61) emphasised that a death in the family often precipitated school phobia although this factor was often only apparent after many interviews. Blagg (1979) and Blagg and Yule (1986) confirmed and extended these findings. The phobics were significantly more concerned than the truants about: 1. separation anxiety in relation to both the mother and the father; 2. general anxiety about leaving home; 3. the death of a relative; and 4. their own or their parents' health. In fact, using a discriminant functions analysis, it was possible to classify truants and phobics on the basis of their pattern of home-related anxieties with a 75.4 per cent correspondence to the groupings based on the original behaviour ratings that used different criteria.

Maternal characteristics

Hersov (1960–61a,b) has noted more maternal rejection and more maternal absence both before and after five years in the truant group as compared with the phobics. In contrast, the mothers of school phobics are most commonly described as over-protective (Johnson, Falstein, Szurek and Svendsen, 1941; Morgan, 1959; Hersov, 1960–61a,b; Chazan, 1962; Blagg, 1979). Some writers emphasise that the mother-child relationship is intense and ambivalent (Goldberg, 1953; Model and Shepherd, 1958; Davidson 1960–61; Kahn, Nursten and Carroll, 1981). Thompson (1948) and Suttenfield (1954) feel that the mother's over-protectiveness stems from underlying feelings of rejection towards the child, whilst Waldfogel et al. (1957) stress that the mother's feelings of inadequacy and incompetence are the driving forces behind the over-protection. Goldberg (1953) points out that many of these mothers have unresolved dependency relationships with their own parents.

Paternal characteristics

Chazan (1962) describes the majority of fathers in his sample as 'patient and sensible'. Blagg (1979) found no difference between phobics and truants with respect to paternal characteristics or attitudes towards schooling. Possibly these findings reflect a wider treatment sample than applies to the more specialist clinics. On the other hand it may also reflect less therapist involvement with the fathers so that paternal characteristics and attitudes were more difficult to judge. Other writers have described fathers of school phobics as 'passive' (Goldberg, 1953); 'dominated by their wives' (Thompson, 1948); and 'ineffectual' (Warnecke, 1964).

Personality characteristics

Tyerman (1968) comments that truants are unhappy, unsociable, lonely children. Blagg (1979) noted that although truants were refusing school without associated, obvious anxiety, many of them seemed rather worried children with elevated neuroticism scores on the Eysenck Personality Questionnaire (EPQ) (Eysenck and Eysenck, 1964). Blagg (1979) and Blagg and Yule (1986) found that phobics produced depressed psychoticism and introversion scores on the EPQ in comparison to truants. This suggests that in general phobics are rather more sensitive and introverted than truants. In addition, the phobics produced significantly higher lie-scale scores on the EPQ suggesting that they were more socially conforming and perhaps more socially naïve than truants.

Berg and McGuire (1971) provide objective evidence to suggest that school phobics are rather more dependent and socially immature than most children. These authors found high immaturity and low sociability scores amongst school phobics on the Highland Dependency Inventory. Clinical studies by Leventhal and Sills (1964) lead them to propose that school phobics commonly over-value themselves and their achievements. Whilst this accords with the clinical findings of the author in certain cases, it is nevertheless difficult to objectify and measure. Nichols and Berg (1970) explored this area using self-evaluation ratings. They found that school phobics showed lower levels of self-evaluation than similar non-phobic children. The finding runs counter to Leventhal and Sill's (1964) hypothesis although it could be argued that a child who frequently over-values himself and his achievements does so as a means of over-compensating for low self evaluation.

Intelligence and attainments

Truants are generally reported to be less intelligent than non-truants as well as academically retarded (Burt, 1925; Murphy, 1938; Tyerman, 1958; Hersov 1960–61a,b, Cooper 1966a,b). School phobia seems to occur across the ability range (Warnecke, 1964; Hersov, 1960–61a,b; Blagg, 1979). However, most investigations report that the large majority of school phobics are of average or above average intelligence and show a high standard of school work (Warren, 1948; Goldberg, 1953; Rodriguez, Rodriguez and Eisenberg, 1959; Hersov 1960–61a,b). However, these findings may be a function of selection bias. Chazan (1962) noted a significant number of school phobics with learning difficulties. Hampe, Noble, Miller and Barrett's study (1973) suggests that a large unbiased sample of school phobics shows a normal distribution of intelligence. Blagg and Yule's (1986) study confirms this suggestion. Amongst the 70 school phobics in this latter study, the WISC-R Verbal Scale IQ ranged from 60–137 with the mean WISC-R Verbal Scale IQ 96.8. Furthermore, Blagg and Yule's (1986) study found no difference between phobics and truants with respect to reading age, although there were significant numbers of children in each of these groups with serious learning difficulties.

Factors relating to the school environment

A series of papers by Reynolds and Murgatroyd (Reynolds 1976, 1978; Reynolds and Murgatroyd 1974, 1977; and Murgatroyd 1974) persuasively argue that the school's general organisation and the attitude of the teachers towards pupils and one another exert an important influence on the level of absenteeism and delinquency within the school. Their research was conducted in a Welsh mining valley having a relatively homogeneous community, thus the schools under investigation shared similar catchment areas. Whilst few of their findings within schools reached statistical significance, the highly consistent relative performance of schools on a range of factors, over a number of years lends support to the role of institutional factors in the aetiology of persistent absenteeism. It would have been interesting to have explored the differential effects of the various school environments on school phobia and truancy. For instance, it might be the case that some schools may be quite good at reducing truancy at the expense of increasing the numbers of school phobics. Of course, research in this area is extraordinarily complicated in that all schools are unique. Furthermore, there is a multitude of factors that make schools what they appear to be to pupils, teachers and parents. Many of these factors are intangible and consequently, difficult to isolate and measure. Much more research in this area over a long period involving many schools will be necessary before firm conclusions can be drawn.

The role of school factors in the development of school phobia has been minimised in the American literature. Eisenberg (1958) stresses that school-related concerns do not seem to differ in kind and intensity to the incidents that most children experience at some time or other in their schooling. However, in the United Kingdom, Chazan (1962) felt that schooling factors were of major importance in his 33 school phobics. Being afraid of other children and dislike of being shouted at or punished were the reasons most frequently cited for not going to school. Other reasons given included dislike of certain lessons; sex play, traumatic events in class as well as fears of crowds, confined spaces and examinations. Apart from this 13 of his 33 cases experienced serious educational difficulties warranting remedial help.

Hersov (1977) concludes from his own studies and a review of the literature that in some children, anxiety is mainly related to some aspects of the school situation rather than leaving home or separating from school. Yule, Hersov and Treseder (1980) suggest that there is nearly always a series of additive stresses relating to both home and school involved in the genesis of school phobia. A change of school has been stated as the most common precipitating factor in school phobia, (Hersov, 1960–61a,b; Davidson, 1960–61; Smith, 1970).

Blagg's (1979) findings reported in Blagg and Yule (1986) add weight to the importance of considering school factors in the aetiology of school phobia. Out of 56 phobics, 23 experienced educational difficulties warranting remedial help. A large proportion of school phobics (42 per cent) expressed anxieties about some aspects of their school work. Educational difficulties and anxieties were not, however, confined to the phobic group. Of the truants, 46.4 per cent were worried about aspects of their school work.

As Hersov (1960–61a,b) predicted, a change of school or a significant upheaval within the same school like a change of class, tutor group or subject set caused considerable anxiety in 46.4 per cent of the school phobics in Blagg's 1979 sample. In contrast, only 8.9 per cent of truants were disturbed by a change of or within school. Blagg (1979) also noted that many phobics were more worried than truants about being bullied, PE and games, exams and tests, reciting in class, being criticised, making mistakes, crowds, travelling on the school bus, a long journey to school and the size of the school. As with home-related anxieties it was possible to predict the original group membership of the phobic and truant groups from the pattern of school-related anxieties. Using a discriminant functions analysis, 65.7 per cent of the cases could be correctly allocated to the original groupings.

TYPOLOGIES OF SCHOOL PHOBIA

A number of workers have attempted to classify school phobia. Coolidge, Hahn and Peck (1957), in a study of 21 cases, presented evidence supporting the existence of two types of school phobia that they termed 'neurotic' and 'characterological'. The neurotic group were younger children, mostly girls, who showed a dramatic and sudden onset of the condition. Apart from their school phobia, these children seemed to be generally well-adjusted. The primary conflict in this group seemed to centre on the child's 'symbiotic tie' to the mother. The characterological group consisted mainly of older boys who were regarded as being generally more disturbed. The onset of the problem was gradual in contrast to the neurotic group. The school phobia was regarded as a 'culmination of a relentless process rather than any marked change'. These authors also noted that the characterological group have invariably shown an early history of the school phobic symptoms which have shown a spontaneous remission.

Eisenberg (1958) supports the notion that school phobia in adolescence represents a much more serious internal disturbance than in the early years. However, Johnson (1957) doubts the validity of distinguishing types of school phobia and feels that the characterological group shows a difference in severity of the condition rather than a difference in kind. In fact, a later paper by Coolidge, Willer, Tessman and Waldfogel (1960) recognises that the original classification was rather crude and somewhat arbitrary, disguising the fact that the condition was probably 'associated with widely varying degrees of emotional disturbance ranging all the way from transient anxiety states — reflecting a developmental or external crisis — to severe character disorders bordering on psychosis'. Nevertheless, Kennedy (1965) developed the Coolidge, Hahn and Peck (1957) typology. He described the general characteristics of school phobia: '(i) morbid fears associated with school attendance (a vague dread of disasters). (ii) frequent somatic complaints (headaches, nausea, drowsiness). (iii) symbiotic relationship with mother, fear of separation, anxiety about many things (darkness, crowds, noises). (iv) conflict between parents and the school administration.' After studying cases of school phobia over an eight-year period, Kennedy believed it was possible to make a differential diagnosis between what he referred to as type 1 and type 2 school phobia. Type 1 represented a modification of the neurotic group and type 2 a development of the characterological group. It was argued that the type 1 group responded to a rapid treatment procedure emphasising immediate return to school whereas the type 2 cases required longer term help. A diagnosis of type 1 or type 2 school phobia depended on the child showing at least seven out of ten of the characteristics of each group. Table 1.1 taken from Kennedy's (1965) article shows his differential symptoms of school phobia.

Although this represents an improvement on the Coolidge, Hahn and Peck (1957) formulation, Kennedy's (1965) differential diagnosis still has some problems. Some of the items are not operationally defined so that diagnosis rests on subjective value judgements. For instance, 'good communication between parents' may be very difficult to evaluate. Also the characteristics of the father in terms of competitiveness with the mother around the house may be open to therapist bias. Just how competitive should the father be for him to be classified as fitting into the type 1 group? Furthermore, the final item 'Parents achieve an understanding of the dynamics easily' is an outcome of treatment rather than a criterion for making an initial diagnosis.

Hersov (1960–61a,b) has classified school phobics into three groups according to their pattern of family relationships as shown in Table 1.2.

However, it is not easy to operationalise terms like over-indulgent, over-controlling, demanding and wilful. Weiss and Cain's (1964) typology can be criticised on similar grounds. These authors make a simpler but similar classification into two basic types characterised by: an over-dependent child with an over-protective mother; an over-dependent child with a rejecting mother.

None of the typologies considered so far are contradictory as they each focus on different aspects of the school phobia problem. Coolidge, Hahn and Peck's (1957) original typology was based upon symptomatology, age group and onset. Kennedy

Table 1.1: Ten differential school phobia symptoms

Type 1	Type 2
1. The present illness is the first episode.	1. Second, third or fourth episode.
2. Monday onset, following an illness the previous Thursday or Friday.	2. Monday onset following minor illness not a prevalent antecedent.
3. An acute onset.	3. Incipient onset.
4. Lower grades most prevalent.	4. Upper grades most prevalent.
5. Expressed concern about death.	5. Death theme not present.
6. Mother's physical health in question: actually or child thinks so.	6. Health of mother not an issue.
7. Good communication between parents.	7. Poor communication between parents.
8. Mother and father well adjusted in most areas.	8. Mother shows neurotic behaviour; father a character disorder.
9. Father competitive with mother in household management.	9. Father shows little interest in household or children.
10. Parents achieve understanding of dynamics easily.	10. Parents very difficult to work with.

Source: Kennedy, 1975.

Table 1.2: School phobias classified in terms of family relationships

Person	Type 1	Type 2	Type 3
Mother	Over-indulgent	Over-controlling	Over-indulgent
Father	Passive	Passive	Firm
Child (at home)	Demanding	Obedient	Wilful
Child (at school)	Timid	Timid	Friendly

Source: Hersov, 1960–61a,b

(1965) broadened this to include parental characteristics and communication patterns. Hersov (1960–61a,b) and Weiss and Cain (1964) dwelt on the child's behaviour at home and the parental management. Each of these typologies has problems with many of the conditions being loosely defined and terminology not operationalised.

Smith (1970) analysed 63 cases of school phobia and grouped the children into three categories:

(i) those showing separation anxiety (used in a descriptive sense). These children were under eight years of age.

(ii) true school phobia in older patients who had not shown a previous incidence of the problem. This group consisted of the eight-year-olds to pre-adolescent children who were approaching the phobic stimulus (school).

(iii) depression and/or withdrawal often associated with fear of failure in adolescence.

Yule, Hersov and Treseder (1980) have taken Smith's ideas further. They suggest that there may be many sub-types of school phobia and outline a crude classification based on likely treatment implications:

1. Separation anxiety at first school entry complicated by poor parental management. It is argued that in such cases some form of *in vivo* desensitisation along the lines proposed by Montenegro (1968) is the most appropriate first step.

2. School phobia occurring in a vulnerable child following a major change in schooling. Frequently, the problem is sparked off by additional home-related anxieties. In these instances systematic desensitisation alongside attention to practical issues in the child's 'physical and social environment' is likely to be the most effective treatment option.

3. School phobia in older children who have attended school regularly for 9 to 10 years is regarded as more sinister, possibly marking the onset of a depressive illness or even schizophrenia. Here treatment work should take account of the adolescent's feelings and reasons for non-attendance and involve the individual in treatment far more than is necessary with younger children. Often the treatment will focus on improving the pupil's coping skills.

4. Cases who have been refusing school for less than two weeks normally respond to a variety of simple straightforward approaches including contingency contracting as used by Vaal (1973) and a rapid return to school approach as advocated by Kennedy (1965).

Kahn, Nursten and Carroll (1981) feel that school phobia can only be fully understood by considering each case from a number of different perspectives: (i) intra-personal considering constitutional, organic, personality and temperamental factors; (ii) interpersonal with particular reference to familial relationships; and (iii) environmental/socio-cultural issues.

An interesting paper by Shapiro and Jegede (1973) also argues the case for moving away from a typology of school phobia in favour of a systems analysis. They suggest four basic areas for logical consideration that should enable one to make an accurate diagnosis allowing for the development of individually structured therapeutic intervention. These authors recommend attention to the following areas:

1. chronological age in relation to developmental factors;
2. transactional involvement with mother, family and community;
3. intrapsychic dynamics; and
4. the personal view of the child towards his symptom as ego-alien or ego-syntonic.

They point out that it is not unusual to regard a three-year-old as too young to attend nursery school. Protests and anxiety on leaving the mother could be quite normal. However, we have somewhat higher social expectations of six- and seven-year-olds in their ability to overcome separation anxiety and cope with school. School phobia in adolescence is regarded as more pathological. With respect to transactional involvements with the school, peers, mother, family and community, Shapiro and Jegede (1973) emphasise that whilst external forces influence a child it is the interaction between the demands of these forces and the individual's personality and vulnerabilities that determine whether a phobia develops. An impulsive, immature five-year-old may find it very hard to cope with a highly structured school programme. On the other hand, a five-year-old from an over-controlled home may become very anxious in an over-permissive class situation. The influence of the peer group becomes crucial during pre-adolescence.

Finally, these authors stress the need to consider the child's own feelings and attitude towards the school phobia. Table 1.3 illustrates this point.

The authors suggest that the child with a true phobia feels anxious about the problem. Difficulties in attending school are unusual and inconsistent with the child's normal way of life. At the other end of the spectrum, the truant is not concerned about a reluctance to attend school. Indeed, the truant may feel school

Table 1.3: The vantage point of the ego

| ALIEN | | | SYNTONIC | |
Suffering Inappropriateness			External Cause Appropriate Indignation	
Phobia Anxiety Clinging	Vomiting Anorexia	Dawdling	Family disapproval of school (overt and covert)	Truancy (group and individual)

Source: Shapiro and Jegede, 1973.

refusal is a reasonable response to various external factors in the home or school. Shapiro and Jegede imply that between these two extremes there may be many children who do not fall into the phobic or truant categories. These children do not show evidence of anxiety symptoms and are not responding in an anti-social way. They may be supported in their non-attendance by overt or covert family disapproval of school.

Some support for Shapiro and Jegede's (1973) analysis comes from Blagg (1979) and Blagg and Yule (1986). It was originally hoped that school refusers referred for psychological help over a given period of time would fall neatly into two groups — truants and school phobics. However, early on in the study it became clear that a third group existed referred to in the study as cultural refusers. These children did not show evidence of a neurotic or conduct disorder. They came from families where schooling was not highly valued. Their absence from school was covertly supported by the family.

THE AETIOLOGY OF SCHOOL PHOBIA

Psychoanalytic theory

Psychodynamically based treatment approaches arise out of psychoanalytic theory advanced by Freud in the early 1900s and subsequently modified and interpreted in varying ways by other workers including Klein (1945), Arieti (1961), Sperling (1961) and Renik (1972). On the basis of treatment studies with Viennese middle class neurotics, Freud formulated his theory of personality development. He proposed three interacting structures; the id, ego and super-ego. The id referred to impulsive, instinctual trends within the personality concerned with the satisfaction of basic emotional needs. The organised, realistic element of the personality was labelled the ego, whilst the controlling critical function was served by the super-ego. These three functions were regarded as being frequently in conflict with the instinctual demands of the id, clashing with what was regarded as socially and morally acceptable by the ego and super-ego. Whenever a conflict arose anxiety was generated signalling impending danger. This in turn organised defensive manoeuvres to keep the id under control whilst allowing the ego to present a normal front to the world. In order to deal with this internal, instinctual danger, a process of externalisation transferred the danger to an external object whilst displacement moved the danger from within the family to a neutral object often outside the home. This object could then be avoided, thus warding off uncomfortable feelings. Freud argued that all phobias arose from conflicts of psychic energy (libido). However, later psychoanalysts felt that aggression and dependence also played an important role.

Johnson *et al.* (1941) were the first to argue that the basis of school phobia was separation anxiety produced by an unresolved mother/child dependency relationship. This viewpoint was elaborated and detailed in a later paper by Estes, Haylett and Johnson (1956).

The dynamic development of the neurosis involves:

1. An early, poorly resolved dependency relationship between mother and child.
2. Inadequate fulfilment of the mother's emotional needs, usually because of a poor marriage.

27

3. A temporary threat to the child's security causing a transient increase in the child's dependency needs.

4. Exploitation of this situation by the mother.

5. A similar relationship between the mother and her own mother.

6. Expression of hostility to the child, not only making him more dependent . . . but also by direct inhibition of any opportunity for the child to express aggressive or hostile feelings . . . and also by seductive behaviour towards the child.

7. Development of strong hostility . . . toward the mother, largely unconscious, and expressed by exploitation of the mother's guilt toward him and also by fears for the mother's safety caused by unconscious destructive wishes, thus forcing him to be with her to assure himself of her safety.

8. Displacement of this hostility toward his teacher, so that she becomes a phobic object.

The theory implied by this line of reasoning involves bringing the unconscious conflicts into the open within the context of a therapeutic relationship. The conflicts are analysed and a more mature way of satisfying dependency needs is sought. There has been considerable disagreement amongst psychotherapists, however, about whether the mother and child should be separated or treated together and how quickly a child should be made to confront reality and return to school. A number of writers have stressed the therapeutic value of separating the mother and child during treatment even to the point where the child is hospitalised (Warren, 1948, 1965; Weiss and Cain, 1964; Barker, 1968; Hersov, 1977). The more traditional view of removing pressure, providing insight and planning an ordered, agreed return to school (Johnson et al. 1941; Talbot, 1957; Davidson, 1960–61; Chazan, 1962; Greenbaum, 1964; Coolidge, Brodie and Feeney, 1964; Hersov, 1960–61a,b) has been challenged by other workers who prefer an insistence on immediate return to school followed by concurrent therapy (Klein, 1945; Warnecke, 1964). A number of family therapists do not separate return to school and therapy. They argue that the process of engineering a confrontation over an immediate return and helping the family to successfully negotiate the resulting crisis constitutes the therapy (Skynner, 1974; Framrose, 1978; Hsia, 1984; Bryce and Baird, 1986).

Self concept theory

Leventhal and Sills (1964) and Leventhal, Weinberger, Stander and Stearns (1967) point out that many of the descriptive findings associated with school phobia do not seem to support an explanation based solely on separation anxiety. They question why the problem is not most frequent at the earliest ages and why separation anxiety is not manifested in other areas of life apart from going to school. They emphasise that many of these children maintain normal lives outside school hours.

Instead, Leventhal and Sills (1964) propose that the main feature relevant to school phobia is the finding that:

> These children commonly over-value themselves and their achievements and then try to hold on to their unrealistic self-image. When this is threatened in the school situation, they suffer anxiety and retreat to another situation where they can maintain their narcissistic self-image. This retreat may very well be a running to a close contact with mother.

Lawrence (1987) in a recent book written for teachers also echoes Leventhal and Sills' remarks when describing a school phobic case. Lawrence (1987) refers to school phobics as having a 'distorted self concept' as a result of being overvalued at home. Feelings of anxiety and insecurity are created when the teacher relates to the child in a way that is not in keeping with the distorted self concept causing the child to retreat home to a more comfortable form of interaction.

The treatment emphasised by self concept theorists involves bringing the home and school environments into balance. The parents need to be more realistic and the teachers more accommodating and at the same time the child needs confronting with reality by returning him to school as soon as possible. The therapist deliberately precipitates a crisis by forcing the family to address the issue of immediately returning the child to school. The therapist uses this situation therapeutically by helping the parents to resist the child's manipulative demands and win the power struggle. Anticipation and detailed planning is called for to ensure that the parents are successful (Leventhal, Weinberger, Stander and Stearns 1967). These authors argue that sometimes practical constraints limit the application of this kind of approach.

29

Learning theory

The principles underlying behavioural treatments are derived from learning theory. In contrast to psychoanalytic theory, learning theory has evolved from experimental studies in the laboratory. Three theories explaining how phobic behaviour is learned compete for attention: Respondent Conditioning, Operant Conditioning and the Two-Stage Theory of Fear and Avoidance.

Under the respondent conditioning theory, phobias are regarded as conditioned fear and avoidance responses to specific stimuli. Previously neutral stimuli can acquire fear-evoking qualities by being associated temporally and spatially with a fear-producing situation. Repetition of the feared situation in association with the newly created phobic stimuli will strengthen the fear and avoidance responses to the stimuli. Generalisation can take place from the original phobic stimulus to other similar stimuli.

Watson and Rayner (1920) were the first to demonstrate that a young child could learn to fear a neutral stimulus (a white rat) by pairing a loud bang with approaches to the stimulus. After only seven pairings, presentation of the rat produced a fear reaction. Furthermore, the newly acquired fear generalised to other furry objects with a similar stimulus configuration. A few years later Jones (1924) demonstrated how learned fears could be eliminated through a process of counter-conditioning. Since that time a voluminous number of studies have confirmed and demonstrated how fears can be learned (see Wolpe's 1958 review).

It was Wolpe's (1954) research that led to the development and refinement of systematic desensitisation (SD) procedures which are now widely used in treating both child and adult phobics. Wolpe (1958) argues that treatment effects are the result of reciprocal inhibition, 'i.e. the complete or partial suppression of the anxiety responses as a consequence of the simultaneous evocation of other responses physiologically antagonistic to anxiety'.

Systematic desensitisation involves taking the child step by step through a carefully graded hierarchy of feared situations. At each stage in the hierarchy the child's fear response is reciprocally inhibited through relaxation techniques or some other procedure. Initially, the child is presented with the lowest item in the hierarchy and then gradually faced with more feared items. Care is taken not to rush the child through the stages. Desensitisation occurs at each stage using imagined or real-life (*in vivo*) situations. In sharp contrast, some workers have favoured implosive therapy (or flooding). This involves confronting the child with the most feared item in the hierarchy and keeping the child in that situation until the fear subsides, desensitising via classical extinction. This approach has been mainly applied to treating adults (Marks, 1972). Once again, treatment can be carried out in fantasy or *in vivo*. However, recent findings suggest that *in vivo* treatments may be more effective with adults (Rachman and Hodgson, 1974).

Thus the conditioning theory of fear acquisition has led to the development of a range of treatment techniques that have proved successful with certain cases. Nevertheless, in recent years serious weaknesses in the respondent conditioning analysis of phobias have been pointed out by Seligman (1971) and Rachman (1977). Seligman (1971) draws together a number of experimental findings that do not seem to fit in with laboratory studies of fear conditioning. In particular, unlike laboratory conditioned fears, most phobias are: 1. highly resistant to extinction; 2. confined to a limited set of objects; 3. often acquired in one trial; and 4. resistant to change by 'cognitive' means. Seligman (1971) shares the view put forward by Marks (1970) that most potentially phobic events are probably non-arbitrary and somehow related to the survival of the species. Phobias are seen as highly 'prepared' instances of learning.

In an earlier paper Seligman (1970) states:

The relative preparedness of an organisation for learning about a situation is defined by the amount of input (e.g. numbers of trials, pairings, bits of information, etc.) which must occur before the output (responses, acts, repertoire, etc.) which is construed as evidence of acquisition, reliably occurs . . . If the organism makes the indicated response consistently from the very first presentation of the CS, such 'learning' represents a clear case of instinctive responding, the extreme of the prepared end of the dimension. If the organism makes the response consistently after only a few pairings, it is somewhat prepared. If the response emerges after many pairings, the organism is unprepared . . . Typically ethologists have studied situations from the prepared side of the

31

dimension while general process learning theorists have largely restricted themselves to the unprepared region.

In a later paper Rachman (1977) reiterates some of Seligman's (1971) arguments, but in addition highlights the fact that: 1. the clinical histories of phobic patients often fail to reveal any specific trauma that could have initiated the phobia; and 2. fears can be acquired in the absence of direct contact with fear stimuli. Rachman (1977) referring to work by Bandura (1969) and Rachman (1972, 1976) on the vicarious reduction of fear, argues that fears can be learned vicariously as well as by a process of conditioning. In addition, Rachman (1977) feels that fears can also be acquired through information transmission and instruction.

The fundamental principle that lies behind operant conditioning theory is that behaviour is influenced by its consequences. Behaviour that is rewarded is likely to occur more often whereas behaviour that is punished will decrease in frequency. On the basis of this theory, one can argue that phobias and associated behaviours like temper tantrums are maintained through positive reinforcements from significant others in the child's environment (especially parents and teachers). Any form of attention, whether aversive or affectionate can serve as positive reinforcement. Over-concern on the part of parents can make them over-responsive to normal cautiousness, thus strengthening an avoidance response leading to a stronger parental reaction and the development of a mutually reinforcing circle of behaviour between the parents and child. In a similar way tantrum behaviour that may be regarded as normal in the three-year-old can be strengthened and maintained and carry on into adolescence. This would account for the manipulative, tyrannical behaviour observed in school phobics by Leventhal and Sills (1964).

Yates (1970) in his chapter on phobics explains the development of separation anxiety in behavioural terms. He also answers Leventhal and Sills' (1964) query about why separation anxiety may only occur in certain specific situations. The young pre-school child is very dependent on the mother who acts as a strongly reinforcing stimulus. Separation from the mother at the pre-school age may result in anxiety and protests that lead to the mother returning. As a consequence any separation situation that produces anxiety will result in protest behaviour. If, however, the child can learn that separation experiences are rewarding, he will be more likely to cope with separation anxiety and less likely to exhibit it in the future. Undue anxiety on the part of the mother about the child's safety away from home may lead to the generation and maintenance of separation anxiety in the child. Thus, whether or not a child develops school phobia will depend on: 1. the strength of the separation anxiety and consequent dependence on the home; and 2. the nature of the school experiences, i.e. the extent to which they are rewarding or aversive.

The two-stage theory of fear and avoidance was introduced by Mowrer in 1939. He suggested that fear could motivate behaviour and was not merely a conditional reaction to stimuli associated with pain. He further argued that fear reduction became an operant reward for avoidance of the noxious stimulus. Later formulations of the ideas particularly emphasised the motivating qualities of fear (Miller, 1951). However, in the past ten years a number of experimental and clinical findings have cast doubt on this theory.

In the first place, as outlined earlier, there are serious inadequacies in the classical conditioning theory of fear acquisition on which stage 1 of the theory rests. Apart from this, Seligman and Johnston (1973) point out three other major research findings that seem incompatible with the two-stage theory: 1. avoidance responses are resistant to extinction; 2. avoidance behaviour often persists long after fear has dissipated; 3. it is often difficult to specify relevant conditioned stimuli. Certainly points 1 and 2 apply to the more difficult school phobia cases although thorough diagnostic work usually highlights possible relevant conditioned stimuli. Seligman and Johnston (1973) argue that if avoidance behaviour is reinforced by fear reduction, it seems reasonable to expect a gradual extinction of fear over time, followed by a weakening of the avoidance behaviour. This frequently does not happen. Gray (1971) cites experimental evidence showing the persistence of avoidance behaviour in the absence of fear. In an attempt to account for these findings Gray (1971) introduces the notion of safety signals. He suggests that reinforcement can accrue from any approach to safety signals. Furthermore, he argues these signals can have secondary rewarding properties, even when fear is low. Numerous studies by Herrnstein (1969) demonstrate instances of avoidance responding which do not appear related to specifiable stimuli. However, Rachman (1976) queries whether our experimental techniques are sufficiently refined to allow for the identification of a relevant conditioned stimulus.

In addition to these problems, evidence has been amassed from clinical studies that clearly show that fear arousal and avoidance behaviour are not always synchronous (i.e. do not always co-vary as the two-stage theory would predict (Rachman 1976)). Rachman and Hodson (1974) have discussed these matters in some detail and point out fresh implications for theory and practice. The possible combinations of the three major components of fear (i.e. subjective experience, avoidance behaviour and physiological disturbance) are given in Table 1.4. Hodgson and Rachman (1974) argue that 'Concordance or desynchrony between response systems (in fear) is a function of the intensity of emotional arousal, level of demand, therapeutic technique and length of follow-up.'

It is postulated that concordance will be high during strong emotional arousal whereas discordance will be more likely with low levels of emotional stimulation. They also suggest that discordance will increase under high levels of treatment demand. With regard to therapeutic techniques, it is anticipated that considerable desynchrony will be observed during 'implosion' or 'flooding' treatment (with avoidance behaviour diminishing rapidly whilst subjective fear shows a cognitive lag). On the other hand, they expect synchrony between response systems when using a modelling treatment. If the authors' fourth hypothesis regarding length of follow-up is confirmed, the therapist will be able to reassure the patient receiving flooding treatment that, given sufficient time, newly learned behaviour will cease to be

Table 1.4: A matrix of possible combinations of 3 components of fear, where + indicates 'present' and − indicates 'absent'

Possibility	Subjective fear	Avoidance behaviour	Physio. disturbance
1	+	+	+
2	+	+	−
3	+	−	+
4	+	−	−
5	−	+	−
6	−	+	+
7	−	−	+
8	−	−	−

Source: Rachman, 1976.

accompanied by fear.

The authors stress that it is important for the behavioural psychotherapist to know: 'which response system is initially modified by a particular treatment technique, and the extent to which this change generalises to other systems. An effective technique should lead eventually to change across all response systems'.

As Chapter 3 demonstrates, a wide variety of behavioural techniques have been developed arising out of classical and operant paradigms as well as social learning theory. Increasingly behavioural treatments encompass a problem-solving approach to therapy (Yule, 1977). Although behavioural approaches concern themselves with the immediate problem of returning the child to school, arguments surrounding the preparation for and the timing and pacing of the return parallel those in the psycho-dynamic camp. Increasingly therapists employ a mix of approaches tailored to take account of the unique range of child, family and school-related issues that may be involved in any one case (Kennedy, 1965; Hersov, 1977; Blagg, 1977 and 1979; Yule, Hersov and Treseder, 1980; Phillips and Wolpe, 1981; Blagg and Yule, 1984). Moreover, in varying degrees these authors acknowledge the need to go beyond the immediate confines of the behavioural framework and address many subtle process and pragmatic issues likely to hinder or enhance treatment progress.

2

Psychodynamic Approaches to the Treatment of School Phobia

INTRODUCTION

Early treatment work with school phobia was largely psychoanalytically based (Johnson, Falstein, Szurek and Svendsen, 1941; Klein, 1945; Warren, 1948; Thompson, 1948; Van Houten, 1948; Bornstein, 1949; Sperling, 1951; Suttenfield, 1954; Coolidge, Hahn and Peck, 1957). The publication of Wolpe's (1954, 1958) work stimulated interest in behavioural techniques but for many years the majority of large-scale treatment investigations utilised therapeutic approaches derived from psychoanalytic theory (Talbot, 1957; Rodriguez *et al.*, 1959; Glaser, 1959; Hersov, 1960–61a,b; Davidson, 1960–61; Chazan, 1962; Warnecke, 1964; Weiss and Cain, 1964; Barker, 1968; Berg, 1970; Skynner, 1974). Nevertheless, beneath the psychoanalytic umbrella, strategies and styles of intervention have varied enormously. In particular there have been major differences of opinion with respect to: who to treat; where to treat; whether to insist on an immediate return to school before, during or after treatment and finally the extent to which factors outside the family should be considered in aetiology and treatment.

Much of the pioneer work was concerned with the psychopathology of the child although most studies broadened the treatment focus to include the mother-child relationship. In a detailed literature review Malmquist (1965) highlighted the fact that although many studies discussed the nature of family dynamics in the aetiology of school phobia, very few therapists actively involved the fathers in treatment. More recent papers including those by Skynner (1974), Framrose (1978) Hsia (1984) and Bryce and Baird (1986) argue strongly that treatment should be based on a family system model with the father occupying a crucial role in therapy. Will and Baird (1984) and Bryce and Baird (1986) take the systemic approach further and argue the case for 'an integrated approach to dysfunction in interprofessional systems'.

Psychodynamic treatments have generally emphasised community-based or out-patient treatment. The drastic and sudden separation experiences involved in hospitalisation seem to run counter to the general principle of developing insight and understanding as a way of resolving difficulties. Nevertheless, in certain circumstances, admission to a hospital in-patient unit has been recommended (Warren, 1948; Hersov, 1960–61a,b; Weiss and Cain, 1964; Barker, 1968; and Berg, 1970).

The majority of dynamically oriented therapists have regarded an early return to school as fundamentally important to the successful management of school phobia (Klein, 1945; Talbot, 1957; Eisenberg, 1958; Rodriguez et al., 1959; Glaser, 1959; Weiss and Cain, 1964; Warnecke, 1964; Leventhal, Weinberger, Stander and Stearns, 1967; Skynner 1974; Framrose, 1978; Hsia, 1984). Most therapists emphasise the need to organise the return to school in carefully agreed, manageable steps as specified by Berryman (1959) although some therapists argue for immediate confrontation using the threat of legal action if necessary to provide therapeutic leverage over the family and child (Eisenberg 1958; Rodriguez et al., 1959; Warnecke, 1964; Skynner, 1974). In contrast a few therapists have favoured a delayed return to school (Thompson, 1948; Talbot, 1957; Hersov, 1960–61a,b; Davidson, 1960–61; Sperling, 1961; Greenbaum, 1964; Radin, 1967). Thompson (1948) feels that any form of pressure is likely to be dangerous, making the phobia worse and more difficult to treat. Talbot (1957) argues that the psychological needs of both mother and child should be evaluated in timing the child's return to school. However, the first step must involve removing the pressure to attend school to enable treatment to begin. Waldfogel, Coolidge and Hahn (1957) claim that rapid return to school may lead to the child and family withdrawing from treatment leaving emotional conflicts and issues unresolved. Sperling (1961) echoes these views and states:

If psychotherapy is planned, it is better to uncover the

dynamics underlying the phobic behaviour in treatment, and when this is achieved, the child will return to school voluntarily and assume responsibility for doing so himself. Any other method exempts the child from this responsibility and places it instead on parents, teachers, principal, truant officer or therapist.

In the main, psychodynamic treatments have either ignored or de-emphasised the role of school factors in the aetiology and treatment of school phobia. However, a few writers have emphasised the importance of co-ordinating the family-based treatment with the school personnel (Waldfogel, Tessman and Hahn, 1959; Eisenberg, 1958; Davidson, 1960–61; Chazan, 1962; Framrose, 1978; Hsia, 1984; Bryce and Baird, 1986). Waldfogel, Tessman and Hahn (1957), dealing with incipient cases of school phobia, put forward a number of therapeutic advantages in operating directly in the school situation:

> The therapist can offer direct support to the child in the feared situation. In addition, he can help the principal and the teacher by relieving them of their sense of helpless bewilderment and guilt. By modifying their feelings toward the child he is able to work with them towards altering whatever reality factors exist to aggravate the child's fears. Sometimes adjustments need to be made, such as reducing the pressure of work and allowing the child to attend only part of the day. On rare occasions, the child must be transferred to another class.

The above issues will be returned to later in this chapter as a range of significant treatment studies are reviewed. The literature will be considered under the following headings:

a. Traditional Psychodynamic Treatment Studies
b. Traditional Psychodynamic Treatment Studies involving hospitalisation
c. Family Therapy Studies

TRADITIONAL PSYCHODYNAMIC TREATMENT STUDIES

Studies reviewed in this section will include hospital out-patient cases as well as community-based treatments. Traditional psychodynamic studies are interpreted as those focusing treatment on the individual child or the mother–child relationship.

In a collection of papers Jung (1911) describes the treatment of what appears to be a school phobic. The eleven-year-old girl could not cope with school because of sudden nausea and headaches and refused to get out of bed in the mornings. The analytic treatment was focused entirely on the child. Her problems were viewed in terms of an incest complex which had become displaced onto a male teacher. The child's family were not mentioned nor even the girl's relationship with either parent.

Bornstein (1949) provides a detailed account of the analysis of Frankie a five-and-a-half-year-old boy who was in therapy for three years. Treatment was primarily focused on the child but Bornstein does acknowledge the need to develop and maintain a continuous relationship with the boy's parents so that unconscious material could be interpreted against reality events.

The classic article by Johnson, Falstein, Szurek and Svendsen (1941) was the first to emphasise the importance of treating both the mother and child. It was recommended that two psychiatrists were involved so that the child and mother could be treated separately by two different therapists. The father's contribution to the child's problem was regarded as indirect, by adding to the mother's disturbance. Treatment with respect to the father was felt to be most efficiently handled by helping the mother clarify and restructure her feelings about her husband rather than dealing with the father direct. The treatment details are summarised in Table 2.1.

Table 2.1: The treatment outcome in a number of traditional psychotherapy studies that favour 'insight' before return to school

Study	N	Age range	Length of treatment	Number and % of children returning to school	
				N	%
Johnson, Falstein, Szurek and Svendsen (1941)	8	6–14 yrs	5–12 mths	7	87.5
Talbot (1957)	24	5–15 yrs	2–24 mths	20	83.33
Davidson (1960–61)	15	7–10 yrs	Not stated	25	83.33
	15	11–14.5 yrs			
Chazan (1962)	15	5.5–10 yrs	2–5 mths	25	75.75
	18	11–14 yrs			

Van Houten (1948) reported on 12 children where the treatment centred on the mother-child ambivalent relationship. Nevertheless other wider issues were referred to including: the mother's relationship with her husband and society; the child's attitudes to the father, siblings and peers; and the child's feelings about the school phobia symptomatology.

Robinson, Duncan and Johnson (1955) describe the case of a 14-year-old school phobic girl with severe separation anxiety. The mother and daughter were treated collaboratively but the authors noted that neurosis in the father often played a sufficiently significant role in the problem that three therapists were sometimes needed to deal with a 'threeway interlocking family neurosis'.

Talbot's (1957) paper stresses the dangers of putting too much pressure on the phobic child. She argues that the timing of the return to school determines the success or failure of treatment. Most of the 24 cases (aged 5–15 years) received some treatment before school return was considered. Five of the cases were allowed to remain off school for one to two terms and given home tuition. It would be interesting to know how many of her failures received this form of help. The paper does not make clear the extent to which fathers were involved in therapy although the author seems keen on them 'participating' in treatment. Talbot recognises the need to consider the child's 'total reality adjustment' in evaluating outcome. However, she does not offer criteria to assess this. Furthermore, treatment is not broken down by age. The results are summarised in Table 2.1.

Davidson's (1960–61) study of 30 cases is difficult to interpret. Treatment is divided into: practical measures dealing with the environment and psychotherapy. School factors are considered and where possible the child is offered a 'better bargain' in return for full- or part-time attendance. Timetable alterations and a change of school are regarded as being useful on some occasions provided they follow treatment. Home tuition is also recognised as a valuable measure together with in-patient treatment and residential school placement where necessary. It is not clear from Davidson's study whether all of these approaches were used and whether the outcome was affected by these different practical measures. As Table 2.1 shows, 25 out of 30 children returned to school. However, Davidson does not state whether all of the 25 children who went back to school managed to do so without residential placement. Furthermore, outcome is not broken down by age. If only 10 of the 15 older children returned to school the figures for this group would not seem that impressive.

Chazan's (1962) paper acknowledges the usefulness of a number of treatment measures. Educational factors are given particular significance. In his 33 cases there were 19 changes of school and 9 cases where remedial reading was provided at a special centre. Apart from this, 5 cases were given sedatives and 2 cases received hospital in-patient treatment. Psychotherapy was conducted on a group and individual basis with 9 cases attending for group sessions and 16 cases being seen individually. With all of these measures operating it is difficult to know which were of significance. It would be interesting to know why certain cases needed to be placed in residential schools.

One of the few long-term follow-ups reported in the literature was conducted by Coolidge, Brodie and Feeney (1964) at the Judge Baker Guidance Centre. This paper reports a follow-up 5–10 years later of 66 children diagnosed as 'school phobic' between 1953 and 1958. However 10 of the 66 children could not be located and of the remaining 56 cases 7 were eliminated 'because in retrospect it seemed that their difficulties in going to school were either part of a more pervasive disorder . . . or related primarily to external overwhelming events, rather than to anxiety motivated by internal conflicts'. This retrospective elimination of cases seems a dubious procedure that highlights the lack of explicit behavioural criteria for selecting cases of school phobia. With these limitations in mind, their results need to be interpreted with appropriate caution. Of the 49 cases followed up 47 returned to school and continued to attend. However, 50 per cent of the cases were still exhibiting various problems relating to the original school phobia: e.g. over-anxiety about exams; absences due to feigned illness; longer absences for minor illnesses than is normally expected. It should be remembered that all 49 cases were treated between the ages of 4–11 years.

Leventhal, Weinberger, Standen and Stearns (1967) feel that the key to successful treatment involves the child being forced to reappraise an unrealistic self-image by losing a carefully engineered showdown between the child and parents over school avoidance. They described two cases in which the child's resolve crumbled as soon as the parents were seen to be fully in control. Furthermore both children seemed relieved at the parents being in charge. These authors feel that a major confrontation is in itself therapeutic, providing the parents win. In contrast Radin

(1967), who views the aetiology of school phobia in rather similar terms, suggests that 'premature pressure to return to school may precipitate or release an underlying psychosis'. In fact, a number of earlier treatment studies (Rodriguez *et al.*, 1959; Glaser, 1959; Warnecke, 1964) suggest that Radin's fears are unfounded. None of these authors noted ill-effects resulting from rapid return to school procedures.

The classic paper by Rodriguez *et al.* (1959) represented the first major trial (with long-term follow-up) of a therapeutic method involving immediate return to school. Their approach represented a 'sharp deviation from traditional methods of treatment which tended to emphasise insight before action'. The method was supported by reference to an earlier paper by Eisenberg (1958) who had observed that the school phobic's symptoms were a response to 'contradictory verbal and behavioural cues provided by his parents'. The involved parent 'initiated and reciprocated the child's anxiety'. Apart from breaking the circle of anxiety the therapeutic advantages of insistence on an early return to school were argued in these terms:

> to begin with, it brings into sharp focus the primary issue of separation and dissociates the therapist from the family's displacement on to fantasised dangers in the school situation. Secondly, it emphasises our recognition of the core of health in the child; the fact that we *act* upon this premiss constitutes effective reassurance to a panic-stricken family. A de-emphasis on school attendance and a plan for prolonged therapy tend to signify to the family that the physician, too, is uncertain and regards the child as being sick as they do despite verbal formulations to the contrary. Finally, the return to school restores the child to a growth-promoting environment and removes him from his immersion in the cycle of mutually reinforced anxieties in the home.

They also point out the dangers of secondary fears developing the longer the child remains off school. Of the 41 cases, 32 were treated in less than 12 clinic visits. Only one-sixth of the cases were in treatment for as long as six months. The authors do not clearly define school phobia, however they indicate that the 41 cases include all school phobics seen at their clinic between 1952–1957. Follow-ups were limited to school and family reports. The children themselves were not interviewed. Outcome was considered successful if the child was regularly attending school. As in most studies, regular attendance was not defined. As Table 2.2 shows, 71 per cent of the cases were successful. However, a more detailed analysis revealed that for children younger than 11 years there was a success rate of 89 per cent whereas for children 11 years or older the success rate dropped to only 36 per cent. There were no significant differences in outcome related to sex when age was taken into account. Furthermore, no relationship was demonstrated between duration of the school phobia and treatment success rate. With regard to academic progress and social adjustment 23 of the 29 successful cases were reported to be making satisfactory social and educational progress at follow-up. It should be emphasised that of the 12 failures, three and possibly four were schizophrenic. Most other studies have excluded cases of psychosis from their treatment series. The other eight treatment failures showed a longer history of 'emotional maladjustment' before treatment than the rest of the group.

Glaser (1959) also adopted a rapid return approach supported on similar theoretical grounds. He produced quite impressive results with 36 out of his 38 cases returning to school. However, once again no criteria are stated for adequate attendance. Furthermore, Glaser does not give the precise age range for the children in his study. Sixteen cases were aged between 6–9 years and 22 cases were 10 years and older. If this latter group was

Table 2.2: The treatment outcome in a number of traditional psychodynamic studies emphasising an immediate (forced) return to school

Study	N	Age range	Length of treatment	Length of follow-up	Number and % of children returning to school	
					N	%
Rodriguez, Rodriguez and Eisenberg (1959)	41	5–13 yrs	12 sessions	15–80 mths	29	71
Glaser (1959)	38	6–10 yrs	5–10+ sessions	12–24 mths	36	94.7
Warnecke (1964)	47	5–11+ yrs	Not stated 1–14 yrs (n=44)	>1 yr (n=3)	40	86.9

swamped with 10-year-olds it would make the treatment outcome less impressive. Finally, the follow-up period was one to two years as against a mean follow-up period of three years in the previous study.

A later paper by Warnecke (1964) reports on the treatment and long-term follow-up of 47 cases of school phobia. Treatment was modelled on the approach adopted by Rodriguez et al. (1959). Cases of school refusal were treated as emergencies with the primary concern being the return of the child to full-time schooling. Dealing with background psychopathology was put in second place. The diagnostic interview was concerned with considering what steps would be needed to secure the child's return to school. Sometimes discussions with general practitioners were required to clarify medical issues. One of the 41 cases was excluded from school on medical grounds against the wishes of the clinic. However, when medical cover was withdrawn after six months, the same school refusal and panic reaction remained. Eventually, it was agreed to apply pressure in all cases. Sometimes parents were brought before an attendance committee and on occasions legal action was taken. Warnecke argues that it is often necessary for an Education Welfare Officer (EWO) to call for the child in the mornings and states that there are times when force is necessary. A change within school, like transfer to another class may be indicated.

The child and the parents are encouraged to live with their emotions in an active way. It is suggested that immediate confrontation can play an important part in treatment in that:

> in dealing with these situations the ego of the child is supported and the feeling of inadequacy in the parents is diminished. Such an approach does not imply that unconscious determinants are ignored but that they should be dealt with at the proper time.

Warnecke emphasises that the mothers need help in achieving separation from their child and separation from their own mothers. The treatment results in this study were very encouraging. Out of the 46 cases where a follow-up was possible, 40 returned to 'satisfactory' attendance at school. With regard to 'adjustment' in the 39 cases where information was available, 36 were regarded as 'adjusted or improved'. However, it should be remembered that these terms were not objectively defined and no individual assessment was carried out at follow-up. Warnecke does not state the full age range although he does report that 24 of the cases (64 per cent) were over the age of 11 years. The six failures all fell into this older age range which means that for the children of 11 years + successful outcome in terms of satisfactory school attendance was 80 per cent.

Studies considered so far have placed a high reliance on return to school as an indication of treatment success. Nevertheless, increasing attention is being been paid to the child's general emotional adjustment and performance in school. An interesting study by Baker and Wills (1979) followed up 71 school phobic children beyond school leaving age. The cases chosen were school phobics as defined by Berg, Butler and Hall (1976), seen at a Child Guidance Clinic over a ten year period. Information was gleaned from clinic records, a postal questionnaire and a lengthy interview with the child at home. The authors explored a number of issues including the relationship between work or further education records at follow-up and: 1. duration of the child's absence from school; 2. whether or not the child had returned to school; 3. the clinical assessment of the child during treatment. Baker and Wills (1979) concluded that: 'Whether or not the child returned to school had no relationship to future performance at work or in further education.' In comparison to the general population, children with a history of school phobia had on average a slightly poorer work record. The authors noted that there was no difference in the original patterns of the disorders between those that were subsequently working and those that were non-working. Thus Baker and Wills (1979) argue that: 'Adequate treatment of the underlying conditions appears to be more important than returning the child to school.'

TRADITIONAL PSYCHODYNAMIC TREATMENT STUDIES INVOLVING HOSPITALISATION

Warren's (1948) paper was the first to advocate hospitalisation as a valuable treatment measure. He argued that in some cases out-patient treatment was highly problematic and time consuming. Three of the eight cases reported in this study were hospitalised. Two of the three cases returned to school satisfactorily. However, the third case was eventually placed in a boarding school after several discharges, relapses and readmissions.

Warren states that hospitalisation relies heavily on parental co-operation and the child's acceptance of hospitalisation. In two cases that were unresponsive to out-patient care the mothers would not agree to hospital admission.

Hersov (1960–61a,b) reports that 29 of his 50 cases required in-patient treatment. Twenty-two of these cases were direct admissions that had failed to respond to a lengthy period of out-patient treatment elsewhere. Seven other children were taken into hospital after out-patient treatment 'because of acute family tensions with depression on the part of the mother and child'. Elsewhere Hersov (1977) argues that in-patient treatment is indicated when alternative methods have failed and where it is assumed that 'the family environment is itself such a pathogenic factor in supporting and maintaining the disorder that it blocks effective treatment'. In a later article Hersov (1980) develops these arguments but does not distinguish clearly between reasons for out-patient versus in-patient hospital treatment.

Hersov's (1960–61a,b) study is particularly significant in that it is one of the largest treatment series in the literature. Furthermore, the majority of the children fell into the older age group (10–16 years). Sixty-eight per cent of the children returned to school after treatment of between 6–12 months duration. As Table 2.3 shows, follow-up 6–18 months later revealed that successful outcome in terms of regular school attendance had dropped to 58 per cent. Hersov does not compare outcome figures for the in-patient and out-patient groups. However, one suspects that the success rate for the in-patient group was considerably worse than 58 per cent. Treatment outcome was not related to age, sex, IQ or quality of family relationships.

Weiss and Cain's (1964) study involved 16 adolescents who had proved highly resistant to community based psychotherapy. All 16 cases evidenced separation anxiety although observations of the children and their parents suggested two styles of relationship and interaction. One group were regarded as demonstrating 'symbiotic' parent-child relationships whereas the children in the other group were noted as being 'parasitically' dependent on their parents. The former group were very reluctant to agree to hospitalisation with many last minute tears and protests. In contrast, the latter group entered hospital without any signs of distress. This group did not desperately cling on to the parents but did become quickly over-dependent on substitute mother figures on the ward staff.

The beneficial aspects of hospitalisation were felt to include:

1. Managed separation experiences. The parents were encouraged to visit the hospital according to a planned agreement. It was felt that this forced the child to face that the problem lay at school and not at home.
2. Full-time attendance at the hospital school removed the build-up of secondary worries with regard to falling behind with school-work. Immediate success in attending the hospital school demonstrated to the child that the difficulties were more related to leaving home than going to a school.
3. General benefits arising out of the 'therapeutic milieu' such as the opportunity to develop new relationships with peers and significant adults as well learning to cope with new social situations.

In terms of outcome, Weiss and Cain's (1964) study is not very clearly reported. At the time of writing two of their 16 cases were still in treatment. Of the 14 cases that were discharged, two were greatly improved, eight moderately improved and three mildly improved. One case became school phobic within six months of discharge and showed no improvement thereafter. Thus it would seem that only six cases (37.5 per cent) were able to return home and attend a day school after lengthy hospital treatment. Weiss and Cain (1964) comment on the difficulties in treating hospitalised children. Some children displayed a lack of fantasy life and many found difficulties in relating easily and talking about their feelings. It was suggested that the 'parasitically' dependent group was less accessible to treatment than the 'symbiotic' group. However, a long-term follow-up study by Weiss and Burke (1967) found no evidence to support this view.

Unlike the previous studies in this section, out-patient treatment had not been tried on any of the six cases in Barker's (1968) study. Furthermore, all of the cases were below 12 years of age, with the three cases quoted in detail being only 8–9 years old. Barker (1968) justifies in-patient treatment by claiming that all of the cases were severe, falling into Kennedy's (1965) type 2 category. It was felt that other forms of treatment would not be satisfactory. The major problem in each case seemed to be separation anxiety with the mothers maintaining the pattern through over-protection.

Hospitalisation was not easily accepted by the families so that the therapist often needed to delay admission until a relationship had been established and other alternatives considered and dismissed. Treatment essentially involved a 'parentectomy' with enforced separation. Nevertheless, the parents were encouraged to visit the hospital frequently (even daily) especially in the early stages. This was reassuring to both the child and parents and provided plenty of practice in coping with separation experiences in a supportive environment. Barker (1968) argues that keeping the child busy with hospital schooling and occupational therapy aimed at developing self-esteem helps to mitigate the stress involved in separation. Much importance was placed upon a single case worker being assigned to the family from the early diagnostic stages through to follow-up so that the family could be consistently supported and new material appropriately interpreted and handled as it arose. Discharge and return to mainstream schooling were handled by allowing increasingly longer weekends with lengthening attendance at the mainstream school. Viewed behaviourally, the child was 'shaped up' into a normal school and home routine. Barker (1968) achieved 100 per cent success with respect to return to mainstream school although two of the six children still showed neurotic symptomatology at follow-up. However, bearing in mind the age range it seems highly likely that equally good outcome figures could have been achieved via out-patient or community-based treatment.

Berg's (1970) treatment study was at the time unique in offering explicit behavioural criteria for diagnosing school phobia (see Chapter 1 pp. 7–8). However, the authors do not state whether any of their cases had received out-patient treatment before hospitalisation. The in-patient unit was organised along therapeutic community lines. Each child was assigned a particular hospital therapist who acted as a confidant for the child and family and assisted in any difficulties concerned with accepting the hospitalisation. Berg (1970) outlined problems in approximately 50 per cent of his patients such as running off from hospital, persistent requests to contact or return home. In contrast to some hospital in-patient units, all children returned home each weekend from the very earliest stages of treatment. Understandably, some children refused to return to hospital after weekends resulting in some parents being given special help and occasionally children receiving medication.

Children attended the hospital school each day and participated in various social activities and meetings. No formal psychotherapy was undertaken. Return to mainstream schooling required considerable liaison between the hospital staff and teachers, much family support and often a short-term escort procedure normally undertaken by the hospital therapist.

It was possible to follow-up 27 of the 29 cases three months to two years after treatment was completed. Sixteen cases (59 per cent) were attending school or work regularly at follow-up. However, only nine cases (33 per cent) were in addition well-adjusted in relation to home and their contemporaries.

In a later paper Berg, Butler and Hall (1976) report on a follow-up study of 125 school phobics treated in a psychiatric in-patient unit over a seven year period. One hundred cases were reviewed on average three years after discharge. Berg states that the findings were consistent with previous outcome studies. One third had improved very little in that they still showed evidence of impaired social functioning and severe emotional disturbance. Another third showed an appreciable improvement but still presented with neurotic symptomatology. The remaining third had shown a marked improvement. Approximately 50 per cent of the cases still showed school attendance difficulties although subsequent work difficulties were not so great.

As mentioned earlier many studies evaluate treatment efficacy in terms of immediate measurable indices like: normalised school attendance; the disappearance of somatic complaints and avoidance routines; social and academic progress. Relatively few studies consider long-term adjustment into adulthood. A recent investigation by Valles and Oddy (1984) has attempted to do this building on the example set by Baker and Wills (1978). Valles and Oddy (1984) identified 108 school phobics admitted to an in-patient adolescent unit over a one year period. Berg, Butler and Hall's (1976) criteria were used in selecting cases and only those children fourteen-and-a-half-years or less on admission were included in the target group. Only 76 of the 108 pupils could be traced at long-term follow-up. Of these cases 66 per cent of the males and 25 per cent of the females agreed to be interviewed (34 cases). The age range of the subjects was 18 years 2 months– 26 years 8 months (mean age 20 years 9 months). A number of objective measures were used to assess social and emotional adjustment including: a structured social adjustment question-naire (Weissman and Paykel, 1974) the Leeds Anxiety and Depression Scale, (Snaith, Bridge and Hamilton, 1976); the Rosenberg (1965) Self-Esteem Scale and finally a dependency

Table 2.3: The treatment outcome in a number of studies involving traditional psychotherapy and hospitalisation

Study	N	Age range	Length of phobia	Length of treatment	Number returned to day school N	%	Follow-up period	Number in school at follow-up N	%
Warren (1948)	8	9–14 yrs	Not stated	Not stated	4	50	Not stated	–	–
Hersov (1960–61b)	8 42	7–9 yrs 10–16 yrs	2 mths–2 yrs	6–12 mths	34	68	6–18 mths after discharge	29	58
Weiss and Cain (1964)	16	8–16 yrs	2 mths–2.5 yrs	Mean=9 mths	6	37.5	No follow-up	–	–
Barker (1968)	6	All <12 yrs	Not stated*	3–14 mths	6	100	6–12 mths	6	100
Berg (1970)	29	10–15 yrs	3 days–2 yrs+	1–19 mths Mean = 9 mths			3–24 mths Mean = 13 mths	16	59

* Details were given for only three cases

questionnaire developed specifically for the study.

Sixteen of the subjects had successfully returned to school following discharge whereas the other 18 cases continued to show major attendance difficulties. The authors reported that there were differences between the two groups at the start of treatment. Those that succeeded in returning to school were younger on admission and experienced more stable family relationships than those that failed to return to school. Apart from this the two groups were remarkably similar on a large number of important indices. Accordingly, the adjustment of the two groups was compared at long-term follow-up.

With respect to the pattern of employment, work-attendance rates and relationships there were no differences between the two groups, supporting Baker and Wills' (1979) findings. The failed return group did however, seem less well-adjusted socially although many of the results were not statistically significant. Failed return-to-school cases were more inclined to boredom, less interested in dating, had fewer friends and were more sensitive to criticism than the successful cases. The failed return group also showed significantly more anxiety on the Leeds Scale with more evidence of depression, significantly higher conviction rates and more visits to their general practitioners in the year prior to follow-up.

Family relationships continued to be strained for the group who failed to return to school suggesting that hospital treatment did little to alter the basic family dynamics for these cases. It should be noted that both groups at follow-up were low in self-esteem and led 'rather impoverished social lives'.

The findings from this study need to be interpreted cautiously. Long-term follow-ups, although very necessary do have a number of inherent methodological hazards, not least the difficulty of tracing and gaining the co-operation of the original treatment group. The 34 cases in this study may not have been representative of the initial treatment sample. Furthermore, it is always risky relating treatment effects to long-term outcomes because of the likelihood of many other uncontrolled variables intervening between treatment and follow-up. Nevertheless, Valles and Oddy's (1984) paper does tend to suggest that although return to school may be important, it does not necessarily guarantee long-term adjustment. The authors argue that there is a 'need to bring about changes in family dynamics to secure a satisfactory and lasting solution'.

FAMILY THERAPY STUDIES

Family therapy approaches transcend the parent-child dyad in addressing the entire family system. School phobia is regarded as symptomatic and sometimes protective of faulty family functioning. Treatment approaches consistently emphasise the importance of early return to school although the manner by which this is achieved varies greatly from therapist to therapist.

Skynner (1974) refers to his approach as conjoint family psychotherapy. The central problem within school phobia is seen as the 'parents failure to help their child relinguish omnipotent demands for exclusive possession of the mother'. Hence there is a persisting problem over separation and leaving home with a subsequent need for the child to replicate the exclusive mother-child relationship with the teachers. This is possible in the 'one-parent' primary school but not in the multi-parent secondary school environment.

Skynner (1974) argues that school phobics are protected from the challenges of reality by their mothers. Like Warnecke (1964), he stresses that these mothers maintain exclusive and possessive relationships with their own mothers until they are transferred, in time, to their own children. He believes that the crucial challenge is concerned with:

> the first disruption of the exclusive attachment characteristic of the oral stage, the first weakening of omnipotent posses-sion. However, secure mastery of this earlier stage underpins later achievements so that failure at this level does also create difficulties in the resolution of oedipal and other subsequent conflicts. Thus the symptomatology is often complex with derivatives from various levels simultaneously.

Skynner claims that 'bonds' within these families run vertically from parent to child with a consequent weak relationship between spouses. In an attempt to resolve these apparent difficulties, the following treatment elements are stressed:

1. The whole nuclear family is included in treatment as well as other family members where necessary.
2. An emphasis is placed upon non-verbal communication and confrontation of the parents over their hidden rule system. Attention is directed to the 'here and now' of family

interactions although past events may be considered as and when they arise.

3. There is a focus on an early return to school. However in contrast to many other approaches a few widely spaced interviews are used so that pressure is placed on the family to resolve its own problems.

4. An effort is made to weaken the mother-child bond and strengthen the marital bond by encouraging the father to take on a more active, demonstrative role.

5. In the more straightforward cases, interpretation of the problem develops insight in the parents enabling the family to marshal its own resources and solve the problem. However, in cases where the parents are less co-operative or unable to cope, the missing parental role has to be fulfilled by the therapist or some outside agency, e.g. social services or the court.

6. In contrast to the other rapid treatment procedures, Skynner advocates the use of drugs to help in the confrontation stage. In addition, excessively timid pupils are occasionally helped by attendance at psychotherapy groups whilst some mothers are helped to become more independent of their children by attending psychotherapy groups for mothers.

7. Only minimal attention is paid to school factors.

Skynner (1974) feels that 'school phobia is best understood as a psychosocial problem rather than a purely medical intrapsychic or even intrafamilial disorder'. Thus in the resistant families the therapist must adopt a 'real authority role' by either introducing a clear value system about the nature of the parental responsibilities or temporarily taking over the parental role. Like Rodriguez *et al.* (1959) and Warnecke (1964), Skynner (1974) sometimes uses the threat of court or residential placement to help the family overcome previously unsurmountable developmental hurdles.

In a retrospective study of 20 school refusers seen over a one year period at the Queen Elizabeth Hospital, Skynner (1974) reports the following outcome details. One case returned to school before the initial assessment. A further 15 returned within a month of consultation. Most cases only needed one interview. One case needed four interviews spread over a ten month period before *regular* attendance was resumed. Of the three cases that failed, one was classified as a truant and one was diagnosed schizophrenic. If these two cases are excluded initial favourable treatment outcome reaches 94.1 per cent and drops to 88.2 per cent on long-term follow-up. The limited findings on general adjustment were obtained from school reports via the education welfare service. Apparently two of the 15 successful cases had experienced slight relapses since treatment. One case was resolved by placement in a day unit for maladjusted children whilst in the other case, encouragement from an education welfare officer sufficed. One other girl was reported as remaining over-attached to the mother. There did not appear to be major problems with the other successful cases at follow-up. Fifty per cent of the treatment group were 11 years or older and yet there were no differences in outcome related to age.

Skynner (1974) recognises the similarities between his approach and other explicitly behavioural rapid return approaches such as that advocated by Kennedy (1965). He suggests that the success of Kennedy's approach may well be the result of implicitly addressing crucial faulty family mechanisms.

Nevertheless, there are important differences between Skynner's approach and the rapid return approaches advocated by Kennedy (1965) and Blagg (1977). The latter consistently communicate an optimistic message emphasising the child's normality and core of good health whereas Skynner's willingness to use drug therapy seems likely to imply there is something wrong with the child, undermining the intended message that the child is fit and well enough to return to school. Both Kennedy (1965) and Blagg (1977) strongly emphasise the role of the school in treatment. Furthermore, the additive stress model employed in Blagg (1977, 1979) and Blagg and Yule (1984) implicates the school in the aetiology of school phobia.

Framrose (1978) who describes himself as a structural family therapist takes on a much more vigorous active role in therapy. As such his approach overlaps considerably with Warnecke's (1964). Framrose's (1978) emphasis on an immediate return to school, escort system and collaboration with school and other agencies has much in common with Blagg's (1977) rapid behavioural approach. The main therapeutic tasks are seen to centre around actively challenging the child's omnipotence, dealing with very genuine anxiety symptoms, and altering pathological family interaction patterns. Framrose (1978) provides detailed treatment accounts of four cases that fit

Skynner's (1974) description of the more resistant collusive families. The three main treatment elements are:

1. *Active therapeutic intervention* reminiscent of *in vivo* systematic densensitisation to be described in Chapter 3. Framrose describes the need to 'force' some adolescents out of the home and 'escort' them to school so that they come face to face with the feared situation. The quality of the relationship between adolescent and therapist is seen as the key to success. For a short time the adolescent should be 'able to borrow elements of determination and conviction from the therapist'.

2. *Concurrent family work* to bring about the necessary shifts in family functioning. Framrose (1978) suggests that a 'therapeutic trial of confrontation' can be helpful in the first family interview as a way of assessing the family's willingness and ability to change. He illustrates this by referring to 'Brian' a grossly over-protected and over-indulged 15-year-old. His mother dominated the initial interview from the start whilst the father remained silent and detached. Constantly, Brian looked to his mother to answer the therapist's questions and always she obliged. Eventually, Framrose angrily challenged this behaviour. The father woke up and became interested; the mother protested and the boy made a small gesture in self-defence. The boy was then seen on his own and agreed a treatment contract with respect to returning to school. Brian re-entered the family room quite relaxed and both he and his father were thereafter more actively involved in the discussions. By the end of the session unresolved marital issues were aired and subsequently followed up with another therapist. Brian received two individual office interviews; a preparatory school visit and three weeks of diminishing escorting. At six-months follow-up the family had adjusted to Brian's normality. He was leading an active independent social life with no evidence of the previous difficulties.

Framrose (1978) refers to Minuchin's (1970) work in summarising the family changes. The over-close mother-son bond was disrupted by the initial confrontation. The therapist then developed an alliance with the boy creating a temporary boundary between the parents and child allowing the marital relationship to strengthen and normal adaptive adolescent separation to occur.

55

3. *Liaison with other agencies.* In the case of highly collusive families close collaboration with other agencies is essential. Occasionally, external authorities like the courts may need to intervene to reinforce the therapeutic confrontation. In some cases residential education may be necessary in the short-term. Framrose pays relatively little attention to school factors in the aetiology and maintenance of school phobia but does emphasise the importance of 'a preparatory rehearsal' visit to school and the need to establish a 'watertight system of attendance checks'.

In an earlier article Framrose (1977) makes the point frequently stressed by metacognitivists that adolescents are very accessible to therapeutic change. Self-awareness and the general state of adolescent change can be the 'start and subsequent consolidation of maladaptive identity-choices', but on the other hand, 'it can be the beginning of a new and more adaptive adjustment in young adult life'. Success rests heavily upon persistent determination and conviction on the part of the therapist.

Hsia (1984) also argues for a family-systems approach with the main therapeutic aims expressed in similar terms to those outlined by Skynner (1974) and Framrose (1978). Nevertheless, the treatment described incorporates many behavioural elements and once again bears remarkable similarities to the behavioural treatment packages described by Kennedy (1965) and Blagg (1977, 1979, 1981). Hsia (1984) provides a detailed account of the diagnosis and treatment of a 12-year-old girl who had missed many days of schooling the previous year before finally refusing school altogether. She suffered aches and pains without evidence of physical cause and complained of excessive teasing. She was described as overweight and sloppily dressed and highly self-conscious of her glasses with lenses 'as thick as the bottom of a coke bottle'. The girl bargained that she would only go to school in West Virginia where she could live with her paternal grandmother and attend a smaller school with her heavily bespectacled cousins. The therapist hypothesised that the child's continual requests to live with the paternal grand-mother were implicitly encouraged by the mother as they served the important function of enabling the mother to maintain contact with her divorced husband.

Nevertheless, the mother was motivated towards treatment

because of the threat of residential placement. Accordingly, she was receptive to taking control of the situation by addressing and eliminating the grandmother option and reasserting her authority with the child by insisting on immediate return to school. Hsia (1984) states that the mother was helped to 'reframe' her daughter's problems. Thus incapable, helpless behaviour became interpreted as defiant 'school refusal'. Other treatment measures included: contact lens fitting; the mobilisation of the younger sister and older brother to defend their sister against teasing; an organised welcome by classmates, teachers and the school counsellor; and assistance with missed schoolwork. In addition, the mother removed some positive gains for being off school (TV, stereo and the child's bike) and allowed access to them only when the child attended school regularly. Finally, in the early stages of treatment the mother took the child to school by car. After 17 individual therapy sessions over a seven week period, normal school attendance was resumed. At six months follow-up the attendance gains were maintained and the child was reported to be a 'different' girl happily adjusted at school and more agreeable and helpful at home. She wore contact lenses, had lost weight and even experimented with a little make-up.

There were so many treatment elements involved in this case that it is difficult to evaluate the relative contributions of the various aspects. Although the therapeutic approach was theoretically explained in family-system terms, many other factors were attended to outside this frame of reference.

Will and Baird (1984) argue that school phobic families often provoke inter- and intra-professional conflict that mirrors the dysfunctional processes operating in the families. The school phobic is seen as both a victim of separation anxiety and a manipulative omnipotent product of faulty family functioning. Accordingly, the authors argue that it is not surprising these dual characteristics create ambivalence and confusion amongst the therapists and professionals. Will and Baird (1984) present the case for an integrated approach to combat this problem based on appreciating the interplay between: (1) personal characteristics and vulnerabilities of particular professionals; (2) specific familial factors likely to cause discord; and (3) genuine differences of opinion between professionals. A number of behavioural studies including Kennedy (1965) and Blagg and Yule (1984) see the need to consider these same issues, referring to good communications between professionals as a prerequisite to successful treatment. Both Kennedy (1965) and Blagg (1977) argue strongly in favour of one professional taking on responsibility for treatment ensuring that other key workers are kept informed and involved where necessary. In this way families are presented with a consistent co-ordinated approach. In contrast to Will and Baird (1984) both Kennedy (1965) and Blagg (1977, 1979) place as much emphasis on working with the school system as the family system. As Chapters 6, 7 and 8 show, attention to detail at the individual and systems level is crucial.

An interesting paper by Bryce and Baird (1986) outlines a multidisciplinary family therapy approach to school phobia illustrated by samples from the case histories of a series of ten secondary-aged school phobics. The approach outlined has its roots in Skynner's (1974) techniques but uses Will and Wrates (1985) problem-centred style. In common with the majority of family therapy papers, the school system is largely ignored and the role of school factors in the aetiology of school phobia is overlooked. Nevertheless, the authors' emphasis on an immediate return to school and the techniques described to elicit coping strategies in the families overlaps considerably with Blagg and Yule's (1984) approach more fully described in part 2 of this book. Regrettably, Bryce and Baird (1986) do not provide systematic, comprehensive data on the ten cases. Thus it is not possible to compare the effectiveness of their work with the findings from other treatment studies.

DISCUSSIONS AND IMPLICATIONS

At first sight the results from traditional psychotherapy (outpatient or community-based) and family therapy look quite impressive. However, serious shortcomings in information supplied casts doubt on the significance of many of the findings:

1. None of the studies quoted supply explicit behavioural criteria for diagnosing school phobia, making comparisons between treatment studies difficult.
2. Many authors do not clarify whether they are reporting on genuine treatment series or selected treatment samples.
3. Whilst the dynamics of individual cases are often discussed in great detail the systematic data about number of treatment

sessions, duration of treatment, follow-up times, etc. are often omitted.

4. Treatment success has often been judged rather loosely in terms of whether or not the child returns to school without specifying required attendance rates, etc. Furthermore, important details of the child's emotional adjustment and academic performance have been either ignored or not operationalised.

5. Most treatment studies have included a wide age range. However, the majority of studies fail to break down outcome figures by age making it difficult to compare like with like.

6. The majority of studies acknowledge the importance of a range of different practical treatment measures to complement psychotherapy sessions. However, the extent to which such procedures are used is often not fully reported or systematically evaluated.

It is interesting to note the earliest psychodynamic studies favoured 'insight' before confrontation of the feared situations. However, a number of later studies favoured immediate, even forced, return to school, equally well-justified in psychodynamic terms. These latter studies are in general more specific about their treatment groups and more thorough in detailing number and duration of treatment sessions. Furthermore, most managed to achieve long-term follow-ups. In spite of the weaknesses in much of the data, the evidence does suggest that, on balance, approaches favouring a rapid return to school do not produce any adverse effects in the children. Indeed, rapid return treatments seem at least as effective but far quicker than delayed return treatments.

Family therapy studies add further weight to these arguments even when considering older more disturbed cases. The very process of confrontation is seen to be beneficial to family functioning provided it is properly handled. Increasingly, attention is being directed towards making explicit the many subtle procedures involved in engineering and managing the confrontation. The focus is on the 'here and now' of family interactions although the significance of school and community factors is gaining recognition. In many ways structural and strategic approaches to treatment have much in common with comprehensive behavioural packages emphasising immediate return to school.

Traditional psychodynamic studies involving hospitalisation suffer for many of the methodological problems outlined above although the majority have recorded treatment duration and achieved long-term follow-ups. Treatment outcome figures for hospitalised cases seem generally worse than for out-patient or community-based psychodynamic treatments except for Barker's (1968) study dealing exclusively with younger children. Hospitalisation is a rather extreme and expensive treatment measure normally justified by the fact that community based or out-patient treatment has failed or is unlikely to work. In theory it might be anticipated that hospitalised school phobics would be generally more disturbed and difficult to treat than non-hospitalised cases. If this were the case it would explain the poorer outcome figures for hospitalised treatment samples. However, in the absence of explicit behavioural criteria defining cases selected for treatment this must remain a moot point. Blagg and Yule's (1984) comparative treatment study reported in Chapter 4 sheds some light on this matter.

3

Behavioural Approaches to the Treatment of School Phobia

INTRODUCTION

This chapter will review the ever-expanding literature on the behavioural treatment of school phobia. The majority of evidence in support of the use of behavioural approaches has stemmed from single case studies. A review by Berecz (1968) found that up until then behavioural studies were over-simplistic 'one-shot attempts to prove the effectiveness of certain techniques'. Early studies inspired by the work of Wolpe (1954, 1958) and Lazarus (1960) were mainly concerned with the application of systematic desensitisation procedures to young children. Since then a wide range of techniques arising out of both classical and operant paradigms have been developed and applied to both young children and adolescents.

As Yule (1977) has pointed out, sound behavioural work encompasses a problem-solving approach to therapy. The presenting difficulties are objectively described and clarified; hypotheses proposed to account for observations; and clear deliberate therapeutic interventions introduced, tested and evaluated. More recent studies have placed increasing emphasis on treatment strategies that draw upon a range of behavioural techniques and principles in order to deal with an extensive range of child, family and school related issues (Kennedy, 1965; Hersov, 1977; Blagg, 1977, 1979; Yule, Hersov and Treseder, 1980; Phillips and Wolpe, 1981; Blagg and Yule, 1984).

Nevertheless, although the behavioural art has become increasingly sophisticated, the literature continues to be dominated by 'one-shot' single case studies with just two papers reporting behavioural treatment series (Kennedy, 1965; Blagg

61

and Yule, 1984). Thus relatively little attention has been paid to the comparative efficacy of the many different behavioural techniques currently employed. Indeed, there have been no formal research investigations of this area. Furthermore, the current trend towards comprehensive behavioural management utilising a mix of approaches makes it difficult to evaluate the significance of the various aspects of treatment. The question of the relative merits of behavioural and psychodynamic approaches in the treatment of school phobia will be dealt with in Chapter 4.

In the interests of clarity, the literature review will be categorised into four sections according to the rationales underlying the treatment approaches:

    a. treatments based on the classical conditioning paradigm;
    b. treatments based on the operant conditioning paradigm;
    c. treatments based on social skills training; and
    d. mixed treatment approaches that include techniques from both classical and operant conditioning paradigms.

A final section will discuss the key issues and implications of the research carried out to date.

TREATMENTS BASED ON THE CLASSICAL CONDITIONING PARADIGM

The basic assumption underlying classical conditioning is that some form of anxiety is responsible for school phobia. The major treatment techniques developed from this model include: systematic desensitisation, emotive imagery, flooding and implosion.

Systematic desensitisation

This approach involves working the child through a carefully graded fear hierarchy starting with the least feared situations, building up to most feared situations. At each stage the child is helped to overcome any anxiety by concentrating on a behaviour that is antagonistic (i.e. reciprocally inhibiting) to the anxiety (Wolpe, 1958). The approach is highly dependent on skillful analysis and clarification of the anxiety-provoking circumstances involved in the school phobia. In reality, many children find it hard to put their worries and fears into words so that the therapist needs to rely on a combination of teacher and parent reports together with careful observation of bodily changes in the child when questioned on potentially sensitive areas.

The earliest reported behavioural treatment of a school phobic (Lazarus, 1960) provides a vivid example of systematic desensitisation (in imagination). The case considered is that of a previously well-adjusted nine-and-a-half-year-old girl who suddenly developed school phobia with associated stomach pains, night terrors and enuresis following three closely spaced traumatic events. A school friend drowned, a second friend died of meningitis and the child also witnessed a motor accident in which a man was killed. It was established that the primary problem was the child's fear of losing her mother. A seven-item hierarchy related to lengthening separation experiences was worked through in imagination with each stage being paired with muscle relaxation. The child returned willingly to school after 10 days and the night terrors and enuresis soon disappeared. Apart from occasional incidents of bedwetting, the therapeutic gains were maintained over a 15 month period. No details were given of the child's attendance figures, academic progress and overall social adjustment. There was no reference to the role of school staff in treatment.

Chapel (1967) describes how systematic desensitisation (in imagination) was also applied to a case where separation anxiety was seen as the main feature. Relaxation at each stage of the hierarchy was achieved through hypnosis. Prior treatment involving individual psychotherapy had not met with success. Eventually, the boy was placed in a hospital day ward school. This resulted in further distress and anxiety which was treated via daily 30 minute sessions of hypnosis. A week later when the boy was more relaxed, treatment started on his separation fears via graded exposure to hierarchies relating to distance from home, travelling to school and arriving home to find his parents out. Eighteen 20–30 minute desensitisation sessions over a six week period enabled the boy to return to school although unspecified out-patient treatment continued for the rest of the academic year. The school phobic symptoms recurred with a change of class at the start of a new year after a long summer holiday. A further 15 sessions were required to overcome the problem.

Thereafter the boy attended school freely although he remained timid and shy with his peers. This study points out the need for vigilance after a holiday period, especially where a change of class is involved. The treatment approach is not that clear-cut. Although the paper focused on the desensitisation aspects, it is possible that 'flooding' played a significant role as the boy was forced to stay at school throughout the day.

A more recent paper by Croghan (1981) also reports on the successful application of systematic desensitisation (in imagination). A 17-year-old boy who had been phobic for five years was initially treated by desensitising to current worries and issues like preparing for school in the mornings. Later Croghan discovered that the boy still harboured painful memories of a major 'show down' with two boys five years earlier. Apparently, the subject had refused to fight feeling outnumbered. In view of this the boy was desensitised to this incident through a series of 12 sessions. Alongside the desensitisation sessions, the boy was helped to restructure the incident and view it as an intelligent, reasonable response rather than a cowardly act. The treatment gains were fully maintained at a one year follow-up.

Croghan's (1981) paper raises an important diagnostic point. In cases where the child has been out of school for a prolonged period, the initial precipitating issues are often buried and difficult to uncover. Sometimes anxiety over the initial problem will have waned with other secondary issues being the main obstacle to treatment. On the other hand, the original precipitant may still be a major concern. It is always important to systematically explore the events leading up to the school phobic episode even if they were a long time ago. With respect to the treatment approach it is worth noting that the desensitisation sessions relating to painful memories were not graded in difficulty and not paired with relaxation, thus departing somewhat from the traditional reciprocal inhibition paradigm. The discussion and restructuring of the boy's row could be interpreted in cognitive behaviour therapy terms.

A number of studies have combined desensitisation treatments involving both real life (*in vivo*) and imagined situations (Scherman and Grover, 1962; Eysenck and Rachman, 1965; Miller, 1972). Scherman and Grover (1962) describe the case of a verbally bright, tense, ten-year-old boy whose school phobia was precipitated by a genuine illness. The boy was trained in a simplified form of relaxation which was to be practised at home whenever he felt anxious. He was initially excused school for a few days and told that he would be returned in easy stages. An eight stage hierarchy was worked through *in vivo* with each stage in the hierarchy followed by a relaxation and discussion session in the clinic. The boy returned to full-time school attendance without protest in six weeks. No other treatment outcome details were supplied and no follow-up was reported.

A similar approach was adopted by Eysenck and Rachman (1965). They treated a 13-year-old boy who had been off school for almost a year. School refusal had been precipitated by a number of unfortunate incidents coinciding with a change from primary to secondary schooling. The boy had been unable to attend school for the first four days of term because of toothache. On the fifth day he was injured on the games field losing two teeth. As well as refusing school he also refused to attend at out-patients and was therefore hospitalised for treatment. Initially he was able to attend his school from the ward, however, the attendance soon broke down. An *in vivo* desensitisation programme was started in the mornings backed up by desensitisation sessions involving imagined scenes combined with relaxation training in the afternoons. By the ninth day of treatment he was able to go to school alone and remain there for almost a whole day. The boy was discharged after two weeks but readmitted for one week's 'top up' treatment just before the beginning of the new term. He experienced a slight relapse after two months of regular attendance, requiring further treatment, but attended well for the next three months.

This case provides an interesting example of behavioural treatment involving hospitalisation. The decision to hospitalise seems to be based more on therapist need and convenience than clinical necessity. Presumably, in-patient treatment was easier to administer than a series of home visits. It would have been interesting to know how this was explained to the parents and grandparents and how they reacted to it. In some ways hospitalisation runs counter to a learning theory interpretation implicitly communicating that the child is 'sick' in the medical sense. It also makes parental involvement in treatment more difficult to engineer.

In a much later paper, Miller (1972) also reports on the combined use of *in vivo* and imaginal systematic desensitisation. A ten-year-old boy with numerous problems including separation anxiety, death phobia, school phobia, sleep difficulties and enuresis was treated via multiple hierarchies constructed to deal with various symptoms. Training in muscle relaxation was enhanced by positively reinforcing appropriate responses using sweets and verbal praise. Visual imagery was employed to desensitise the child to separation experiences and prepare him for a return to school. Sleep difficulties resulting from death fears were handled by encouraging the child to ring the therapist when necessary whereupon muscle relaxation was induced over the telephone. The enuresis gradually disappeared even though it was not specifically treated. Finally, desensitisation *in vivo* was used in effecting a return to full-time school attendance. The boy was expected to spend increasingly longer periods of time near and eventually in school. Follow-up at three months and 18 months showed that he was still attending school regularly. The early improvement that had been noted in the school grades was also maintained and no new problems had emerged.

There are some drawbacks to systematic desensitisation using imagined scenes. The technicalities of the approach effectively minimise the role of the parents and school in treatment placing the responsibility for success firmly in the hands of the therapist. Treatment can be quite a lengthy process making enormous demands on therapist time. In addition, desensitisation (in imagination) sometimes does not work, as described later in the paper by Tahmisian and McReynolds (1971). Lazarus (1960) has commented that some children show 'poor visual imagery' so that real life situations need to be used. Yule (1977) points out that it can be difficult to find any behaviour that is both reciprocally inhibiting (antagonistic to anxiety) and easily controlled by the child at the therapist's request. Some children do not seem to experience anxiety in response to imagined stimuli whilst other children do not easily learn relaxation techniques. Whether these problems reflect fundamental skill weaknesses in the child or inadequate therapist skills is debatable (Yule, Hersov and Treseder, 1980). Desensitisation sessions in real life do at least overcome the problems associated with poor visualisation and do perhaps offer more scope for parental involvement.

Papers by Garvey and Hegrenes (1966) and Olsen and Coleman (1967) cite examples of the effective use of systematic desensitisation (*in vivo*). Both studies utilise the therapeutic relationship as the means of reciprocally inhibiting the anxiety responses and both studies actively involve the father in treatment.

Garvey and Hegrenes (1966) describe the case of Jimmy, a ten-year-old school phobic who had failed to respond to six months traditional psychotherapy. He was a sensitive boy with a high level of aspiration. His school phobia had been triggered by a chest infection but the long absence from school had created secondary problems including avoiding friends and peers. Jimmy was worked through a carefully graded fear hierarchy on 20 consecutive days with each session lasting 20–40 minutes. On the twentieth day, the therapist was replaced by the father. The boy quickly adjusted to being in the classroom with the other children present. Progress was fully maintained over a two year follow-up period.

In vivo treatments lend themselves more easily to the involvement of the school in treatment. On the other hand, they can also create the problem of highlighting the school phobic's plight. If other children see the anxious child coming and going each morning it could easily lead to further embarrassment and worry. In Jimmy's case this issue was dealt with by having him arrive at school early *before* the other children arrived. These authors were also ingenious in ensuring that some form of progress was made each day in spite of set backs. Thus when Jimmy felt unable to go nearer the school, he was instead asked to remain at the same spot for longer than on the previous occasion. Garvey and Hegrenes (1966) emphasise that it is important not to push the child through the fear hierarchy too quickly. They suggest that it is common for the child to suddenly feel confident and want to tackle more than the agreed stage. In such cases, children should be helped to be more realistic and take things steadily. Although these authors conceptualise their treatment as *in vivo* systematic desensitisation the approach does, nevertheless, resemble 'shaping', based on the operant conditioning paradigm. This issue will be discussed in more detail in the section dealing with mixed approaches utilising both classical and operant conditioning techniques.

Olsen and Coleman (1967) treated a six-year-old boy whose school phobia was a function of separation anxiety. He refused to stay in the class without a member of his family being there. The father, who was somewhat ineffectual was encouraged to take on a major therapeutic role. He took his son to a clinic for desensitisation sessions involving lengthening separation experiences.

The boy was eventually able to walk off with the psychologist for 30 minutes. On the first day back at school he was accompanied by the psychologist who remained in the classroom for the first 20 minutes. There were no further problems subsequently.

Emotive imagery

Emotive imagery is a technique that some behaviour therapists have found to be a powerful alternative to normal relaxation procedures used in conjunction with systematic desensitisation. In this approach the therapist develops imagined scenes that conjure up feelings of excitement, self-assertion and general 'positive effect' as a means of inhibiting anxiety.

An interesting paper by Lazarus and Abramovitz (1962) illustrates this procedure. They report on an eight-year-old girl who had developed enuresis and a phobic avoidance of school following a series of emotional upsets in class. A hierarchy of feared school situations was created in which the Enid Blyton character Noddy was placed. The child was asked to protect and actively reassure Noddy helping him overcome his fear. The treatment was highly successful. The child returned to school after only four sessions. The enuresis disappeared within two months although it was not specifically treated. The authors comment that the child continued to improve. However, no long term follow-up is stated and no reference is made to the child's scholastic progress and overall social adjustment.

A later case study reported by Van der Ploeg (1975) makes use of emotive imagery in addition to traditional systematic desensitisation with relaxation. The author details the treatment of a fourteen-year-old boy with school phobia and associated urinary frequency problems. The boy was trained in deep relaxation and systematically desensitised imaginally using both relaxation and stories of sailing experiences designed to create powerful emotive images. Following 15 office sessions, the treatment shifted into an *in vivo* mode involving increasing exposure to school. One month later the school phobia was overcome and the urinary frequency symptoms had disappeared. Follow-up at 18 months indicated that the treatment gains were maintained. Once again this study demonstrates how related symptoms can improve with the systematic desensitisation of another symptom.

A further instance of this phonomenom is given in a report by

Galloway and Miller (1978). They report on the classic case of an eleven-year-old boy who regularly refused school on certain mornings. He seemed a vulnerable unpopular boy with a weak mother. Diagnostic interviews revealed that he feared showering in public and thus he avoided school on games days. The problem was quickly treated by systematic desensitisation using imagined shower scenes followed up by *in vivo* desensitisation activities. The problem was overcome in four 40-minute and three 15-minute sessions. The boy no longer feared showering after games and the attendance pattern normalised.

Flooding or implosion

These procedures involve immediate confrontation of the maximally feared situation without any careful preparation via graded exposure to less threatening circumstances. The subject is maintained in the intense feared situation until the anxiety shows visible signs of waning on the classical extinction model (Stampfl, 1967, 1968; Stampfl and Levis, 1967; Levis, 1967). The assumption here is that if the subject feels anxiety as a result of prior classical conditioning the vivid presentation of the conditioned stimuli (CS) in the absence of any primary aversive stimulus (UCS) will eventually lead to the extinction of the anxiety response. Flooding normally refers to a direct *in vivo* approach as in Kennedy (1965), Rines (1973), Blagg (1979) and Blagg and Yule (1984). Implosive therapy carries out the confrontation in the client's imagination, vividly exaggerating the individual's worst fears.

The latter approach is exemplified in a paper by Smith and Sharpe (1970). These authors argue that implosive treatment in imagination is preferable to flooding as it avoids the possibility of the child being ridiculed by peers for demonstrating anxiety in class. They present the case of a thirteen-year-old boy who had been refusing school for 60 days. He was quite unable to say why he was anxious. The therapist asked him to visualise and describe in great detail a typical school day. By observing body posture, tone of voice and other physiological signs it was possible to deduce that fear of failure in mathematics and literature classes was the main source of anxiety. In particular he was especially anxious at the thought of 'being called in class; being unable to correctly answer the teacher's questions; and anticipating being

69

made fun of by his teacher and classmates'. Treatment consisted of the boy holding in imagination highly threatening scenes involving returning to school facing derision and ridicule from teachers and pupils. There was no escape for the boy. The mother was described as 'cold and rejecting, grim and silent'; the school Principal as 'leering' with a 'sadistic tone of voice'. The literature classroom scene was presented thus:

> The room is dark and strange and the chairs have been pushed to the sides of the room. Students begin silently filing into the room. It is too dark to identify them. Tension grows as Billy wonders what will happen. The students encircle him, pressing ever closer and begin to murmur 'Crazy Billy' and 'stupid, stupid, stupid'. They then begin to jostle and strike him.

The approach produced very rapid results. Billy received six consecutive daily sessions of implosive therapy. After the first session he was able to attend the maths class the next day. By the fourth session he was attending school full time. A follow-up 13 weeks later showed that he was still attending school regularly, achieving better grades in his schoolwork and enjoying improved social relationships.

This study raises a number of interesting points. The need for careful behavioural analysis is emphasised in order to isolate the main areas of concern. In addition, the authors stress the importance of gaining the *total* cooperation of the parents and school staff. In this connection, the therapists went to some lengths to explain the principles of treatment to the parents. They also gave them a written description of implosive therapy to read at home. Although understandably hesitant, the parents quickly grasped the principles and were eventually highly motivated towards the treatment approach. The parents were seen on a daily basis separate from the child and frequent long distance phone calls were made to the school Principal and Billy's teachers. As in many other studies the treatment regime is less tightly defined than is implied in the write up. Although the imagined implosion was intense, the introduction to school was graded into four stages. In addition, operant factors may have been more important than the authors suggest. The parents were urged to remove secondary gains at home for being off school (like watching TV and going to bed late) and the school staff were advised on contingency management.

Direct confrontation of maximal fears in real life (flooding) is a highly demanding and often stressful treatment. Parents and teachers naturally need a lot of convincing that forced confrontation is the best way ahead and many practical management issues need careful consideration. If mishandled, flooding can easily backfire on the therapist resulting in an even more anxious child and unco-operative parents. The process of classical extinction often means a temporary worsening of the problem before it begins to wane. Giving up treatment in the face of more anxiety could 'shape up' the problem by effectively reinforcing protest behaviour. For these and many other reasons, flooding has often been reported as one part of a more complicated treatment package. In view of this, studies by Kennedy (1965), Rines (1973), Blagg (1979) and Blagg and Yule (1984) will be reported later in the section dealing with mixed treatment approaches.

TREATMENTS BASED ON THE OPERANT CONDITIONING PARADIGM

Operant-based treatment approaches are concerned with changing the reinforcement contingencies affecting an individual's behaviour. In the treatment of school phobia this essentially involves: 1. maximising the incentives for being in school by building into the school programme extra positive reinforcements; and 2. minimising incentives for remaining at home during the school day by removing positive reinforcements (like greater personal freedom, extra adult attention). In order to encourage greater likelihood of the generalisation and maintenance of treatment gains, natural reinforcers in the individual's life are reorganised and rescheduled in preference to the introduction of more artificial reinforcers like sweets. Nevertheless, in certain cases, tangible reinforcers may be necessary in the early stages of the treatment programme.

In view of these considerations, operant approaches naturally involve parents and school personnel in treatment. Frequently, a 'shaping' procedure is used in which the child is introduced to schooling through a series of graded approximations eventually building up to full time attendance. The focus of treatment centres on reinforcing the child for each step taken towards normal school attendance. The operant approach does not assume that anxiety has caused the school phobia and thus, although the approach is reminiscent of *in vivo* systematic desensitisation, no formal fear hierarchies are established and the child is not trained in relaxation procedures.

The operant approach is particularly well illustrated by Ayllon, Smith and Rogers (1970) who provide one of the most detailed accounts in the literature of the behavioural analysis and treatment of a school phobic. They describe the case of an eight-year-old girl who had shown a gradual onset of school phobia. Eventually any attempts to take the child to school resulted in severe temper tantrums with screaming and crying fits. Traditional styles of questioning and diagnostic work failed to reveal any relevant information that would guide treatment. In view of this the therapists observed the child at home over 13 days and noted that she was being strongly reinforced for staying off school. She appeared to enjoy a very close relationship with her mother. She always tried to follow her to work but ended up staying with an undemanding neighbour each day.

The treatment plan ultimately involved four distinct procedures: 1. prompting and shaping of school attendance; 2. removal of pleasant social consequences for not attending school; 3. the development of a home-based motivational system; and 4. the production of aversive consequences in the mother whenever the child stayed at home.

Initially, a graded return plan was formulated. After playing with school materials at the neighbour's house the child was subsequently taken to school each day by the therapist or therapist's assistant. The approach was reminiscent of systematic desensitisation (*in vivo*) in that the child was obliged to spend increasingly longer periods of time in school each day starting with the last hour of the day. Gradually the child was taken to school earlier and earlier spending progressively longer periods in school. The backward chaining approach allowed natural contingencies like home time to reinforce school attendance. Primary reinforcers in the form of sweets were also utilised as added incentives. By the seventh day she was able to stay at school without the support of the therapist, however she was still unwilling to dress herself in the mornings and go to school voluntarily. When the pressure was taken off for five days she did not attend school.

At this stage, it was realised that the child was being reinforced by the individual attention from the mother after the siblings had gone to school. Accordingly, it was arranged for the mother to leave for work at the same time as the other children left the house. Nevertheless, even though a significant reward for remaining at home had been removed the child still refused school for a further ten days, spending each day at the neighbour's house.

The home-based motivational system was now introduced. The mother was given a large chart and all of the children were put on a star system. Each star was earned by going to school voluntarily for one day. Five consecutive stars signified perfect attendance for one week and resulted in a special treat (sweets). Although the attendance improved, the child was still not fully established in a normal school attendance routine.

The therapist now put more pressure on the mother by expecting her to leave 10 minutes before the children. If they arrived within 15 minutes of the mother they earned their star. If not the mother was greatly inconvenienced by having to walk back home (one mile) and then bring the child to school. This was necessary on only two occasions. In the second instance the mother was clearly very irritated and literally pushed the girl to school denying her the opportunity to discuss the matter or offer an explanation.

Normal attendance was resumed thereafter and maintained when the star system was faded out after one month. A follow-up nine months later showed no evidence of symptom substitution; the child's attendance was excellent and her schoolwork and social behaviour had shown a dramatic improvement.

This study has been reported in considerable detail as it shows how the treatment intervention was developed, tested and adapted to the needs of the case. Although the treatment can be construed in operant terms, it can also be interpreted within the classical conditioning paradigm. It could be argued that the therapist acted as a desensitiser in the 'shaping' procedure and that treatment was finally effected by 'flooding'. The child was finally forced to attend school and probably did not dare risk the mother's wrath thereafter. The report does highlight the crucial importance of assessing the parent's motivation to resolve the problem at the outset. In this case, the mother was ultimately provoked into a more committed stance by being in effect punished for the child's poor attendance. One wonders whether treatment would have been more efficient if the mother had been obliged to take a more forceful stance in the very early stages. This issue is discussed more fully in Chapter 5.

An earlier study by Hersen (1968) places so much emphasis on the parent's role in maintaining the school refusal pattern that treatment was directed entirely towards the mother. Hersen (1968) describes the case of a twelve-year-old boy who showed irregular school attendance with accompanying complaints like dizziness, headaches, colds, etc. The mother was trained in contingency management over ten one-hour sessions spread over ten weeks. During these sessions the mother was helped to recognise and alter her pattern of reinforcements. Initially, she was extremely resistant to change and very anxious that she might accidentally send the boy to school when he was genuinely ill. This problem was overcome by telling the mother to keep the child off school only if his temperature rose above 100°F. Six months later the mother reported that her son's attendance was normal and physical complaints rare. The boy was also noted to be more assertive and independent.

In a later paper Hersen (1970a) outlines a more elaborate treatment approach in dealing with Bruce, a twelve-and-a-half-year-old school phobic. The boy's five elder siblings had also shown a history of attendance difficulties creating a well-established familial pattern. Unfortunately, the school counsellor had unwittingly reinforced the boy's problems by allowing him to stay in his office whenever he cried in class.

On this occasion the mother was trained in contingency management over 15 half-hour weekly sessions. Over the same period the boy was seen independently for 15 individual sessions in which coping behaviours were verbally reinforced and inappropriate behaviours like crying were extinguished via planned ignoring. Bruce was also given the opportunity to vent hostile feelings. In addition to this the school counsellor was warned against reinforcing dependent and avoidance behaviour. He was directed to be supportive but firm in returning the child to class within a maximum time of five minutes. Resistance to the behavioural approach on the part of the mother was dealt with by giving her a simplified lecture on operant principles.

The tripartite treatment programme eliminated the school avoidance behaviour in 15 weeks. Follow-up, six months later showed that attendance was normal and 'previous forms of deviant behaviour remained extinguished, academically the previous year Bruce had earned above average grades'. In two later publications Hersen (1970b, 1971a) further explores the problem of resistance to behaviour treatment.

The importance of involving both parents in treatment was stressed by Doleys and Williams (1977). The mother and father were trained in contingency management and the boy was introduced back into school via a 'shaping' procedure. Inappropriate behaviour in school was dealt with by summoning both parents who punished the child by placing him in a small room until he was willing to go back to class. Treatment was effected within three weeks. A follow-up four months later confirmed satisfactory academic performance and attendance. Once again, although treatment was reported from an operant viewpoint, it seems likely that incidental desensitisation accompanied the 'shaping' procedure and extinction occurred as a result of forced school attendance.

Several studies have demonstrated the usefulness of contingency contracting (Cantrell, Cantrell, Huddleston and Woolridge, 1969; Welch and Carpenter, 1970; Vaal, 1973). This approach involves the careful selection of reinforcers and punishers. A tightly defined behavioural contract is developed and agreed upon between the child and other appropriate parties.

Cantrell *et al.* (1969) highlighted the great detail necessary in specifying steps leading towards the target behaviour of full-time school attendance in a school phobic girl of unspecified age. Rewards were made contingent on the achievement of each step. A return to full-time schooling was managed in eight treatment sessions. Progress was maintained over more than one year.

A similar sequential approach was adopted by Welch and Carpenter (1970) in the treatment of an eight-year-old school-phobic boy. Following an interview with the mother in which careful consideration was given to available punishers and reinforcers a detailed contract was formulated and progress was carefully recorded. The treatment was entirely implemented by the parents. Treatment was very successful. The boy returned to school the next day and the programme was stopped after three weeks. No follow-up was reported. This case is surprising in that the boy was not interviewed by the therapist even at the diagnostic stage.

Vaal (1973) employed a similar contract with a thirteen-year-old boy who had not responded to traditional psychotherapy. He had been absent from school for six months. Three targets were set: a. attend school without tantrums; b. go to all classes; c. remain in school until the appropriate time. Activity reinforcers (basketball, bowling and visiting) were made contingent on the achievement of these goals. One hundred per cent attendance was managed immediately the contract was set up. Excellent attendance was maintained for the next three months and continued after the summer holiday. The contract was only in force for six weeks.

King (1987) comments that antecedent stimulus control has been largely ignored in the operant management of school phobia. Certainly the majority of case studies report on the consequent reinforcement of desired behaviours. However, Blagg (1977) in a short paper on the rapid treatment of school phobia does comment on the importance of contingency management of antecedents as well as consequences. Thus he stresses the importance of the parents modelling 'calm, firm behaviour' and avoiding long circuitous discussions about the pros and cons of school attendance. These issues will be returned to in more detail in Chapter 7.

More particularly, King (1987) argues that in some cases school phobia can be regarded in part as a failure to comply with parental instructions over school attendance. This seems a particularly pertinent point with respect to those school phobics who are omnipotent with ineffectual parents. In such instances, the parents may need help in the nature and quality of their instructions. King (1987) suggests that Forehand's (1979) parent training model may be very helpful here. Attention is paid to issues like: the need to gain the child's attention; the importance of firmness of voice; the avoidance of long chains of instructions and too many explanations accompanying commands. Improved command-giving can be trained through structured learning situations involving modelling, performance feedback and behaviour rehearsal.

TREATMENTS BASED ON SOCIAL SKILLS TRAINING

Many schools phobics have quite major problems in relationships with both peers and teachers. Chapter 5 makes clear that whilst some children may need sheltering from ridicule and unfair demands, others need help in improving their coping skills. Close behavioural analysis often reveals significant social skills deficits. As King (1987) points out, it is surprising that in spite of a growing body of research on social skills training, there is little evidence of its application in the treatment of school phobia. A recent paper by Esveldt-Dawson, Wisner, Unis, Matson and Kazdin (1982) may be the first to redress the balance.

These authors provide a fascinating account of a twelve-year-old girl treated for school phobia and extreme fear of unfamiliar males. The child suffered multiple somatic complaints and limited interaction with peers. She was hospitalised in a psychiatric unit. Very detailed assessments were taken noting the fine minutiae of avoidance behaviours and the absence of appropriate 'prosocial approach responses'. Treatment involved attention to many areas including:

1. body posture especially the subject's stiffness and lack of mobility in the trunk and limbs;
2. nervous mannerisms such as giggling, facial grimacing, tone of voice;
3. eye contact;
4. appropriate emotional affect in social interactions; and
5. the verbal content of messages and responses.

Training involved 'participant modelling' as suggested by Bandura (1969) and Mateson (1981). The subject was required to act out the same ten role-play situations in each of the treatment sessions. Role play was preceded by a five minute general chat on phobias and how the training programme could help. The therapist then modelled the appropriate behaviours before asking the child to act out the scene. The child was socially reinforced for progress and specific advice given on areas needing improvement with further modelling where necessary. The whole scene was then rehearsed. The next scene was then introduced with treatment following a similar pattern until all ten scenes had been worked through. Twenty-four treatment sessions produced rapid improvements in a multiple baseline design. Treatment gains were fully maintained at 7 week and 21 week follow-ups. The child was attending school quite happily and performing well. There had been a marked improvement in her social skills. She was interacting more normally with her peers and had been appropriately assertive with a stranger. Social skills improvements had generalised beyond the school to other everyday situations.

MIXED TREATMENT APPROACHES THAT INCLUDE TECHNIQUES FROM BOTH CLASSICAL AND OPERANT CONDITIONING PARADIGMS

Many of the studies reported so far implicitly involve a mixture of treatment techniques whilst explicitly referring to only one or two approaches. Whilst the theoretical underpinnings to the operant and classical conditioning paradigms are fundamentally different, the treatments derived from these models often overlap. This section will report on those studies that openly acknowledge the combined involvement of quite different treatment elements in the effective management of particular cases.

Patterson (1965) was the first behaviour therapist to acknowledge the importance of selecting principles from a variety of learning theories in order to suit the needs of the individual case. Procedures derived from both classical and operant paradigms were employed in the treatment of a seven-year-old boy refusing school because of separation anxiety. The boy's anxiety was so severe that he was unwilling to leave his mother in the clinic even for a few minutes. Using Skinnerian principles (Skinner, 1953) Patterson 'shaped' the child's behaviour towards greater independence from the mother. Successive approximations to the target independent behaviour were reinforced tangibly in the form of M and Ms. and paired with verbal reinforcement. (M and Ms. were employed because initial behavioural testing revealed that the boy was relatively unresponsive to social reinforcers). A form of systematic desensitisation (imaginal) was then introduced, supported theoretically by reference to Guthrie's concept of interference. A graded series of separation situations were acted out with dolls centering around a character named 'Little Henry'. The child was asked how Little Henry felt in the various situations. Assertive, independent responses were reinforced through M and Ms. and praise. On the eleventh session, systematic desensitisation (*in vivo*) was implemented and backed up by clinic sessions. Each day the child was taken to school by the therapist and left alone in school for increasingly long periods. Each *in vivo* session was followed by conditioning sequences in the clinic playroom. The parents had been trained to selectively reinforce coping behaviours. By session 23 the boy had returned to full-time schooling. A repeat of the initial behavioural testing demonstrated that the boy's behaviour was 'now under the control of social reinforcers dispensed by a wide variety of social agents'. A follow-up three months later showed a marked improvement in general adjustment.

Lazarus, Davidson and Polefka (1965) deliberately set out to demonstrate the value of using both classical and operant conditioning procedures at different stages in the treatment of a nine-year-old boy with a long history of unresolved separation anxiety in school situations. A series of additive stresses finally precipitated the school phobia. The boy underwent a serious operation with complications and post-operative pain; he witnessed a drowning and then at the start of fourth grade was distressed by the death of a close friend of his sister.

The study is particularly interesting in that the authors recognise and attempt to resolve the inherent conflicts in using classical and/or operant procedures. Systematic desensitisation (imaginal) was tried and abandoned because of the boy's 'inarticulateness and acquiescent response tendency'. Apparently, he was more concerned with earning therapist approval than describing his true feelings. Desensitisation in real life was, therefore, implemented. Distraction, humour, relaxation, coaxing, encouragement and emotive imagery were all used as desensitisation agents. A mild tranquilliser was also prescribed by the family doctor to reduce anticipatory anxiety first thing in the morning. Attempts were made to make school more attractive (by giving the boy special jobs), and being out of school less desirable (by not allowing him in the house during school hours).

Beyond step 15 the boy appeared minimally anxious and accordingly an operant strategy was employed to secure school attendance independent of a therapist. A comic book and tokens (to be later exchanged for a baseball glove) were given contingent on the child returning to full-time schooling. However, it was still necessary for the therapist to be on the school premises even though out of sight. Eventually, the mother discussed the reality of the situation with the boy, emphasising that school attendance was compulsory and would be enforced if necessary by agents beyond her control. This enabled the therapist to withdraw. Three weeks later tangible reinforcers were no longer necessary. A ten-month follow-up revealed that Paul had maintained his gains and made further progress.

The theoretical implications in this study are worth considering in detail, as they apply to many of the other behavioural studies. Viewed in operant terms, (*in vivo*) systematic desensiti- sation sessions may be actively reinforcing dependent behaviour and strengthening avoidance responses by allowing the child to return home after the arousal of anxiety during each treatment session. Furthermore, the special attention and support given over such a long period may have highlighted the child's difficulties in the eyes of his friends, possibly strengthening avoidance responses to peers. Finally, the adjunctive use of drugs may have reinforced the view that the child was 'sick' and in need of very special treatment.

However, the authors argue that an operant approach in which attention is withheld until the child returns to the classroom might be therapeutically disadvantageous if one views the problem within a classical conditioning paradigm. Premature exposure to the maximally feared situation could lead to an increase in anxiety and consequent strengthening of the avoidance response if escape is possible. On the other hand, the authors do not point out that if the escape route is effectively blocked and the child is held in the fear-provoking situation, desensitisation should occur through a process of extinction. If operant procedures were then implemented to reinforce regular attendance, the classical and operant approaches would not be in conflict. Instead, the authors propose that the level of anxiety as judged by the therapist should determine which strategy should be employed. They suggest that high levels of anxiety indicate the need for desensitisation whereas low levels of anxiety call for the use of operant procedures. However, apart from the fact that this line of reasoning does not resolve the inherent conflicts in the treatment procedures, it raises the further problem of how the therapist should judge the level of anxiety. As Lang (1970) has demonstrated, observed levels of anxiety do not necessarily correlate with subjective self reports and physiological measures. It is not always easy for the therapist to distinguish between genuine fear responses specific to leaving home or going to school from long-standing operant-derived tyrannical and tantrum behaviour that can be produced whenever the child's wishes are thwarted.

This study took up an inordinate amount of therapist time. Furthermore, in the end it was necessary to threaten the boy with the consequences of not coping alone with regular school atten- dance before the therapist could withdraw. Clearly the model proposed by the authors for deciding on the maximally effective treatment approach at any particular time has yet to be demonstrated more convincingly.

Tahmisian and McReynolds (1971) present the case of a thirteen-year-old girl with separation anxiety triggered by attendance at a summer camp. A twelve step desensitisation hierarchy involving imagined scenes was completed. However, the child made no progress towards returning to school. It was noted that the parents constantly gave in to her when she was upset. In view of this the parents were given a major therapeutic role and systematic desensitisation *in vivo* was employed. The parents took the child through a 15 step hierarchy. Contingency management was also acknowledged as an important feature in treatment. Co-operative behaviour was rewarded and there was no giving in to the child's protests. After three weeks regular school attendance was resumed and maintained at a four-week follow-up. There were no long term follow-ups reported.

Yule, Hersov and Treseder (1980) in their review of behavioural treatments, selected six cases to illustrate their own treatment style. The authors work in a teaching hospital setting and many of the cases seen are dealt with by students under supervision. The cases chosen for discussion were not a treatment series, nor even a random selection from those cases seen during a given period. Instead, the authors chose cases that raised some of the issues and problems involved in treatment.

The case histories clearly demonstrated the common themes associated with school phobics, whilst also emphasising the uniqueness of each case. Like Blagg (1977) the authors place great importance on thorough, wide-ranging diagnostic work. Cases are treated as quickly as possible. Assessment work includes close attention to: the history of the problem; family structure and way of life; and the intellectual and personality assessment of the child. As far as possible, both parents are given a principal role in treatment and much effort goes into helping the parents to understand the rationale and reasons for each treatment step. The authors are eclectic in their behavioural approaches adapting a range of techniques to suit the needs of each case. They tend to favour various forms of graded re-entry with detailed consideration of the practical family and school issues, especially likely areas of resistance. The paper also brings out the importance of being flexible, adapting to new facts and situations as they emerge. Although, predominantly behavioural, the authors do acknowledge the need to attend to many personal

81

and family factors outside the specific treatment programme. In certain cases, parents may be offered therapy separate to the child to remove a potential burden from the child.

Phillips and Wolpe (1981) describe a highly complex and lengthy treatment programme applied to a twelve-year-old boy suffering from 'severe separation anxiety and obsessive compulsive disorder'. Prior to their involvement the subject, who had been regarded as school phobic, received two years of unsuccessful psychoanalytic treatment. Careful behavioural analysis revealed that the subject was fearful of separating from the parents in nearly all circumstances and not just school situations. Apart from playing football with friends in the back-yard, Rob could not let the parents out of his sight. Thus Phillips and Wolpe (1981) did not regard the problem as a true school phobia even though the boy had been refusing school for five and a half months with irregular attendance for the two previous years.

Treatment involved systematic desensitisation both imaginal and *in vivo* with muscle relaxation training; a written contract between Rob and his parents along the lines advocated by Vaal (1973); contingency management and parent training modelled on Patterson's (1975) work; and a gradual reduction of repetitive ritualistic behaviours as suggested by Azrin and Nunn (1973). The latter approach involved substituting muscle relaxation for rituals; self-monitoring and recording of rituals with interim and long-term rewards for achievement of reduction and ultimate elimination of rituals. After two years and 88 sessions, the boy was able to attend school without anxiety and could even go on holiday to Europe with schoolfriends. All therapeutic gains were maintained at two year follow-up.

The authors comment that the treatment programme was long and tedious because of the 'father's alcoholism, the mother's agoraphobia and the interference of a tyrannical grandmother'. Unfortunately, however, they do not specify precisely how these family issues affected treatment. It would have been useful to know how the grandmother interfered and in what way this was handled by the therapists. Phillips and Wolpe (1981) were at pains to ensure that the boy's problems were overcome gradually with the minimum of agony. The previous treatment, although argued on psychoanalytic grounds, had in a sense involved 'flooding' but *without* close attention to the practical details. The boy had been dragged to school and left there by the parents who promised to stay on the school grounds but promptly left the premises. The breakdown in treatment and trust resulted in a worsening of the problem thus making Phillips and Wolpe's (1981) task much more difficult.

In the first large-scale behavioural treatment series in the literature Kennedy (1965) describes the application of a treatment package to 50 cases of type 1 school phobics (see Chapter 1, p. 23). Kennedy's approach draws from both the classical and operant models yet appears to avoid the difficulties noted in the study by Lazarus, Davidson and Polefka (1965). Essentially Kennedy blocks the escape route and forces the child to attend school (desensitising via classical extinction). At the same time school attendance is positively reinforced by giving the child special privileges in school and treats at home. Finally, somatic complaints are handled in a low key, matter-of-fact way so that they gradually peter out. In order to achieve these aims, good relations between the various professionals and the ability to inspire confidence in the parents are fundamentally important. The results were extremely impressive, as shown in Table 3.1.

All 50 cases returned to school with only three days treatment. Follow-ups conducted by telephone at 2 weeks, 8 weeks and annually for between two and eight years after treatment revealed that every case remained symptom free. Kennedy argues that five of the cases might be considered as semi-controls in that they were longstanding type 1 cases or cases that had failed to respond to a previous treatment intervention. However, a number of points need to be borne in mind. Firstly, 37 out of the 50 cases were 11 years or younger. Secondly, Kennedy gives the impression that most of his cases had been out of school for only a few days. He admits that the majority of the cases would probably have returned to school no matter what treatment was given. Thirdly, no true diagnostic evaluation was made at follow-up. Kennedy (1965) concludes his paper by recommending his approach for only type 1 school phobics. He indicates that the prognosis for type 2 cases is much worse and suggests that long term supportive therapy is required. This raises a final point about Kennedy's work. He gives no details of the original population of school phobics on which he based his type 1 and type 2 classifications. It is not clear whether he originally applied his behavioural package to all cases of school phobia, or whether he only tried it out on type 1 cases. If his cases were assigned to type 1 and type 2 groups *after* treatment, this would cast some doubt on the validity of his findings. As pointed out in Chapter 1,

Table 3.1: Details of treatment and outcome for the behavioural treatment studies reviewed in this chapter

Study	No. of cases	Age	Sex	Length of treatment	No. of sessions	Type of treatment	Return to school	Follow-up period	Attendance satisfactory at follow-up
Lazarus (1960)	1	9 yrs	F	10 days	5	SD (imaginal)	Yes	15 mths	Yes
Lazarus and Abramovitz (1962)	1	8 yrs	F	Not stated	4	SD (imaginal) and emotive imagery	Yes	Not stated	Yes
Schermann and Grover (1962)	1	10 yrs	M	6 weeks	8	SD (in vivo) and SD (imaginal)	Yes	No follow up	–
Patterson (1965)	1	7 yrs	M	6 weeks	23	SD (imaginal) and contingency management	Yes	3 mths	Yes
Lazarus, Davidson and Polefka (1965)	1	9 yrs	M	4.5 mth	Not clear	SD (imaginal), SD (in vivo), operant techniques and drug therapy	Yes	10 mths	Yes
Kennedy (1965)	50	4–16 yrs	M F	>13 days	Not reported	Enforced school attendance, contingency management	Yes	2–8 yrs	50/50
Garvey and Hegrenes (1966)	1	10 yrs	M	6 weeks	20	SD (in vivo)	Yes	2 yrs	Yes
Chapel (1967)	1	11 yrs	M	6 weeks	18	SD (imaginal) with hypnosis	Yes	Not stated	1 breakdown responded well to extra treatment
Hersen (1968)	1	12 yrs	M	10 weeks	10	Contingency management	Yes	6 mths	Yes
Cantrell, Cantrell, Huddleston and Woolridge (1969)	1	Not stated	F	8 days	8	Contingency contracting	Yes	1 year +	Yes

Study	N	Age	Sex	Duration	No.	Technique	Follow-up	Follow-up period	Success
Ayllon, Smith and Rogers (1970)	1	8 yrs	F	70 days including initial baseline observations		SD (in vivo) and operant techniques	Yes	9 mths	Yes
Hersen (1970a)	1	12.5 yr	M	15 weeks	10	Contingency management techniques	Yes	6 mths	Yes
Smith and Sharpe (1970)	1	13 yrs	M	1 week	5	Implosive therapy and contingency management	Yes	13 wks	Yes
Welch and Carpenter (1970)	1	8 yrs	M	3 weeks	*	Contingency contracting	Yes	No follow up	–
Tahmisian and McReynolds (1971)	1	13 yrs	F	3 weeks	27**	SD (imaginal), SD (in vivo) and contingency management	Yes	4 wks	Yes
Miller (1972)	1	10 yrs	M	Approx. 17 wks	Not clear	SD (imaginal) and SD (in vivo)	Yes	18 mths	Yes
Rines (1973)	1	12 yrs	F	Not clear	Not clear	Kennedy treatment approach	Yes	1 year +	Yes
Vaal (1973)	1	13 yrs	M	6 weeks	*	Contingency contracting	Yes	5 mths	Yes
Van der Ploeg (1975)	1	14 yrs	M	4 weeks	15**	SD (imaginal), SD (in vivo) and emotive imagery	Yes	18 mths	Yes
Galloway and Miller	1	11 yrs	M	Not clear	7	SD (imaginal) and SD (in vivo)	Yes	5 wks	Yes
Croghan (1981)	1	7 yrs	M	Not clear	12	SD (imaginal) and cognitive restructuring	Yes	1 yr	Yes
Phillips and Wolpe (1981)	1	12 yrs	M	2 years	88	SD (imaginal and in vivo), operant techniques, contingency contracting	Yes	2 yrs	Yes

Table 3.1: (cont.)

Study	No. of cases	Age	Sex	Length of treatment	No. of sessions	Type of treatment	Return to school	Follow-up period	Attendance satisfactory at follow-up
Esveldt-Dawson, Wisner, Unis, Matson and Kazdin (1982)	1	12 yrs	F	Not clear	24	Social skills training involving instructions, participant modelling, behavioural rehearsal, performance feedback, social reinforcement	Yes	7 wks 21 wks	Yes
Blagg and Yule (1984)	30	11–16 yrs	M F	Mean = 2.53 wks		Enforced school attendance with comprehensive behavioural management	29/30	Mean = 1.71 yrs	28/30

* Treatment programme carried out by the parents on a continuous basis.
** 15 of the 27 sessions were implemented by the parents.

a number of the items differentiating type 1 and 2 school phobics seem to be open to therapist bias and, furthermore, one item appears to be an outcome of treatment rather than a criterion for initial diagnosis. On the other hand, if Kennedy categorised his school phobics *before* attempting any treatment, how can he argue that type 2 cases require long-term supportive therapy rather than a direct behavioural approach?

In fact, an interesting case study by Rines (1973) contradicts Kennedy's views. Rines successfully applied Kennedy's package approach to a twelve-year-old girl who showed seven or eight of the ten type 2 features. At the time of the referral, the parents were at the end of their tether. They had reluctantly come to the conclusion that hospitalisation was necessary and indeed their feelings were endorsed by the majority of clinicians at the Psychological Service Centre, University of South Carolina. Nevertheless, it was decided to try a direct behavioural approach for two months before finally deciding on disposition. The parents somewhat sceptically agreed to give it a try, but felt that the whole approach was far too simple to be effective. Rines gained the support of the school and the parents were advised in contingency management along the lines advised by Kennedy (1965).

Within two months the child's behaviour was back within tolerable limits. Regular group therapy was offered but the mother sabotaged this treatment. A follow-up at the end of the year and beginning of the subsequent year revealed that the child was attending school regularly and achieving excellent marks. However, the family pathology continued and the child still showed deviant social relationships with her peers. Rines suggests that a direct behavioural approach should be the first course of action even in severe cases where hospitalisation seems almost inevitable.

In two brief papers Blagg (1977, 1981) describes a comprehensive strategy for the rapid diagnosis and treatment of school phobia. The strategy is based primarily on behavioural principles and draws from both the classical and operant conditioning paradigms. The approach is fully described in Chapters 6, 7 and 8. However, at this stage it is probably helpful to draw out the main elements in the procedures. These include:

i. a detailed, wide-ranging analysis and clarification of child, school and family issues surrounding the school phobia;

ii. informal desensitisation of child, teacher and parental worries at the diagnostic stage through humour, emotive imagery, discussion and brief behaviour rehearsal;

iii. flooding, i.e. immediate full-time school attendance facilitated through an escort procedure where necessary (effectively blocking the avoidance behaviour);

iv. contingency management at home and school to eliminate factors likely to maintain fear reactions, protests, psychosomatic complaints and avoidance behaviours;

v. engineering and maximising home and school based ways of positively reinforcing regular school attendance.

Although not particularly emphasised in Blagg's (1977 and 1981) papers, certain aspects of the strategy could be construed in cognitive behaviour therapy terms as described by Beck (1976) and more recently McAdam and Gilbert (1985). The approach not only emphasises the identification of key anxiety-provoking circumstances, but also how they are perceived by the child, parents and teachers. Some circumstances may be open to change through environmental manipulation; others will be no longer significant or worrying; whereas others may need desensitising through discussion, rationalisation and restructuring. Blagg (1977) states that successful treatment is dependent upon 'establishing good relationships, reducing anxiety, rationalising guilt feelings and inspiring confidence. Resistance to treatment is dealt with by continuing support whilst confronting the parents with the reality of the situation.' These areas are clarified and developed in Chapters 6, 7 and 8.

The approach was tested on a treatment series of 30 cases and compared against 20 school phobics who received home tuition and psychotherapy and 16 who were hospitalised (Blagg and Yule 1984). Details of these latter treatments and the overall comparative implications of the study are considered in Chapter 4. The diagnostic criteria for inclusion in the treatment groups were similar to those proposed by Berg, Nichols and Pritchard (1969). There were five ten-year-olds in the behavioural treatment series with the rest of the group aged between 11 and 16 years. The mean age of the group at the start of treatment was 12.95 years. Applying Kennedy's (1965) criteria as far as possible, bearing in mind the subjective nature of some of the items, 13 out of the 30 cases fell into the type 2 category and 17 were deemed type 1.

In considering outcome, it was felt important to determine what was meant by 'returned to regular school attendance'. Many of the low-achieving children from older age groups came from classes where some regular absenteeism was the norm. Furthermore, although many children in the treatment study returned to full-time schooling, not all children remained there until follow-up and some needed additional booster treatment.

In view of this, the following stringent, behaviourally operationalised criteria was applied to each of the treatment groups. 'Success' was defined as the child returned to full-time schooling without any further problems or, if there was one breakdown in attendance, the child responded quickly to booster treatment and showed no further difficulties. A 'partial success' was judged if the child returned to day-school for at least one year but then had attendance breakdowns before leaving school and did not return to school thereafter. Failure was judged if the child did not return to day-school or returned for less than 3 months and then broke down thereafter and did not respond to further treatment.

Applying these criteria at follow-up (mean follow-up period for the behavioural group 1.71 years) 28 out of 30 cases were 'successful' with one case 'partially successful'. Examining the actual attendance rates for the year prior to follow-up, 25 out of the 30 cases in the series attended school more than 80 per cent of the time. Those classified as type 1 were 100 per cent successful on both sets of criteria. One of the 13 type 2 cases was regarded as a treatment failure with 4 cases attending school regularly but still having quite a lot of time off. It is important to recognise that the 5 cases showing poor attendance were all girls, over 13 years with IQs below 85 on the WISC-R Verbal Scale. Some of these pupils came from classes where poor attendance was the norm. Of the 5 cases, 4 had siblings who were also poor attenders and parents who were far from co-operative in treatment. Nevertheless, the overwhelming success of the majority of the type 2 cases casts further doubt on Kennedy's assertion that only type 1 cases can benefit from a rapid behavioural approach.

As Baker and Wills' (1979) paper demonstrates, return to school may not be the most important outcome measure with respect to long-term adjustment. The clinical state of the client on discharge from treatment seems more important (Berg, Marks, McGuire and Lipsedge, 1974). In this connection, none of the 30 behavioural cases showed evidence of separation anxiety at follow-up. Furthermore, 23 out of the 30 cases showed no signs of a behavioural disorder as assessed by both teachers and parents on the Rutter and Yule (1968) Behavioural Scales. Finally, on the Eysenck Personality Questionnaire (1975), extroversion scores increased and neuroticism scores decreased significantly in the group following treatment. Average treatment time for the behavioural group was only 2.53 weeks making the approach extremely cost effective.

DISCUSSION AND IMPLICATIONS

It is clear from the foregoing that many behavioural techniques have been usefully employed in the treatment of school phobia. However, it is difficult to draw firm conclusions for the following reasons:

i. The majority of treatment studies consist of single case reports. Whilst most indicate successful treatment outcomes, it is impossible to know whether the cases referred to were truly representative of the clinical experience of the various authors or just carefully selected examples from less successful treatment series.

ii. As Chapter 1 points out, the term school phobia has been interpreted in a variety of ways by different workers. Although most behavioural reports provide detailed descriptions of cases, many fail to list explicit behavioural criteria defining school phobia. Thus it is difficult to make comparisons between the separate treatment studies.

iii. Treatment outcome has often been loosely defined and inadequately evaluated. The majority of studies evaluate outcome in terms of whether attendance is satisfactory or not. However, only Blagg and Yule's (1984) study operationalised 'satisfactory attendance'. Furthermore, it is only recently that researchers have made a point of considering the child's attainments and social adjustment following treatment. Finally, there have been relatively few long-term follow-ups.

iv. There have been no research investigations comparing the relative efficacy of different behavioural approaches.

v. As behavioural treatment approaches have become more complex, many therapists have developed broad-based strategies employing a mixture of different behavioural techniques. In addition, some authors admit that many factors outside the behavioural treatment framework often need dealing with. Thus it becomes very difficult to know which elements and facets of treatment are essential and which are superfluous; and of those that are essential, which techniques are most efficient and in what combinations and circumstances.

In many ways, the search for a definitive behavioural technique or group of techniques to suit all cases is inappropriate. Above all the review clearly demonstrates the complexity and range of issues involved in treating school phobics. Although there are common themes, every case in unique and will require slightly different emphases in treatment. Furthermore, the vagaries of the referral system, therapist personality and place of work often seriously limit treatment options. A hospital-based worker may not have the scope, freedom or time to offer home and school visits. Thus if the parents cannot be helped to cope with clinic sessions and advice, hospitalisation may be necessary. A clinic-based worker covering a large geographical area may find a lengthy systematic desensitisation procedure impossible because of the pressure of other duties. *In vivo* approaches may be difficult to organise and supervise if the therapist works a long way from the child's home. Some therapists may not be very good at creating imagined scenes so that systematic desensitisation (imaginal) may not be workable. Others may find reciprocal inhibition procedures like hypnosis and muscle relaxation difficult to manage. On the other hand, many therapists may not be able to handle or support the intense short-term distress that often accompanies an immediate forced return to school.

Nevertheless, in spite of these problems, some tentative generalisations do seem possible:

1. Some children avoid school with mild anxiety and are unwittingly reinforced in this pattern by parents and/or teachers. If these cases are dealt with quickly, simple techniques like contingency management and contingency contracting can be highly effective (Cantrell *et al*. 1969; Welch and Carpenter, 1970; Vaal, 1973) involving relatively little time and effort. Rapid-return treatment packages as advocated by Kennedy (1965) and Blagg and Yule (1984) can also be very successful with such cases.

2. More longstanding cases with additional problems often require more sophisticated treatment procedures of longer duration. Systematic desensitisation, imaginal and *in vivo*, combined with other approaches has proved helpful in such cases. Flooding via enforced school attendance has also worked well but not without careful preparation and attention to many school, family and child factors (Blagg and Yule 1984).

3. Systematic desensitisation (*in vivo* or imaginal) does seem to be a tedious long-winded procedure involving considerable therapist time. Furthermore, it seems possible that two mutually opposing effects may be operating during treatment. On the one hand, the child's fear reaction is being reduced through reciprocal inhibition whilst the avoidance response is being strengthened through the secondary reinforcing properties of the anxiety reduction that is likely to ensue at the end of each treatment session. If this is the case, the extent to which the reciprocal inhibition effect overrides the operant strengthening of the avoidance behaviour would decide the length of the treatment.

4. As Table 3.1 shows, approaches involving a strong implosive or flooding component have produced more rapid results than studies relying heavily upon systematic desensitisation procedures. Smith and Sharpe (1970) using implosive therapy produced a positive therapeutic change in a 13-year-old girl in one week. Kennedy's (1965) treatment series required only 3 days treatment. Blagg and Yule's (1984) behavioural treatment series, which included many type 2 cases, required a mean treatment time of only 2.53 weeks. Under the circumstances, there seems to be strong evidence to suggest that approaches involving flooding or implosion are worth considering as the first treatment choice in the majority of cases.

5. Interventions derived from social skills training and cognitive behaviour therapy have received very little attention in the literature on the treatment of school phobia. Both areas offer considerable scope and may well feature more explicitly in future flexible treatment packages.

4

A Comparison of Behavioural and Psychodynamic Approaches

This chapter will review comparative treatment studies before going on to consider similarities and differences between behavioural and psychodynamic approaches. A final section will summarise the issues and findings. Controlled comparative treatment studies with randomly allocated treatment groups are difficult to justify on ethical grounds. Clinical work is extremely time-consuming and long-term follow-ups pose another time burden on the therapist researcher. Under the circumstances, it is perhaps not surprising that there have been relatively few large scale treatment studies, hardly any comparative investigations and only two studies that have included a control group (Waldfogel, Tessman and Hahn, 1959; Miller, Barrett, Hampe and Noble, 1972).

COMPARATIVE TREATMENT STUDIES

The study by Waldfogel et al. (1959) is the sole investigation (dealing exclusively with school phobics) to have included an untreated control group. These authors set up a field unit for the early identification and treatment of school phobics. Less severe (neurotic) cases were treated in the school situation whilst the more seriously disturbed (characterological) types were referred to the clinic for intensive treatment. During the two years that this field unit was in operation a total of 36 children were referred with the majority of the cases occurring during elementary school grades. In five cases spontaneous remission had taken place between referral and intervention. A further eleven cases received no treatment either because of a lack of time or because the parents were not co-operative. Sixteen children were given brief therapy in school whilst the remaining four were treated in the clinic.

A follow-up was carried out 6 to 18 months after the termination of treatment. Of the 16 cases that received brief focal treatment, 14 cases were attending school regularly whilst two showed recurring difficulties. All 16 cases showed superior or satisfactory academic performance. However, 10 cases exhibited minor problems in classroom adjustment. Three of the four clinic-treated children were still in treatment at follow-up, although all of them had returned to school. Only one out of five of the spontaneous remission group showed any recurrence of phobic symptoms, and none of the group showed learning or social adjustment problems. In contrast at follow-up 8 of the 11 untreated cases still showed recurring or persistent problems in attendance. Furthermore 10 out of the 11 cases showed minor or serious problems in classroom adjustment. Two of the cases were also producing unsatisfactory schoolwork.

However, conclusions can only be very tentative. Cases were not randomly assigned to the control and treated groups. The fact that the parents of 7 of the 11 untreated cases were unco-operative suggested that there may have been a greater proportion of more difficult cases in the untreated group which in turn suggests that in a larger unselected sample of school phobics the spontaneous remission rate might be higher.

Miller *et al.* (1972) conducted a comparative treatment study of children's phobias in which 46 out of the 69 cases were school phobics. The study aimed to compare the relative effectiveness of behaviour therapy, psychotherapy and waiting list control as treatment methods of phobics aged 6–15 years. Pre- and post-treatment measures were taken with follow-up at 6 weeks by both parents and an independent evaluator. Subjects were randomly assigned to the three groups. Both treatment groups received 24 one-hour sessions, three times a week over eight weeks. It is difficult to draw conclusions from this study with regard to the treatment of school phobics as outcome was not broken down according to the type of phobia. Furthermore, no specific criteria were stated for diagnosing school phobia. It should be noted that of the 46 school phobics included in the study 13 were attending school irregularly, whilst 7 were attending regularly but with distress. Most treatment studies have concerned themselves with cases where attendance has broken down altogether.

It is however worth recording that on the total sample of phobics there were no significant differences in treatment outcome on the basis of the primary evaluators' ratings. In other words there was no evidence to suggest that psychotherapy was superior to behaviour therapy or vice versa. Furthermore, neither treatment procedure seemed more effective than the waiting list control. Parental ratings also showed no evidence of differential outcome for the two treated groups. They did however, indicate a better outcome for both treated groups in comparison to the waiting list controls. Miller *et al.* (1972) point out that these latter findings could be accounted for in terms of an expectancy or cognitive dissonance following treatment. In the final analysis one is forced to choose between the seemingly objective observations of an outsider and the emotionally tinged observations of the parents. The principal factor affecting treatment outcome was found to be age. For younger, phobic children (6–10 years) there was a 96 per cent success rate. This is in line with treatment studies dealing solely with school phobics. However, when it came to the 11–15-year-olds, the treatment outcome was poor for both treatment groups and no better than for the waiting list controls. The precise findings are given in Table 4.1.

In addition to age, initial parental motivation was also related

Table 4.1: Results of a comparative treatment study on a group of children suffering from a variety of phobias

Age	Treatment Reciprocal inhibition therapy	Psycho- dynamic therapy	All treated subjects	Waiting list control	Al Ss
Younger success*	11	12	23	8	31
(6–10) failure	1	0	1	6	7
Older success*	5	4	9	4	13
(11–15) failure	4	7	11	5	16
N	21	23	44	23	67

Source: Miller *et al.* (1972, p. 275).
* Success means that the child received a primary evaluator severity score rating of 2.9 or less on a 7-point scale (1–7) at a 6-week follow-up after the treatment.

to treatment outcome. Children with highly motivated parents responded better to treatment than those whose parents were rated initially as being low in motivation. Unfortunately, the authors do not state criteria for deciding on the level of motivation. Sex, IQ and socio-economic status were all unrelated to treatment outcome.

To some extent the lack of differential treatment effects could be explained by the short-term follow-up period and the overlap in treatment methods. The behaviour therapy treatment principally involved systematic desensitisation (imaginal) but in addition operant techniques were utilised and treatment was coordinated to include significant individuals in the child's life. Psychotherapy mainly concentrated on the 'child's inner experience', his hopes and his fears, particularly his aggressive and sexual fears and dependent needs. However, in addition, behavioural strategies were formulated to cope with stress, operant techniques were employed to remove secondary gains likely to maintain the phobia and, where necessary, contacts were made with individuals outside the family.

Blagg and Yule's (1984) study is the only reported comparative treatment investigation dealing exclusively with school phobics. In view of this it will be described in some detail. A rapid behavioural treatment approach (BTA) was systematically applied to a treatment series of 30 school phobics occurring in north-west Somerset over a three year period. At the time of the study, two other traditional treatment approaches were favoured by professional colleagues working in different geographical areas. Accordingly, it was possible to compare the treatment time and outcome for the BTA group with 16 hospitalised children (HU) who attended a psychiatric unit and hospital school and 20 home-tutored cases (HT) who also received psychotherapy at a child-guidance clinic.

Neither the HU or the HT groups were randomly allocated to treatment groups and neither constituted treatment series from specific geographical areas. Nevertheless, care was taken to compare like with like. Every case of school phobia treated by hospitalisation or home tuition with psychotherapy was investigated over a given period of time. All cases that satisfied the same initial selection criteria (as in Berg, Nichols and Pritchard, 1969) for inclusion in the BTA group were utilised in the comparative study. A subsequent comparison on an extensive range of variables showed the three treatment groups to be remarkably well matched. There were no statistically significant differences between the groups on sex or social class (as assessed by the Registrar General's (1970) classification).

As Table 4.2 shows, the three groups were also similar in intelligence characteristics according to the Verbal Scale from the Wechsler Intelligence Scale — Revised Version (WISC-R: Wechsler, 1974). In addition the groups were similar with respect to pattern of associated symptoms, school and home-related anxieties, family size, parental attitudes and employment rates. Applying Kennedy's criteria as far as possible given the subjective nature of some of the items, half the children in the BTA group, three quarters of the HU group and one quarter of the HT group were classified as the more disturbed Kennedy type 2 school phobics. These variations were not statistically significant.

Apart from five ten-year-olds in the BTA group and one in the HU group, all of the children in the study were in the 11-16-year-old age range. The BTA group was significantly younger (t = 2.86, P<0.01) than the HU group at the beginning of treatment.

Many of the children in the study received some form of prior treatment ranging from drug therapy to a variety of environmental changes. However, there were no significant differences between the groups with respect to history and type of prior

Table 4.2: Characteristics of the three treatment groups

Variable	BTA Group	HT Group	HU Group
Age at start of treatment (years)	N = 30 $\bar{X}$ = 12.95 SD = 1.90	N = 20 $\bar{X}$ = 14.28 SD = 1.27	N = 16 $\bar{X}$ = 13.52 SD = 1.92
Age of onset of attendance problems (years)	N = 30 $\bar{X}$ = 9.33 SD = 3.76	N = 20 $\bar{X}$ = 11.20 SD = 3.38	N = 16 $\bar{X}$ = 11.69 SD = 1.81
WISC-R Verbal Scale IQ	N = 30 $\bar{X}$ = 94.27 SD = 16.31	N = 13 $\bar{X}$ = 100.08 SD = 18.04	N = 15 $\bar{X}$ = 99.67 SD = 16.40
Time off school before treatment (weeks)	N = 29 $\bar{X}$ = 11.48 SD = 28.52	N = 16 $\bar{X}$ = 14.47 SD = 17.31	N = 16 $\bar{X}$ = 12.56 SD = 29.16
Number of periods of school refusal	N = 30 $\bar{X}$ = 1.47 SD = 0.68	N = 18 $\bar{X}$ = 1.44 SD = 0.78	N = 16 $\bar{X}$ = 2.06 SD = 2.08

treatment. The BTA and HU groups completed self esteem scales (Lawrence, 1979, 1981) and Eysenck Personality Questionnaires (EPQ; Eysenck and Eysenck, 1975). Finally the parents and teachers of these children completed the appropriate Rutter Behaviour Rating Scales (RBRS; Rutter and Yule, 1968). Once again, there were no significant differences between the groups on any of these variables. As Table 4.6 shows, both the BTA and HU groups were significantly more introverted, sensitive, socially conforming and naïve than the standardisation sample. Both groups evidenced neurotic disorders on the parent and teacher RBRSs. Thus any variations in treatment outcome could not be accounted for in terms of different selection criteria or varying compositions of the groups.

The BTA which has been described in Blagg (1977, 1979, 1981) and summarised in Chapter 3, is fully documented in Chapters 6, 7 and 8.

The HU treatment involved:

1. physical separation of the child and parents via hospitalisation;
2. therapeutic milieu (high staff-patient ratio; daily group psychotherapy, accepting emotionally neutral environment;
3. educational and occupational therapy;
4. drug treatment (occasional use of tranquillisers);
5. carefully managed discharge with attendance contract.

The HT group were regarded as too 'ill' to return to school immediately. Home tuition was arranged where possible at the tutor's house or in a small tutorial class, two hours a day, so that the children spent some time away from home each school day. The intensive personal help was intended as a confidence booster as well as an opportunity to remediate any specific learning difficulties or worries. Psychotherapy was supplied on a fortnightly basis at a child-guidance clinic although some children received rather less of this form of help as they became 'clinic refusers' as well as school refusers during the course of treatment. Under normal circumstnaces, the child would see the psychiatrist whilst the parents talked to the psychiatric social worker. However, in cases of severe separation anxiety, parents and child would be jointly interviewed at first and then gradually separated for increasing lengths of time over a number of sessions. Either way, the sessions would finish with a family

Table 4.3: Comparing treatment outcome for each group after one year

Child attending school at follow-up	HU		HT		BTA		X^2 Values and significance levels		
	N	%	N	%	N	%	HU × HT	HU × BTA	BTA × HT
Failure	10	62.5	18	90	1	3.3	No	$X^2=20.21$	$X^2=38.27$
Partial success	0	0	0		1	3.3	significant	$P<0.001$	$P<0.001$
Success	6	37.5	2	10	28	93.3	difference		
Total N	16		29		30				

Table 4.4: Comparing treatment outcome for each group in terms of % attendance at follow-up

Attendance at follow-up (%)	HU		HT		BTA		X^2 Values and significance levels		
	N	%	N	%	N	%	HU × HT	HU × BTA	BTA × HT
0–80	11*	68.8	20	100	5	16.7	$X^2=4.88$	$X^2=10.29$	$X^2=30.08$
81–100	5	31.3	0		25	83.3	$P<0.05$	$P<0.001$	$P<0.001$
Total N	16		20		30				

* Three cases in this group were attending boarding school at follow-up. They had been placed in residential schools because their return to normal day school was not possible. In the circumstances, they were placed in the 0–80 per cent attendance group.

discussion involving professionals, parents and child with a view to developing insight and understanding.

Treatment outcome was objectively defined using behaviourally-operationalised criteria as noted in Chapter 3 (p. 89). The results are summarised in Table 4.3. On these criteria, highly significant differences were noted between the groups with 93.3 per cent of the BTA group being judged successful as against only 37.5 per cent of the HU group and 10 per cent of the HT group. Exploring the data in terms of actual attendance rates the BTA group continued to show superiority over the HU and HT groups. As Table 4.4 shows whereas 83 per cent of the BTA group were attending school more than 80 per cent of the time, only 31 per cent of the HU group and 0 per cent of the HT group achieved the same levels of attendance.

A similar outcome pattern significantly favouring the BTA group occurred when type 2 cases alone were considered. The pattern also endured when cases below the age of 11 years were excluded from the analysis. Finally, there were no significant

Table 4.5: Separation anxiety at follow-up

Separation anxiety at follow-up	BTA N	BTA %	HT N	HT %	HU N	HU %	X^2 Values and significance levels BTA×HT	BTA×HU	HT×HU
Present	0		8	66.7	1	7.1	$X^2=19.96$	Not	$X^2=7.66$
Absent	30	100	4	33.3	13	92.9	$P<0.001$	Significant	$P<0.01$
Total N	30		12		14				

differences in outcome favouring either sex.

As Berg, Butler and Hall (1976) and Baker and Wills (1979) have emphasised, the child's clinical state on discharge from treatment may be more important than success at returning to school. Behavioural treatments are often criticised for treating symptoms without dealing with underlying causes. Treatment is often said to be narrowly defined so that whilst there may be improvements in some areas, deterioration in other areas is often missed. Accordingly, Blagg and Yule's (1984) study systematically explored other indices of adjustment. There was no evidence of symptom substitution in the BTA group at follow up. Furthermore, Table 4.5 shows that none of the behaviourally treated children showed evidence of separation anxiety at follow-up. In contrast, 66.7 per cent of the home-tutored group still showed major problems in this area.

Data on personality, self-esteem and behavioural ratings could only be gathered on the BTA and HU groups who were recruited prospectively. Interestingly, both groups showed significant positive changes on the EPQ, with extroversion scores increasing and neuroticism scores decreasing following treatment. Similar post-treatment changes in EPQ scores have been previously observed by Hallam (1976) in adult neurotics. In that study the largest changes in personality scores were paralleled by the greatest clinical improvements. As Table 4.6 indicates a significant increase in self-esteem scores was confined to the HU group.

Not all teachers and parents co-operated in completing behavioural rating scales. Nevertheless, on the basis of the available evidence shown in Table 4.7 it would seem that whilst the majority of BTA and HU cases showed a neurotic disorder prior to treatment, most were rated as having no disorder after treatment.

Table 4.6: Changes in EPQ scores; and Lawrence Self-esteem Inventory scores before and after treatment for both the BTA and HU groups

Variable	BTA Group				HT Group			
	Before	After	t-values	P	Before	After	t-values	P
EPQ 'P' scale Z scores	N = 14 $\bar{X}$ = -0.75 SD = 0.55	N = 14 $\bar{X}$ = -0.35 SD = 1.10	-1.61	NS	N = 12 $\bar{X}$ = -0.37 SD = 0.81	N = 12 $\bar{X}$ = -0.10 SD = 0.60	+1.64	NS
EPQ 'E' scores Z scores	N = 18 $\bar{X}$ = -1.37 SD = 1.39	N = 18 $\bar{X}$ = -0.30 SD = 1.08	-3.64	P = 0.01	N = 12 $\bar{X}$ = -1.73 SD = 1.74	N = 12 $\bar{X}$ = -0.23 SD = 1.60	-2.86	P = 0.01
EPQ 'N' scale Z scores	N = 18 $\bar{X}$ = +0.25 SD = 0.75	N = 18 $\bar{X}$ = -0.56 SD = 1.08	+3.17	P = 0.01	N = 12 $\bar{X}$ = +0.26 SD = 0.80	N = 12 $\bar{X}$ = -0.34 SD = 0.80	+2.22	P = 0.05
EPQ 'L' scores Z scores	N = 18 $\bar{X}$ = +0.83 SD = 1.35	N = 18 $\bar{X}$ = +1.05 SD = 1.53	-0.57	NS	N = 12 $\bar{X}$ = +0.96 SD = 1.32	N = 12 $\bar{X}$ = +0.62 SD = 1.33	+1.47	NS
Lawrence Self-esteem Inventory scores	N = 14 $\bar{X}$ = 24.07 SD = 3.94	N = 14 $\bar{X}$ = 24.07 SD = 3.54	-1.02	NS	N = 11 $\bar{X}$ = 22.27 SD = 7.42	N = 11 $\bar{X}$ = 27.09 SD = 4.11	-2.25	P = 0.05

Table 4.7: The number (and %) of children in the BTA and HU groups showing evidence of a neurotic disorder on the Rutter and Yule Parents' Behaviour Scale (A2) and Teachers' Behaviour Scale (B2) before and after treatment

Treatment	Treatment stage	Parents' Behaviour Scale A(2)				Teachers' Behaviour Scale B(2)					
		No disorder		Neurotic disorder		No disorder		Neurotic disorder		Not* applicable	
		N	%	N	%	N	%	N	%	N	%
BTA	Before	3	21.4	11	78.6	7	43.8	9	50.3		
	After	23	95.8	1	4.2	23	88.5	3	11.3		
HU	Before	6	60.0	4	40.0	1	10.0	9	90.0		
	After	11	84.6	2	15.4	7	50.0	1	7.1	6	42.9

* Child does not return to school.

Table 4.8: Total treatment time (weeks) and number of interviews with the child, parents and teachers for each group

Treatments	BTA	HT	Hu		
C.A. at follow-up (yr.)	$\bar{X}$ = 14.66 SD = 2.08 N = 30	$\bar{X}$ = 15.84 SD = 0.79 N = 20	$\bar{X}$ = 14.66 SD = 1.73 N = 16	BTA × HT	t = 2.93 P < 0.01
Total treatment time (weeks)	$\bar{X}$ = 2.53 SD = 3.23 N = 30	$\bar{X}$ = 72.1 SD = 55.75 N = 20	$\bar{X}$ = 45.31 SD = 31.01 N = 16	BTA × HT BTA × HU	t = −5.57 P < 0.001 t = −5.50 P < 0.001
Number of interviews with: child	$\bar{X}$ = 2.40 SD = 2.43 N = 30	$\bar{X}$ = 7.61 SD = 5.91 N = 13	$\bar{X}$ = 3.70 SD = 4.27 N = 10	BTA × HT	t = 3.08 P < 0.01
parents	$\bar{X}$ = 2.57 SD = 2.43 N = 30	$\bar{X}$ = 9.00 SD = 5.69 N = 13	$\bar{X}$ = 4.00 SD = 3.27 N = 10	BTA × HT	t = −3.93 P < 0.01
teachers	$\bar{X}$ = 2.13 SD = 2.38 N = 30	$\bar{X}$ = 1.20 SD = 2.02 N = 13	$\bar{X}$ = 1.90 SD = 1.37 N = 10	No significant differences	

* t-values and significance levels are only recorded where differences between the groups reach a level of significance of 1 per cent.

Finally, Table 4.8 presents data showing that the behavioural treatment was by far the most economic form of intervention in terms of therapeutic time. The average length of behavioural treatment was 2.53 weeks compared to 45.3 weeks for hospitalisation and 72.1 weeks for home tuition. These dramatic differences conceal even greater variations in terms of financial costs. The cost of hospital in-patient treatment may run into hundreds of pounds per week per child. Home tuition with psychotherapy may be cheaper than hospitalisation but is still an expensive option that may need to go on for many months and even years.

In summary the behavioural treatment approach adopted in this study achieved a better treatment outcome than any other reported study dealing with children in the 11–16 year age range. This applied using stringent behaviourally operationalised criteria relating to (1) whether the child returned to full-time day-schooling and remained there until follow-up and (2) whether the child showed an overall attendance rate in excess of 81 per cent in the year prior to follow-up. Using the same criteria, the hospital group showed a much poorer treatment outcome than that reported by Hersov (1960–61) and Berg, Nichols and Pritchard (1969), although it is difficult to make accurate comparisons as these previous studies have not broken outcome down by age. Somewhat curiously, no other investigations using home tuition and psychotherapy were located in the literature. This is surprising as it does seem to be a commonly used procedure in many local education authorities in the United Kingdom. The progress of the home tutored group was so uniformly poor in Blagg and Yule's (1984) study that one wonders whether home tuition with psychotherapy actually inhibited spontaneous remission. In the absence of a control group and any other previous clear-cut studies on spontaneous remission rates for school phobics in the 11-16-year-old range, this must remain a debatable point.

Treatment improvements in the BTA group were not confined to narrow behavioural gains relating to attendance. Although many of the parents and children found the rapid return approach stressful in the short term the remarkably quick adjustments in the majority of cases more than justified the heightened initial anxiety. There was no evidence of separation anxiety or symptom substitution at follow-up. Furthermore, the EPQ scores for the BTA group normalised between treatment and follow-up suggesting that the children were generally less worried about everyday events at home and at school and more outgoing in their social behaviour after treatment. These trends were confirmed by both parents and teachers and substantiated by RBRSs where it was possible to obtain such data.

On some of these wider outcome indices the hospital unit group did not peform too badly. These results may be misleading as only two of the treatment failures returned home during the course of the study. The others remained in hospital or transferred to carefully selected boarding schools where the children would receive considerable nurture and sensitive handling. Accordingly the apparent improvements in RBRSs could have reflected the child's adjustment to the somewhat artificial regime or even to the different thresholds for deviant behaviour existing in specialist treatment facilities. The improvement in self-esteem in the HU group might also reflect unrealistic self-appraisal in the context of rather sheltered environments. It also points up the fact that self-reported attitudinal gains are not necessarily associated with changes in observable behaviour.

The findings in this study are contrary to Kennedy's (1965) suggestion that rapid flexible treatment packages are only applicable to less severe type 1 school phobics. All of the type 1 cases and the majority of the type 2 cases were successfully treated by the BTA approach. Nevertheless it should be emphasised that some of the older, more seriously disturbed children, did take longer to treat as the case studies in Chapter 8 demonstrate. The one treatment failure and the four cases that were only partially successful with respect to attendance figures were all Kennedy type 2 cases. It is important to note that some of these children came from families where poor attendance amongst other siblings was the norm and from school classes where the general attendance rate was poorer than the rest of the school. All of these cases were girls over 13 years with well below average academic attainments and WISC-R Verbal Scale IQs below 85.

The Behavioural Treatment Approach was carried out by an educational psychologist as part of normal everyday duties as opposed to a team of researchers or clinicians. The effectiveness and economy of this approach strongly suggests that flexible behavioural treatment packages emphasising rapid, and if necessary enforced, return to school should be the first treatment option considered in dealing with school phobics, even those more seriously disturbed long-standing cases.

SIMILARITIES AND DIFFERENCES BETWEEN BEHAVIOURAL AND PSYCHOTHERAPEUTIC APPROACHES

A number of authors (Patterson, 1968; Hersen, 1971a,b; Miller, Barrett and Hampe, 1974) have commented on the overlap between behavioural and psychotherapeutic approaches.

Within the context of traditional psychotherapy, fear hierarchies may be informally and incidentally worked through via discussion with desensitisation taking place in a variety of ways. A non-specific desensitisation effect may accrue from the relationship the child establishes with the therapist. As Miller, Barrett and Hampe (1974) point out, the interpretation of unconscious material may involve 'a psychic shock process which combines emotional arousal with flooding of ideational material similar to that employed in implosive techniques'.

Hersen (1970b, 1971) stresses that behavioural therapists often overcome resistance to treatment by utilising support, interpretation and reality confrontation techniques that would normally be associated with traditional psychotherapy. Cautela (1968) comments that behavioural treatment studies tend to report on certain aspects of treatment and often omit crucial details relating to therapist/patient interactions.

The accounts of the earlier behavioural studies reported in Chapter 3 lend support to Cautela's comments. Nevertheless a number of later behavioural studies (for instance Yule, Hersov and Treseder, 1980; Blagg and Yule, 1984) do acknowledge the need to address issues that fall outside the immediate focus of the treatment programme. Nevertheless, the pursuance of academic tidiness and limitations on journal space results in the majority of treatment accounts still being selectively reported to fit the theoretical framework and linguistic style of the therapist.

In addition, important information relating to previous treatment attempts may not be reported. This often applies to therapists working in clinic settings or hospitals, especially those offering specialised forms of treatment. In certain parts of the country, where such specialist resources exist, there may be a tendency on the part of some more eclectic therapists to make an initial diagnosis and treatment intervention, but refer on after initial treatment failure. For example, some educational psychologists may not be confident in working with resistant families but feel at ease in relation to school issues. In this way many family therapists may receive referrals where much of the spade work in relation to school issues has already been completed so that family issues can be safely and almost exclusively focused upon. Subsequent journal reports may then highlight all of the important family factors without even mentioning any school issues. Indeed some family therapists imply that school issues are irrelevant.

A further overlap between the different schools of thought becomes apparent when considering the problems associated with confrontation. All treatments inevitably involve confrontation at some stage in some form or other. It is interesting that the arguments concerning the timing, nature and management of confrontation are mirrored in both the psychoanalytic and behavioural camps. Traditional psychotherapists tend to favour a gradual process of interpretation with a view to developing insight before organising a planned return to school. Some of these therapists believe that the process of interpretation will in itself lead to a spontaneous desire on the part of the part of the child to return to school. In contrast, many other psychotherapists prefer an immediate reality confrontation with concurrent ego support. The process of confrontation is seen to provide essential material for the therapist to work with. Similarly, many behaviour therapists spend considerable time at the diagnostic stage ensuring that all of the essential issues are aired before treatment planning proceeds. Once again, many therapists prefer a careful, gradual reintroduction to school over a number of weeks using some form of systematic desensitisation or else a shaping procedure. In contrast, other behaviour therapists favour an immediate confrontation on an implosive or flooding treatment basis, desensitising via classical extinction.

It is interesting that both the earliest psychodynamic and behavioural studies were over-simplistic with the former focusing exclusively on the mother-child interactions, ignoring family dynamics and school considerations and the latter attempting to demonstrate the effectiveness of specific techniques. Over the years both psychodynamic and behavioural interventions have broadened their base to address a wide range of child, family and school factors to the point where some strategic family therapists adopt very similar treatment approaches to some behaviour therapists working with comprehensive flexible treatment packages. Although the theoretical starting positions are different, similar practical home and school issues are commonly addressed. In their impressive chapter entitled 'Phobias of Childhood in a Prescientific Era', Miller, Barrett and Hampe (1974) point out that treatments from all theoretical persuasions can be reduced to four essential basic elements: a. establishment of a relationship; b. clarification of the stimulus; c. desensitisation to the stimulus; d. confrontation of the stimulus. Different approaches satisfy these four basic elements in various different ways.

Nevertheless, in spite of these similarities and common issues in treatment, significant differences remain between the behavioural and psychotherapeutic approaches. There are still many traditional psychotherapists who concern themselves primarily with unconscious emotional processes relating current problems to the child's psychosexual development and early history. Likewise, there are many behaviour therapists who still focus exclusively on observable behaviour and attempt to establish those factors in the child's environment that have caused the problems and those factors that may be maintaining the difficulties. Some behaviour therapists would not see the value of understanding the cognitions and emotional perspectives of their clients.

Although some strategic family therapists share much in common with certain behaviour therapists, the focus of the family therapists is still very much on communication and hidden rule systems within the family with schooling issues *sometimes* considered under the guise of additional practical measures. On the other hand, many behaviour therapists nowadays consider child, family and schooling issues as equally important areas for exploration. Patterns of influence and control within families may be analysed in order to select key family members for important treatment roles. Similarly, understanding the school system enables key teachers to be recruited to important therapeutic roles.

In contrast to psychotherapists, behaviour therapists have been rather more rigorous in evaluating and reporting treatment outcome details with greater reference to clearly measurable indices and longer term follow-up periods.

5

Treatment Approaches —
Summary and Conclusions

Even though the majority of studies are bedevilled by methodological flaws, a picture does emerge from Chapters 2, 3 and 4 allowing for some tentative conclusions:

1. The treatment outcome for younger children (of 10 years and below) is extremely good irrespective of the treatment approach. This applies to behavioural, psychodynamic, community based and in-patient treatment. Studies that have dealt exclusively with younger children (Glaser, 1959; Barker, 1968) and investigations that have broken down outcome in terms of age (Rodriguez, et al., 1959; Warnecke, 1964; Miller, et al., 1972) consistently report that for the 5–10-year-olds there is a treatment success rate of 95 per cent or more. This certainly accords with the clinical experiences of the author and explains why Blagg and Yule's (1984) study was confined to children 10 years and older. Many younger children were successfully treated during the period of the study but were not included in the treatment sample as they did not pose a significant treatment challenge.

2. The treatment outcome for older children (in the 11–16 years age range) seems far less predictable and has varied widely from study to study. In general the outcome for this age range is far less favourable. Thus, Rodriguez et al., (1959) report only a 36 per cent success rate with their older children. Hersov (1960–61a,b) managed a 58 per cent success rate with his 50 hospitalised cases. Treatment was not broken down according to age although 42 out of the 50 cases fell into the 10–16 years age range. If the 8 younger cases were eliminated from the analysis, a much poorer outcome seems likely. Berg et al., (1969) achieved only a

59 per cent favourable outcome with 29 cases aged 10–15 years. Miller *et al.*'s (1972) comparative study tentatively suggests that for older phobics (most of whom were school phobics) neither systematic desensitisation with contingency management or psychotherapy were any more effective than being placed on a waiting list. In Blagg and Yule's (1984) comparative treatment study, the 16 hospitalised children produced a 37.5 per cent favourable treatment outcome. However, the group that received home tuition with psychotherapy produced a poorer treatment outcome than any other reported study. Only 10 per cent of the home tutored group returned to school.

3. Although the prognosis for older school phobic children looks poor a few studies have produced remarkably impressive results with this more difficult age range. All of these studies emphasise a vigorous energetic approach to treatment in which fears and anxieties are exposed and uncompromisingly confronted. In every case enforced school attendance is advocated where necessary. Escort systems are favoured and the explicit or implicit threat of legal intervention is regarded as a legitimate therapeutic lever. The papers describing these more successful approaches are characterised by an optimistic stance and a powerful commitment to ensuring that treatment does work.

Kennedy (1965) reported a 100 per cent success rate with 50 cases using a behavioural approach emphasising a rapid return to school. However, it is important to remember that only 13 of his cases were above 11 years. Furthermore, the cases were not a treatment series but rather a selected sample of less severe (type 1) cases. Indeed, Kennedy argued that such an approach would not be appropriate to more disturbed type 2 cases. Nevertheless, a similar behavioural approach was subsequently applied by Rines (1973) to an older type 2 case with rapid and effective results. In fact, prior to Kennedy's study, Warnecke (1964) published a paper reporting an 80 per cent success rate with what appeared to be a treatment series of older school phobics. Although the treatment approach was framed in psychoanalytic terms, it did have much in common with Kennedy's approach. A variety of practical measures were taken at home and school to ensure an immediate and, if necessary forced, return to school.

In a retrospective study of 20 older school phobics, Skynner (1974) also claims highly impressive outcome figures with 88.2 per cent successfully treated on long-term follow-up. Skynner's results were surprising, given the amount of time devoted to treatment. In most cases only one interview was required. Skynner's (1974) approach is explained as conjoint family therapy with the crucial issue being argued as the need to address faulty family mechanisms. Once again, however, the approach involved enforced school attendance. As noted earlier Skynner (1974) recognises the overlap between his approach and other more explicitly behavioural strategies. Indeed he argues that Kennedy's (1965) success was probably more an outcome of the implicit focus on faulty family mechanisms rather than the explicit focus on behavioural techniques. Framrose (1978) vividly describes the successful treatment of four older, highly disturbed school phobics. One cannot help being impressed by the powerful sense of conviction and intentionality accompanying this paper. Framrose was clearly totally determined that the adolescent phobics would overcome their difficulties in a highly active, vigorous way. Again, the essential treatment elements are expressed in strategic family therapy terms but at the same time explicit use is made of behavioural techniques and a range of school factors are also addressed. Framrose places a strong emphasis on the establishment of a foolproof system of attendance checks once the child is back in school.

Framrose's positive approach and thorough detailed case management is paralleled in Blagg's (1977) description of a rapid behavioural treatment approach. Interestingly, this latter approach applied to a treatment series of 30 cases in Blagg and Yule's (1984) comparative treatment study produced a more successful long-term treatment outcome with children in the 11–16 years age range than any other reported study. Of the behaviourally treated group, 93.3 per cent returned to school and were still attending regularly at long-term follow-up. Treatment was extremely quick in most cases with the majority of children needing no further help beyond three weeks. A high expectancy of success also permeates Blagg and Yule's (1984) paper. Many practical measures are taken to ensure the child is being reasonably and fairly treated at home and school. At the same time a rapid and, if necessary enforced, return to school is organised. Great care is taken to block any avoidance responses. Even at the first point of contact with the child and family there is never any question of 'if' the child will return to school, but only 'when' and 'how' it will be accomplished.

4. Children who have been hospitalised for treatment have

received from 6–19 months therapy. Undoubtedly, hospitalisation represents the most intensive and costly treatment intervention. At the same time there is no conclusive evidence to suggest that this kind of help is reserved for the most profoundly disturbed cases. It seems more likely that hospitalisation is an outcome of patterns of referral and the restrictions and bias of professionals involved than a carefully considered intervention weighed against alternative community-based approaches. Blagg and Yule's (1984) comparative study revealed that the hospitalised cases were closely matched to the two community-treated groups on all significant indices *even though* they were not randomly allocated.

5. In spite of the cost and intensity of provision, the outcome figures for studies involving hospitalisation are no better for younger or older children than many community based approaches and certainly not as effective as strategic family therapy approaches or comprehensive behavioural packages emphasising a rapid enforced return to school. Under the circumstances, it seems wholly unreasonable and uneconomic to subject school phobics to hospitalisation, particularly where intensive, meaningful community-based approaches have not been vigorously pursued. Barker's (1968) study is especially open to criticism in this respect.

6. Home tuition with psychotherapy is commonly used in the United Kingdom as a treatment intervention with school phobia. Apart from Blagg and Yule's (1984) paper, there appears to be no recorded trial of this approach in the literature. This is rather worrying as the treatment outcome for the home-tutored group in Blagg and Yule's (1984) study was so appallingly poor that this kind of intervention may inhibit spontaneous remission or, even worse, reinforce the school phobia pattern. Clearly experimental evidence for these statements is limited but nevertheless the clinical experience of the author suggests that school phobics who have been put on home-tuition and given psychotherapy prior to a more direct attack on the problem are much more difficult to treat than those who have been out of school for the same amount of time but have had no previous treatment. It is not uncommon for the home tutor to become over-involved with the child and the family and to unwittingly become a powerful maintaining factor. Very often the kind of people that take up a home-tutor post are unemployed or retired teachers. Naturally, some of them may have a vested interest in maintaining the

school phobia as their job depends upon it. In view of these considerations there seems to be a good case for avoiding the use of home-tuition with psychotherapy at all costs.

7. As Chapter 3 shows a wide range of behavioural techniques have been usefully employed with many different cases of school phobia. The behavioural purist's search for the most effective technique or combination of techniques is perhaps naïve given the nature of school phobia. Above all, the previous chapters have demonstrated that school phobia cannot be regarded as a specific clinical entity. It is a complex syndrome of varying pathology, symptomatology and severity involving a wide number of child, family, school and social factors. Although there are recurring themes, the complex interplay of factors involved in each case will be unique. Thus the trend towards flexible, comprehensive, behavioural management is to be welcomed. The strength of behaviour therapy lies in its problem-solving approach to treatment and rigorous attention to detail.

8. Even so, there does seem to be a case for building more detailed and comprehensive typologies of school phobia provided this can be linked to the kind and sequence of treatment approaches appropriate to each case. In particular, more attention needs to be paid to the way in which avoidance behaviours, physiological arousal and self-assessed fear-ratings co-vary in different types of problems undergoing different treatment regimes.

9. It is clear from the treatment reviews that pupils who have been refusing school for only a few days are much easier to treat than long-standing cases of school phobia. There seems to be a strong case for heightening awareness of school phobia amongst professionals, especially teachers, family doctors and social workers so that problems can be caught early or even prevented. As yet there has been very little research on screening techniques to highlight those pupils most at risk. However, it is interesting to note that a by-product of the community-based treatment approach adopted in Blagg and Yule (1984) was a lowering of the referral rate for school phobia during the years following the study. There was good evidence to suggest that the numbers of children showing this problem did not diminish over time but that teachers, family doctors and social workers became much more aware of the problem and more confident in dealing with it. Indeed, during the latter stages of the Blagg and Yule (1984) study, it was quite common for teachers to call on help from the

psychologist only after they had carried out much of the diagnostic and treatment planning work. Within each of the secondary schools in the study, a group of teachers at senior management level became very efficient at spotting and handling school phobics.

Part Two

The Rapid Treatment Approach to School Phobia

6

Diagnostic Considerations

INTRODUCTION

The diagnostic and treatment procedure considered in the present and subsequent chapters represents a detailed look at the rapid behavioural treatment approach reported previously in Blagg (1977, 1979 and 1981) and successfully utilised in Blagg and Yule's (1984) comparative treatment study. Whereas previous accounts dwelt upon pragmatic and content issues this present account will also include a careful review of process issues. This chapter will explore the issues and procedures involved in gathering relevant data whilst Chapter 7 will focus on treatment and resistance to treatment. Finally, Chapter 8 provides a series of illustrative case studies.

The diagnostic/treatment approach is based primarily upon behavioural principles but also involves attending to many subtle school, family and personal issues. The approach can be summarised in terms of the four basic stages involved which fit Miller, Barrett and Hampe's (1974) formulation:

a. establishing good relationships with the child, the family and the school;

b. clarifying the real or imagined events that have caused the anxieties;

c. desensitising the child and if necessary the parents and teachers through a variety of techniques including discussion, humour, role rehearsal and emotive imagery; and

d. confronting the feared situations through forced school attendance. In addition, home and school related operant factors are dealt with through advice on contingency management. In essence, the clarification element encompasses systematic problem-solving procedures whilst the other elements involve the application of a comprehensive range of behavioural techniques tailored to the needs of each particular case.

In terms of aetiology, the additive stress model referred to in Yule, Hersov and Treseder (1980) has been found particularly helpful. The vulnerable child faced with a series of home and school related worries arising over a short period of time becomes highly anxious resulting in a school refusal episode. The absence from school leads to the development of other secondary factors which then reinforce and maintain the school refusal pattern.

PREREQUISITES AND PRAGMATICS

If the ideal client existed he or she would be anxious for advice and help; supply all the relevant information you need; entertain new ideas; willingly participate in treatment suggestions and involve any teachers, family members or friends who might help resolve the problem. Unfortunately, ideal school phobic cases from ideal families and ideal schools rarely exist. For many understandable reasons teachers commonly misunderstand the nature of the child's difficulties; school phobics are often highly defensive and their parents reluctant to seek advice and address the problem. In fact many cases are coerced into treatment because of the social and legal pressures associated with school attendance.

Thus clients are often only superficially co-operative. They may be willing to share their views and feelings and agree to a treatment strategy but sabotage plans at the slightest discomfort or excuse. Psychological realities may be entertained but the solutions are often too painful to execute. This may lead to the parents looking for medical alibis. A physical illness is much more acceptable than a psychological problem. If the family doctor does not come up with a medical explanation the parents may request a second opinion from a paediatrician. At this stage there can often be long delays in obtaining an appointment and waiting for the results of tests. Uncertainty can breed more anxiety and secondary problems arising out of absence from school build up. The paediatrician may eventually refer on to a psychiatrist. In the absence of a physical explanation for the child's distressing symptoms the parents may look for other causes.

The school may be scrutinised and criticised. Parents who may have unpleasant memories of their own school days sometimes misinterpret, magnify or distort minor events. Poor communication between teachers and parents can exacerbate the problem by leaving misconceptions and misunderstandings unchallenged. School-related anxieties may be unwittingly reinforced by friends, relatives and professionals who share parental concern but do not have intimate knowledge of the school environment. In view of these considerations the following issues warrant close attention.

Establish good communications between professionals

There are many helping agencies that might become involved with a school phobic case, including family doctors, paediatricians, psychiatrists, teachers, social workers, education welfare officers, clinical and educational psychologists. Each professional is likely to have a slightly different perspective which could lead to conflicting advice. This provides plenty of scope for the anxious parent to become even more confused and uncertain about how to proceed. There is also good potential for resistant families to stall for time and play one professional off against the other. However, these problems can be avoided if the professionals have a common understanding of the nature of school phobia and work together on a consistent, mutually supportive treatment strategy.

Ensure that one professional takes on responsibility for the treatment

Co-operation and communication between professionals can be enhanced if one person works with both the family and the school and co-ordinates the involvement of other professionals where necessary. In many ways educational psychologists are ideally qualified for this key treatment role. Their combined clinical and educational training enables sensitive treatment of child, school

119

and family issues. They normally possess intimate knowledge of the schools in their area so that they often appreciate the child's school context before actively dealing with the case. In many ways, educational psychologists are general practitioners in the school setting, enjoying comfortable and familiar relationships with educational, medical and social work colleagues.

Eliminate medical problems before investigating other factors

School phobics often present with many distressing somatic symptoms. It is therefore crucial that potential physical causes should be eliminated as quickly as possible with the minimum fuss. Unless this happens, health-related anxieties will linger on — making treatment difficult. In any case school phobia can coexist with a genuine physical illness and obviously the latter needs treating before one can proceed with the former. Debilitating viral infections or other illnesses sometimes contribute to the development of school phobia making it difficult to know when the physical problem has disappeared and the school avoidance started. Close liaison with medical specialists is indicated to clarify when it is appropriate to treat the problem psychologically.

If medical investigations have not been carried out, discuss the case with the family doctor advising on your likely involvement. Ensure that the parents take the child for a medical check-up, preferably out of school hours, *before* making an appointment to see them. If the doctor feels there is an organic basis for the child's symptoms, clarify how long the child should be off school. Follow up the case at the appropriate time. If the child is physically fit but still refusing school, arrange an urgent appointment.

Investigate the appropriateness of the child's current school placement

Successful treatment relies heavily upon the full co-operation of the child's schoolteachers. It is important for the principal case worker to have a good working relationship with the school and enough knowledge of educational matters to make a realistic appraisal of the appropriateness of the school placement. In practice many teachers will have worked up quite an expertise with these sorts of cases, whilst a few will prefer to off-load their problems on to other schools or outside agencies. Teacher attitudes, tutor group and timetable flexibility, availability of remedial help, provision of a quiet room, opportunites for special activities over lunch-hours and breaks and pastoral care facilities are just a few of the areas that would need exploring and understanding *before* interviewing the parents and child.

PROCESS ISSUES

In many ways successful treatment hinges upon painstaking attention to detail. It is vital to gather *all* the necessary data *before* negotiating a treatment plan. Therefore, careful attention should be paid to process issues likely to enhance or restrict information gathering.

Assess client motivation

Background information provided by the referrer may give useful clues about teacher and parental motivation for help. If the school, social services or education welfare services have forced the referral on the family because of the child's persistent absence from school, the parents may not want help and fake co-operation or else be openly hostile. On the other hand, the highly perplexed, worried parent, who is desperate for advice, may press the therapist for an instant solution.

In reality one is likely to see the whole range of parents, from those who are inaccessible and antagonistic to those who are open and suggestible. Some may want to co-operate but block treatment plans because they fear treatment will not work and the problem will worsen. From the outset it is necessary to tease out the parents' feelings by listening carefully to what they say as well as noting implicit cues in phrasing, tone of voice and body language.

Speed of intervention

Intervene as quickly as possible whilst the events leading up to the problem are fresh in everyone's minds. Issues and feelings at this stage are likely to be more accessible and open to investigation. Furthermore, if the problem can be tackled early there will have been less opportunity for secondary maintaining factors to have developed making treatment more difficult.

Timing and pacing

As school phobic problems are normally highly complex, thorough, systematic data-gathering across all relevant areas is extremely time-consuming. It is therefore important to allow for plenty of time at the initial diagnostic stage. Telescoping treatment into one or two lengthy sessions can be highly cost effective by reducing the time required for subsequent sessions. A series of flexible shorter sessions closely spaced can also be effective. Both approaches implicitly communicate to the parties involved that the problem is being taken seriously and tackled with some urgency. Allowing plenty of time and being thorough can also inspire confidence in the therapist and facilitate relationship building.

Shorter, tightly-timed diagnostic sessions that finish abruptly can expose anxieties whilst not systematically exploring them — leaving clients more agitated than at the outset. Furthermore, it can communicate to the clients that the therapist has little interest in the problem and is merely meeting statutory obligations. Finally, if the sessions are widely spaced unnecessary delays can occur in planning a return to school. So long as the child is 'under investigation' the parents and child feel safe in not addressing the problem.

If at all possible, it is better not to have a set time for treatment that must be used up. It is more desirable to set aside more time than is necessary and draw the interview to a close at a stage that is comfortable for both clients and therapist. Ideally, a whole morning should be arranged to interview all parties concerned separately and in groups, so that the diagnostic and treatment planning sessions can be continuous.

The interview setting

It is worthwhile investing a lot of effort in organising the initial diagnostic interview(s) in school. If the parents have requested help emphasise that they should bring their child to school *even if it means using force*. In some cases the social worker or education welfare officer can assist in this process, but where possible it is desirable to leave it to the family members to marshal their own resources involving friends or relatives if necessary.

Care needs to be taken to prepare the school environment. A couple of quiet offices must be booked for interviewing and availability of key teachers needs to be ascertained so that they can be involved at appropriate times. Bringing the parents, teachers and child together in the problem situation has a number of advantages:

i. It implicitly communicates an optimistic message. The therapist is saying that in spite of the difficulties it is reasonable to bring the child to school for interview. A home visit or clinic appointment may well imply that the therapist feels the child is too sick to interview in school, thereby reinforcing the problem.

ii. If the parent(s) can manage to bring the child under protest, one already has a good indication of their desire for the child to return to school and their ability to implement an escort procedure if necessary.

iii. It can be good learning experience for the parents, revealing problems that were not expected that can then be discussed with the therapist.

iv. It may reveal information about whether the child's problem involves separation anxiety, and/or fear of leaving home and/or a phobic avoidance of school.

v. The range, intensity and nature of the child's school-related anxieties can be exposed and quickly investigated to the satisfaction of the parents.

vi. Parental misunderstandings about school can be broken down through discussion so that they are less likely to incubate worries based upon misconceptions.

vii. If the problems are clarified and all parties accept a return to the child's present school a treatment plan can be formulated immediately.

Sometimes the parents may attend school for interview but not bring the child. The reasons for this situation need thorough investigation. Some parents may be unable to cope with the child's tyrannical temper tantrums, verbal threats or emotional blackmail. Alternatively, the parents may have a vested interest in maintaining the child's problem. These issues will be explored more fully in Chapter 7. At this point it is sufficient to say that a follow-up visit to interview the child with a subsequent school appointment to plan a treatment approach often resolves the problem. Sometimes the parents may need outside help in taking the child to school.

Occasionally, preliminary referral data indicates a change of school may be necessary. In this case make a school visit to discuss the problem with the child's teachers. Follow up with a home visit to see the child and parents. Establish which school the child should attend. Liaise with and prepare the new school and then invite the parents and child to attend for a joint session with psychologist and teachers.

Consider interviewing each of the parties separately

There are distinct advantages in conducting separate interviews with the child, parents and teachers before bringing the parties together. It is not so much the events leading up to a problem that are important but rather the way in which the participants view them. The child, teacher and parents are likely to have very different perspectives. Each person may selectively attend to aspects of situations, magnifying some events whilst completely ignoring others that on the surface look just as worrying. The problem facing the therapist is to know how to go about eliciting all these various viewpoints so that each of the participants' feelings are fully understood.

Frequently each of the parties involved looks to the therapist for reassurance and support for his or her point of view. Somehow the therapist has to negotiate a tricky path, empathising without necessarily fully agreeing. Individual sessions allow one to enter into a cautious coalition with each of the parties, whereas conjoint sessions would make this very difficult. All too often empathising with one person offends someone else with a conflicting viewpoint. This may lead to arguments with the result that the therapist is side-tracked into group management issues rather than systematic data gathering. Even worse than this, it may lead to some participants withdrawing co-operation and/or concealing feelings and essential information.

Once the therapist has established a clear picture of significant events and peoples' perceptions of them, treatment options can be sensitively explored and each of the participants appropriately prepared for a joint session. The nature of this preparation will be considered in the next chapter.

Occasionally, the therapist is put under unreasonable pressure to agree strongly with a particular view of the problem. In the event of this happening careful use of qualifying language is indicated:

> I would find it very difficult to agree (or disagree) at this stage as I don't have enough information. I do need to understand everybody's point of view — although it does seem as though you are making an important point.

Interviewing style

Different clients have different expectations of the therapist. The very anxious parents who are highly motivated towards treatment may want the therapist to assume the role of the expert offering quick solutions. On the other hand, the family that has been coerced into treatment would certainly not be impressed by the expert role. In this case, the therapist's initial task would be that of negotiating some means of working with the family. It might mean establishing a very different understanding of the problem in comparison to the referrer's viewpoint. At this point the therapist might be involved in saying something along the lines:

> Well, I appreciate your resentment at having to see me. I understand that you did not ask for help but now that we find ourselves together, perhaps we can explore why the referral was made . . .

> I do appreciate your views but it nevertheless does seem that there is a problem with William's attendance. Clearly, if this is not resolved, the school teachers and the Education Welfare Service will continue to make life difficult for you. Now that I am involved I shall be obliged to submit my observations to the Chief Education Officer — who will be expecting me to come up with some suitable advice. If I can't help, the matter will be taken out of my hands and dealt with by the legal

department. The results of that could be very unpleasant for both you and William. It looks to me as though the best thing we can do is to work together and this will keep everybody happy. I should be glad to look at any school-related issues that you are worried about and will do everything I can to try and help.

In many cases this style works quite well. However, in particularly resistant families a more forceful approach is required. This will be outlined in more detail in Chapter 7.

In the early diagnostic stages there are good arguments for adopting a fairly neutral role in which one acts as a collaborative empirical scientist with the clients playing an important and active role in clarifying the problems. The more directive, confident, reassuring expert role can be slipped into at the treatment planning stage or earlier if the situation demands it. It is far easier to move from a neutral to an expert role than vice versa. In the event of being pressed to adopt an expert role prematurely the therapist may need to make statements like:

I realise you want help quickly and I certainly agree that this is necessary. However, we do need to gather all the relevant information before we can be sure of how to proceed.

Reduce anxiety

The distressing symptoms associated with school phobia often suck the child, parents and teachers into a reinforcing circle of anxiety. Thus, by the time outside help is sought, all of the participants are extremely tense and agitated. From the outset the therapist needs to be mindful of establishing relationships and reducing anxiety surrounding the problem. Attention to the following points has been found useful.

a. Communicate a relaxed unhurried manner to the clients.
b. Thoroughly explore all the issues raised. Attention to detail is reassuring and working through the various painful issues can begin the process of desensitising some of the problems.
c. Seek clarification where necessary, e.g. 'I am not sure I understand what you mean. Could you say more about that?'

Reflect your interpretation back to the clients for checking, e.g. 'So what you are saying is . . .' This communicates to clients that their point of view is fully understood and allows for correction where necessary.

d. Help the parents to interpret the problems as transitory and understandable from a normal developmental perspective. Explain the additive stress model and involve them in explaining how the school phobia might have evolved. Encourage the parents to view the school phobia as a learning experience for the child: 'There are many events in life that can be threatening; helping your child through this crisis will be an ideal preparation for coping with future stressful experiences. On the other hand, if the school phobia remains unresolved your child may learn to avoid facing up to other problems that might come along later.'

e. Assist the parents in rationalising guilt feelings. Many parents blame themselves for their child's difficulties. Some will say 'It's all my fault.' At this point it can be helpful to say something along the lines: 'Well, if you wanted your child to be like this and you tried hard to make it happen, it would be your fault.' Normally parents will deny this but say 'I didn't mean it to happen but I still feel it's my fault.' At this stage it can be helpful to explore reasonable explanations for the child's problems that do not necessarily involve the parents, e.g. 'All children are temperamentally different. Some start off in life more emotional and vulnerable than others. Also, one cannot legislate for all circumstances in life. You couldn't avoid going into hospital — it was just one of those things.'

f. Where possible use humour. An over-serious stance can unwittingly reinforce tension and anxiety. On the other hand, an over-jocular style can imply a flippant unconcerned attitude. Nevertheless, sensitive use of humour can be a powerful technique.

CONTENT ISSUES

The previous sections have focused on prerequisites and issues likely to hinder or enhance collecting sufficient relevant information to plan effective treatment. This section will now highlight the kinds of questions that need exploring and the sort of events that commonly trigger and/or maintain school phobia.

The use of a school phobia record form can be an invaluable *aide-mémoire*, as well as an efficient way of recording information. An example of such a form is given in the appendix. In order to make maximum use of the initial interview with the parents and child, it is useful to obtain *beforehand* detailed background information from the school and other agencies that have been involved with the child. This can be noted on the record form and ultimately checked with the parents. Throughout the information gathering stages, the psychologist needs to constantly clarify fuzzy descriptions so that the problems and issues are fully understood and accepted by all of the parties involved. A series of issues relating to the child, family and school will need to be systematically explored.

The child

Attendance pattern and history

The length and severity of the problem should be established. The therapist needs to know how long the child has been off school and whether the problem has arisen dramatically and suddenly in a normally good attender or gradually and incipiently over the years, finally culminating in total school refusal. In cases of sudden onset there are usually a series of trigger factors that can be identified. Once these factors have been made explicit, treatment planning can proceed relatively smoothly.

Cases involving an incipient onset usually require much more work. There may be trigger factors that have finally tipped the child over into total school refusal, but over and above these, other long-standing issues are likely to need much attention. For instance a long history of frequent absences is likely to have caused disrupted peer group relationships and an episodic grasp of the curriculum. In connection with assessing family attitudes towards schooling, it is often helpful to explore the attendance patterns of any other children in the family who are either at school or have left school recently. Other poor attenders in the family can provide very powerful models reinforcing the school avoidance. In addition, a familial pattern of poor attendance often means that the parents do not place great store by education so that they are poorly motivated towards returning the child to full-time schooling.

Parents and children are notoriously unreliable in accurately

128

reporting attendance histories. Even teachers sometimes overlook or underestimate the extent of absenteeism in a particular pupil. Therefore it is important to examine the school registers. Long-term attendance patterns can sometimes give a lead in looking for home or school related factors that may be precipitating or maintaining the problem. For instance, in very occasional cases a specific worry about a certain teacher or an activity like PE and games can lead to a regular pattern of absences on the school days when those subjects occur. Depressed mothers — or those living in isolated circumstances — sometimes encourage absences on certain days when they know they will be alone. In occasional cases a mother with three or four children will keep one child at home all the time, on a rota system.

The psychologist may gain further clues about precipitating factors and client motivation by exploring the issues surrounding earlier incidents of school phobia. For instance, how did the parents and child view the previous difficulties? How long was the child off school and how was the problem overcome?

Associated symptoms

There are many questions and issues that need explaining to obtain a precise description of the problems surrounding the school phobia and the way adults deal with them. Examples: how does the child's refusal to attend school manifest itself? What exactly happens each morning from the time the child wakes up? Is getting out of bed, dressing or eating breakfast a problem? Does the child prepare books and equipment for school? At exactly what point in the sequence of morning preparations does the child's behaviour give cause for concern? If the child is encouraged to proceed with normal preparations for school or to leave for school, what happens then? Are there any physical signs of anxiety e.g. stomach pains, headaches, nausea, pallor, trembling, running off in a panic? Does the child protest and cry? If pressed further will the child exhibit temper tantrums; how severe are these and what form do they take? Does the child throw things or punch and kick, etc.? Has the child ever threatened suicide? If so what was the behavioural context and exactly what was said? Does the child seem to be suffering from a generalised anxiety state? Is there a problem with bowel or bladder control? Are the child's sleeping or eating patterns significantly disturbed? Are there any signs of a generalised depression with the child feeling constantly overtired and sleeping excessively long hours? However the problems manifest themselves, the psychologist needs to know about the events preceding any specific behaviours, how the adults react to them and what the outcome is from both the child's and adult's point of view.

Occasionally, children referred as being physically fit do have an undiagnosed medical problem. Physical symptoms that persist into the school day, evenings and weekends warrant further investigation, especially if there does not seem to be a psychological basis for the school phobia. Rare viral infections are often difficult to diagnose but can be very debilitating. Even if there are psychological explanations persistent physical problems should not be ignored. In this connection the case of a 10-year-old boy referred by his family doctor comes to mind. The boy showed all the classic symptoms of school phobia. The attendance problem was overcome but the stomach pains continued. Several months later stomach tumours were diagnosed. Fortunately, cases like this are rare.

Out of school activities

The extent to which a child engages in normal out of school activities gives the psychologist a good idea about the severity of the problem. The child who is housebound, refusing to leave the mother's side and unwilling to face friends is obviously more generally disturbed than the child who continues to function normally out of school hours. It will be important to ascertain whether the housebound child is exhibiting major separation anxiety or a strong phobic avoidance of schoolfriends. It can also be helpful to establish whether the social isolation was present at the outset of the school refusal problem or whether it has developed as a consequence of being out of school. The child who is able to walk past the school at the weekend without feeling anxious or fearful is unlikely to be exhibiting a generalised phobic avoidance of school.

Attitude towards school refusal problem

Some children may have such negative attitudes about school that they feel their school refusal is a reasonable and rational response. Children who feel this way will be very poorly motivated to change their position unless the basis for their feelings can be challenged. Accordingly, it will be necessary to explore their feelings about all aspects of school life.

More commonly, school phobics place a high importance on schooling and feel guilty about their persistent absenteeism. In these cases the child needs to appreciate how unavoidable and uncontrollable events have added up and caused the problem whilst at the same time giving strong reassurance that the problem can be overcome.

Intellectual functioning and attainments

A significant number of school phobics experience learning difficulties that have not been fully recognised by the school. A thorough assessment of strengths and weaknesses will allow the psychologist to advise on a detailed compensatory programme. In some cases the problems may be beyond the scope of the school's remedial facilities so that additional specialist help will need to be arranged.

Personality characteristics

The child's temperamental traits and personality structure must not be overlooked. Everyday events which most children do not even notice can be very threatening to vulnerable children. For instance the child with low self-esteem may be highly self-conscious and interpret casual light-hearted remarks as painful criticism. The highly introverted child who has led a rather sheltered quiet life may find the hustle and bustle of a large comprehensive school very uncomfortable. The Eysenck (1964) Personality Questionnaire is a useful pre- and post-treatment barometer of the child's introversion and tendency to worry. It also gives helpful information about pupil sensitivity, social naïvety and social conformity.

Peer relationships

It is useful to gain a picture of the child's relationships at school. If the child is highly unpopular and constantly being teased this would provide a very realistic basis for school avoidance. If this were the case it would be important in conversations with teachers, parents and the child to isolate the precise form of the bullying or teasing and possible reasons for it. Is it to do with the child's physical appearance, mannerisms, or sensitivity, etc.? If explanations are forthcoming, remedies often suggest themselves. Occasionally major relationship problems cannot be overcome and a change of school is indicated.

Some children are highly dependent on one or two close friends. In this circumstance a change of teaching group with the resultant loss of a friend could be very distressing.

The Rutter and Yule (1968) Behaviour Rating Scales provide a useful starting point in looking at the child's behaviour. The teacher's version can be completed by the teachers at the time of the referral and compared with the parent's version of the scale completed at the first interview.

Developmental history

School phobics are often over-protected and/or over-indulged. It is worth exploring possible reasons for this. For instance, are there any medical or social explanations to account for the child being treated differently to other children in the family? Is the child a much wanted only child of elderly parents? Did the mother experience a difficult pregnancy and childbirth? Has the child suffered a life-threatening illness? Have there been any unplanned painful separation experiences? Has the mother suffered a post-natal depression? These and many other possible events could led to pampering and over-compensation by some parents, making the child more vulnerable than most children.

Home and school related anxieties

There are a wealth of home and school related issues that warrant systematic investigation. Examples of commonly occurring themes are included in the appendix (pp. 199–201, 203, 205–7). Unfortunately, anxiety created by particular events can be shaped-up and maintained by the reactions of adults. Thus the child who is naturally distressed by the death of a parent, close relative or friend may continue to be upset by a resultant long-term depression in another family member. At the same time a sudden loss can make the child feel insecure and create fears that another member of the family will die. Similar worries can be caused if there is an illness in the family (physical or mental) particularly where parents are always making exaggerated comments about their state of ill-health in front of the child. Children sometimes take metaphorical statements literally. Health-related fears can also be triggered by an illness in the child, particularly if the child feels depressed following an unpleasant viral infection. Once again, problems can be highlighted by constantly talking about the child's physical symptoms without clarifying them. Similarly, minor psychosomatic complaints can be shaped and reinforced by over-attending to them through: i. giving unnecessary medication; ii. constantly enquiring about how the child is feeling; and iii. taking the child on frequent visits to the doctor *during* school hours. Separation fears which may or may not be linked to death or illness worries can be precipitated by a sudden unplanned separation from a parent or other close family member. This can be especially traumatic if the mother or father have disappeared during the daytime whilst the child was at school. In this case, being at school can sometimes be associated with anxieties surrounding the separation. If the separation is the result of a worrying hospitalisation or a desperate visit to a very sick relative, many other issues may be set in train and interact. The extent to which the school is a secure welcoming environment will also have a crucial bearing on the likely development of a school phobia.

Insecurity and social anxiety commonly arise after the major domestic upheaval in moving house. The child may have acquired some of the natural parental tension resulting from selling, buying, packing and moving. In addition, if the move involves separation from close friends, a long unpleasant journey to school and/or a change of school, anxieties may be even more pronounced. Occasionally jealousy over the attention a younger child is receiving at home may be an important factor. The birth of a new child or an illness in a pre-school child can deflect attention away from the vulnerable adolescent.

Parents can contribute to school-related anxieties by having unrealistic expectations or by over-valuing the child leading to an unrealistic self-appraisal. In both instances, failure at school may be hard to cope with. Too much parental attention on any minor school related worries can shape and reinforce them into major issues.

Once the child is out of school, many secondary issues can arise and maintain the problem. The school phobia may be negatively reinforced through the resulting avoidance of disliked activities and people in school. It may also be positively reinforced through:

1. The child enjoying greater personal freedom at home. For example being able to watch TV, stay in bed later and pursue hobbies and special interests.
2. The child being given special treats and extra attention

whilst *off* school. Sometimes parents may even try and bribe children to go back to school by taking them on shopping sprees, buying them new clothes, etc.

3. The parents removing pressure from the child to attend school, resulting in the anxiety symptoms and protests disappearing. This may in turn reinforce parental views that the school is at fault, leading to collusion with the child over the school phobia.

Finally, there may be many practical difficulties involved in taking the child to school so that the problems are not confronted by the parents. Commonly occurring issues include:

1. the father not being present in the morning when the child's difficulties manifest themselves;
2. the mother being unable to physically manage the child's temper tantrums;
3. the presence of other younger children in the family who need taking to school so that the mother feels unable to deal with the school phobic child and manage the other normal family demands as well;
4. the family living a long way from the school and having no means of transport other than the school bus;
4. the parent(s) being unwilling to force school attendance feeling too stressed by the child's distress and worried that confrontation will lead to an acceleration of the difficulties.

With regard to school-related issues a change of school or a major change within school commonly precedes school phobia. Perhaps this is not surprising when one considers the wide range of adjustments involved in such a change. The child often has to become accustomed to new rules and routines, different academic demands and expectations, unfamiliar teaching styles and approaches as well as forming new friendships. The change from the single parent teaching approach of the small primary school to the multiparent impersonal style of the large comprehensive can be especially disturbing to some children. If the new school is situated a long way from home in unfamiliar surroundings the sense of insecurity can be increased. Some children find long coach journeys distressing either because they are poor travellers or because of the general mayhem that sometimes accompanies trips to school. Journeys to and from school also provide no escape from teasing or bullying if this is a problem. Allegations of bullying are quite common and need thorough and careful investigation, especially if the child is too nervous to expose the culprits for fear of reprisals. Of course some highly sensitive children need help themselves in reinterpreting harmless remarks and jokes.

Many different subject areas can create problems for individual children. Difficulties may centre around the work being too hard or too easy, the relationships with the teacher and/or the pupils in the teaching group, and/or the teaching style. Specific learning problems need thorough investigation and remediation. Overweight or poorly co-ordinated children often find PE and games very threatening. Regular failure in physical activities with consequent ridicule and embarrassment can only serve to undermine the child's self-confidence. It is often possible to produce a games programme that allows the child to take exercise in a more enjoyable less threatening way. Avoidance of games can be linked to many problems including fear of physical injury, self-consciousness at showering in public, a teacher who shouts, excessive noise in the gym, etc.. Worries in any area of school life need to be fully clarified so that appropriate action can be taken.

A number of school phobics have very high levels of aspiration so that they set themselves almost impossible targets and then become anxious when they just fail to achieve them. Such pupils are often very high achievers. Other pupils have more specific worries like coping with exams and tests. Many are anxious about performing in front of the class. Reading out loud and answering questions can be embarrassing for some.

Early signs of school phobia are often not noticed. Odd days off school and frequent visits to the school nurse complaining of minor aches and pains often indicate that something is wrong. A little extra help and sensitive handling at this stage can avert a full-blown school phobia. However, once the problem has developed secondary school related issues arise.

The family

Structure and relationships

The school phobia record form (pp. 204–7) provides a quick means of recording essential information. In many families, the

135

mother has an over-close relationship with the child and a rather unsatisfactory, distanced relationship with her husband. This can be even more pronounced when the father works shifts, long hours or is away from home a good deal so that parenting responsibilities lie mainly with the mother. It will be important to understand whom the child feels closest to and the kinds of communication patterns that exist between the family members. It will also be useful to establish the child's status in the family context, for instance is the child the baby of the family? Sometimes there is such a large age-gap between the youngest and the next eldest that the child effectively functions as an only child living in a world of adults. In this situation parents and older siblings may be inclined to over-value and over-indulge the child. Sometimes an eldest child can be put under unreasonable pressure to behave in certain ways in order to set a good example to younger brothers and sisters. Occasionally a middle child may feel neglected especially if there is a much younger sibling receiving a lot of attention and an older sibling having more freedom and excitement in life.

Sources of stress and anxiety

This area has already been touched upon in previous sections in connection with child-related anxieties. It is important to remember that there may be many issues which, whilst not directly concerning the child, may nevertheless cause a build-up of stress and anxiety in other family members resulting in the family unit being less able to resolve its own problems. Relationship difficulties with close friends and relatives, problems at work and redundancy are but a few of the possibilities here. Sometimes where there are multiple family problems the school phobia may not be the main issue causing concern. In this case it would be important to establish support systems for the family in addition to giving assistance with tackling the school phobia.

Costs and benefits

It is worth exploring the costs and benefits of the school phobia to each of the individual family members as well as to the family unit as a whole. Sometimes the problem fulfils a family function like deflecting parents away from looking at more painful issues such as the state of their marriage. An agoraphobic mother living in isolated circumstances may be very glad to have the child at home for company. Issues like this can often result in covert or overt resistance to treatment. Clues may be revealed when the parents are asked to outline how they have tried to resolve the problem so far. Once again, there may be a need to take on individual family members for treatment in addition to dealing with the child's school phobia.

Patterns of influence and control

As far as possible the family should be encouraged to marshal its own resources in overcoming the child's difficulties. If the therapist takes on too much responsibility in treatment a dependency situation may be set up requiring a lengthy weaning process. Accordingly, the therapist will want to know answers to questions like: who are the key authority figures in the family? What role do the grandparents play in the upbringing of the grandchildren? Are there any family members acting as models for the school phobic problem? Are the parents able to exert authority over the child if they really want to or is the child omnipotent and beyond their control? How do each of the family members view the child's difficulties and what kinds of solutions do they think should be tried? This line of enquiry will be particularly important with highly resistant families and will be returned to in the next chapter.

The school

The review of treatment literature outlined in Part 1 of this book highlights the fact that many therapists have ignored or de-emphasised the role of school factors in the aetiology of school phobia. The beginning of this chapter has already emphasised that a prerequisite to successful treatment must surely be that the child's current school placement is deemed to be appropriate both socially and academically.

Many therapists, whilst accepting that many aspects of school life cause certain children anxiety, imply that it is solely the child's perception of school that needs changing rather than anything in the school. It is further implied that as most children do not react to the kinds of events that cause concern to school phobics, their fears must be irrational and unrealistic. The focus in treatment work is how to deal with these irrational fears through desensitisation or confrontation. It is argued that with successful treatment, the child will eventually come to realise that the fears were ill-founded and that school can be an enjoyable experience. A flooding approach based on this rather simplistic view is depicted in the cartoon shown in Figure 6.1.

The therapist prises the child away from the anxious parents and forces the child to face the fear-provoking situation, perhaps with a degree of social and academic support. Although the child's anxiety levels rise in the early stages, the child's avoidance behaviour is blocked until eventually the anxiety subsides and the child realises that the anxiety provoking situations were misinterpreted or distorted. Soon the child is back into a normal routine enjoying school life and everybody including the parents and teachers feels very grateful to the therapist for taking a firm stand. Apart from being a gross over-simplification of the complex issues surrounding successful treatment, the cartoon ignores the fact that sometimes anxiety provoking situations are well-founded and realistic and there are insufficient incentives for being in school. Clearly a crucial part of diagnostic work involves a thorough and sensitive look at the issues surrounding pupils' expressed anxieties. It is often vital to make significant changes in the school environment before dealing with any residual irrational fears.

There are also more general issues to be considered. Some schools may have such multiple problems that a systems approach is strongly indicated alongside any individual treatment work. Schools that have generally poor attendance rates may be especially difficult to work with on an individual case-work level. In some schools it may be just the lower-achieving children in the higher age-groups that show poorer attendance. School phobics from this section of the school may be rather more difficult to treat on a purely individual basis especially if close friends are regularly absenting themselves from school and thereby providing powerful models for school avoidance behaviour in the school phobic.

Schools that suffer from rowdy behaviour and major discipline problems may also pose considerable obstacles to treatment. The highly anxious child who is complaining of persistent bullying may have particular difficulties of readjustment in this kind of environment and may require placement in a more sheltered controlled system. Issues of this kind will be returned to in more detail in the next chapter on treatment.

Figure 6.1

SUMMARY

It must be apparent at this stage that the distinction between diagnosis and treatment is artificial and that in reality the two are inextricably linked. From the outset, the therapist must pay close attention to many fundamental process issues in order to establish trust and confidence and ensure that all of the crucial information relating to the problem is elicited from each of the parties involved. The diagnostic process itself involves many therapeutic elements preparing the way for the eventual painful confrontation stage.

7

Treatment and Resistance to Treatment

INTRODUCTION

This chapter now builds upon the detailed data gathering stage outlined earlier. It assumes that:

a. medical issues have been eliminated;
b. the child's current school placement is appropriate;
c. the therapist has established warm relationships and gained the confidence of the child, parents and school staff; and
d. sufficient information has been elicited to proceed to treatment planning with the therapist taking on a more directive interpretative role.

The sequence of events can now be considered under the following headings:

1. prepare the parties;
2. confirm the mandate;
3. negotiate areas of change required in the school;
4. negotiate areas of change required in the home;
5. find a suitable escort;
6. discuss the treatment plan with the child;
7. support and follow-up arrangements.

Each of these areas will now be discussed in more detail before considering problems and setbacks in treatment.

TREATMENT PLANNING

1. Prepare the parties

The careful diagnostic work outlined in the previous chapter will have exposed many different viewpoints and anxieties. The therapist's job now involves interviewing each of the parties again in the light of all of the information gathered providing a summative feedback to prepare the way for treatment planning. This stage requires extremely delicate handling. The therapist needs to confirm that he or she has received and understood teacher, parent and child viewpoints weaving together all of the information in such a way that each of the parties can accommodate the other's viewpoints and address the essential issues.

The teachers

As the teachers have not necessarily been involved in joint interviews with the parents and child, they may not fully understand all of the family issues involved or any special vulnerabilities in the child. They may have formed faulty impressions of the parents based on limited contact and in certain extreme cases they may have located the child's problems firmly in the home without considering the school's contribution. Expressions like the following are common:

> There is nothing much wrong with Johnny. The problem is his dad doesn't want to know about him and his mother is too over-protective.

> Jane has always been the same. Every time she has the slightest snivel she takes a fortnight off school. I think the problem is that her mother gives in to her too much, perhaps she even likes having her at home. When Jane had a very unpleasant illness recently she missed so much schooling that I think she has found it hard to get back. Now her mother can't do anything with her. The father seems a nice chap but he leaves for work early and arrives home late.

Comments like this can be usefully dealt with by fully agreeing with them whilst at the same time adding extra information to create a more understanding attitude. As noted in the previous chapter there are many potential sources of familial stress and many ways in which a school phobic may be special in the family context. For instance, an only child who has suffered a lengthy life-threatening illness may be more understandably over-protected by the mother.

The issue over the lack of involvement of the fathers in both of the comments above can be put back to the teachers as a problem to be solved. Is it possible to find ways of actively involving a distanced father? If not, are there other family members who can take on the paternal role? Is the family so isolated and fragile that an outside authority like a school teacher or even the psychologist should temporarily assume this role? If so, how can we ensure that the family will become independent of this help during the course of therapy? Fortunately, most teachers are so concerned at the level of distress and anxiety in both the child and the parents that they are only too willing to entertain additional information and consider ways in which they might augment the school environment to facilitate therapy. In these cases teachers are happy to investigate fully concerns about any school issues that may have contributed to the problem or at least be helping to maintain it. Occasionally, with less sensitive teachers it may be necessary to say something along the lines:

Your views on the parental contribution to this problem are quite right but if there is going to be any chance of returning this child to school, we cannot afford to give the parents any room to manoeuvre. So long as they can point to minor issues at school that have not been addressed they can go on using those as a reason for not confronting the real issues. We really must make sure that the child is being fairly treated and that the school is above reproach.

If this kind of reasoning does not result in immediate co-operation it may well mean that a change of school will be indicated where a more sympathetic view of the problem will be ensured. Situations like this should be rare at this stage provided the appropriate diagnostic work was carried out as indicated in the previous chapter.

Provided the teachers are flexible and motivated to help, a quick résumé of school-related concerns may be all that is required as a precursor to bringing the parties together. However, in less flexible school environments, it may be necessary to debate changes in provision, management and handling *before* organising a joint session with the parents so that teachers and therapist can present a united approach.

In some instances the teachers may feel that all of the blame for the problem lies within the school, being totally oblivious of other factors. In such cases, the teachers may feel guilt ridden and need considerable reassurance. At this point it can be very helpful to explain the additive stress model considering each of the contributory factors from home and school. Occasionally, the school does indeed play a very major part in the child's problem and in these circumstances detailed plans will need to be formulated that will desensitise the parent and child anxieties, establish confidence and avoid any likelihood of the issues recurring again. Instances of bullying and/or major personality clashes with certain teachers would fall into this category.

Above all, the teachers need to be encouraged to communicate a relaxed, caring and confident attitude to the parents.

The parents

In many instances, it can be helpful once again to explain the additive stress model in some detail, highlighting the issues and worries that have been elicited or observed during the course of the separate interviews. For the highly motivated parents anxious for advice a summative résumé and working explanation of the problem is all that is required by way of preparation for the next stage.

On the other hand, more resistant, defensive families, with set views about the problems, may be unwilling to entertain alternative viewpoints or extra information. Thus it may be necessary to reaffirm discussions held earlier that unless the problem can be amicably resolved at this level, less palatable interventions are likely to follow on in the near future. The legal implications of non-school attendance may need to be clearly re-stated. It is important to establish that it is not the therapist who is making threats here. The therapist is there to help and is only being fair by pointing out the kind of action that will be taken by the education authority in the event of non-co-operation in treatment. At this point the therapist will draw heavily upon the good relationship that has been established in the early diagnostic work. At all stages the therapist needs to come across as confident, helpful and accommodating but determined that the child should return to full-time school attendance. The only veiled threat from the therapist is the possibility of having to withdraw from treatment leaving the child and family at the mercy of the education authority.

Occasionally, some parents will argue that the child is so 'emotionally disturbed' that normal schooling is quite unreasonable. In such instances, it can be helpful to suggest that if the child is truly psychiatrically ill, hospital in-patient treatment may be appropriate or perhaps some form of special residential schooling. Here again the therapist should not be seen as threatening these possibilities but merely pointing to the logical conclusions if parents pursue that line of reasoning. At the same time, the full implications of hospitalisation or residential schooling can be explored and discussed so that the parents appreciate the potential anguish and distress associated with these alternatives.

If the discussion has needed to go along these lines, it is useful to re-state immediately that the child's problems are perfectly understandable given the series of additive stresses that have occurred over a short period of time. Every effort should be taken to stress the normality of the child's behaviour and the likely speed of recovery provided the parents and teachers are motivated to work together. The possible increased anxiety associated with an immediate return to school is fully acknowledged but is contrasted against far higher levels of anxiety being likely with hospitalisation or residential schooling. Furthermore, a short-term rise in anxiety followed by a speedy return to normality is presented as a preferable alternative to the prolonged if somewhat lessened anxiety associated with graded return solutions.

The child

Finally, the therapist reviews with the child a working explanation of how the school phobia has developed. The child's normality is emphasised and anxiety interpreted as reasonable in the light of the pressures discussed. Whilst empathising with the child the need to return to full-time schooling is addressed. The following alternatives are usually considered:

1. An immediate return to school with as much help as possible to make this bearable. Short and long-term in-school measures can be hinted at and some of the practical issues

involved in coping with school on the first few days can be broached.

2. Hospitalisation with in-patient treatment or residential special schooling with all of the implications that this might have.

3. Some form of legal action by the education authority. Parental responsibilities are explained in detail so that the child understands the pointlessness of trying to manipulate the parents to support the school refusal. If full-time school attendance is not resumed either the parents and/or the child will be taken to court. Ultimately, legal action could lead to some form of custodial care or residential treatment.

The therapist suggests that immediate return to school may be unpleasant in the short run but will be the easiest option in the long run. At this point it can be very revealing to say something along the following lines:

> If you were forced to go to school at gunpoint and the school was surrounded by wild dogs so that you could not escape, what would worry you most about being back at school? What would be the three worst things you would have to face? Can you put them in order according to how frightening they are for you?

This information will be invaluable in planning treatment with the parents and teachers. Typically, the child will give replies indicating worries about:

1. Facing friends after such a prolonged absence.

2. Facing critical or inquisitive teachers fearing remarks like 'Nice to see you've put in an appearance Jones' or 'Good of you to have graced us with your presence today.'

3. Coping with school-work after missing so much. The mere process of discussing each of these issues can help to reduce anxiety, especially if the child is reassured that:

    a. measures will be taken to prevent 2 from happening;

    b. teachers will be very accommodating about school-work.

Facing friends may cause more of a problem, especially in longstanding cases of school refusal. In these instances, role rehearsal is often very helpful. Being prepared for threatening comments and having some rehearsed answers seems more important than the precise nature of the answers. For instance, it is often quite enough for the child quizzed about absences to say: 'I have been ill for a while and I had to undergo lots of tests. I am now fit for school again.' Obviously, the kind of answers chosen will depend upon the type of child and the sort of pupils he or she will be mixing with.

2. Confirm the mandate

The therapist is now in a position to bring the parents and teachers together with a view to actively involving them in treatment planning. At this stage the child is *not* included. Before considering all the necessary details it is essential that both teachers and parents: 1. firmly state that the child's current school placement is appropriate, i.e. that is there are no insurmountable difficulties suggesting a change of school is necessary; 2. agree that an immediate return to school is the best course of action provided the practicalities of the situation can be overcome.

Sometimes parents are quite accepting of the child's current school at a rational level but nevertheless still argue for a change of school as a means of giving the child a fresh start. This attitude is often fuelled by the child agreeing to go to any school except the current one. In these circumstances, the therapist needs to point out all of the problems associated with a change of school including adjusting to new children, differing teacher styles and expectations and in some cases a new syllabus. In addition, it is often useful to state that facing up to frightening situations and learning to overcome one's fears are a good preparation for adulthood. In contrast, denying problems or running away from this simply leads to a worsening situation. If necessary something along the following lines can be said:

> Learning to cope with upset and facing difficulties are all part of growing up. When your child fell over for the first time learning to walk, did you stop him or her from walking in the future? What happens to children who have a fear of dogs and run every time they see one? What happens to children who are frightened of dogs but learn to control their feelings, stay calm and behave normally?

With particularly persistent parents it is sometimes necessary to agree to *consider* a change of school in three months time *if* the child has failed to adjust to the current school.

3. Negotiate areas of change required in the school

Even though the parents have committed themselves to the principle of immediately returning the child to the current school, many will nevertheless harbour fears about how the child will cope with this and how the teachers will handle the situation. In particular, parents will need to feel confident that: 1. realistic areas of concern will be dealt with; 2. irrational fears will be sensitively handled; 3. practical measures will be taken to ensure that the treatment programme works.

Reality issues

Dealing with realistic areas of concern exposed during the diagnostic stage provides a safe starting point for discussions between teachers and parents. It allows the teachers an opportunity to demonstrate their level of concern and willingness to be flexible which, in turn, can build up confidence and trust creating an atmosphere in which more sensitive issues can be explored. The additive stresses to be considered at this stage will vary from child to child although there are likely to be some universal themes. At an academic level, most school phobics will require some hurdle help to catch up on work missed. Very clear plans will need to be specified for this. Some children may need to miss certain lessons in order to catch up on notes in a quiet room. If the child has missed a great deal of work, a series of individual tutorials may be needed over quite a few weeks to pick up on any difficulties experienced in individual subject areas. Some children will need more specific forms of help directed towards particular learning difficulties and contingency plans will need to be organised to ensure that the right amount and kind of remedial help is available. This often means making temporary short term arrangements pending the establishment of more satisfactory longer term provision.

Practical measures to deal with cases of physical bullying or verbal taunting will need to be clearly spelt out. Often the problem arises on the school transport. If realistic measures cannot be taken to overcome this problem, other means of coming to school need to be arranged. Breaks and lunch hours can also be 'high risk' periods for certain vulnerable children and again special arrangements may need to be made. These could include allowing the child access to a private quiet room or giving the child special responsibilities and jobs.

Most school phobics seem to be socially sensitive, introverted and more inclined to worry than most. Being asked to answer questions in class or read out loud can often cause immense distress. In the early stages of a forced return to school, social sensitivity and levels of anxiety are likely to be particularly high, therefore, it is crucial that the child is not singled out in any particular way at this stage. It is a good idea to let the parents know that all teachers will be circulated with a note reminding them of the child's difficulties and warning against querying absences or questioning the child in any way in front of the class.

Minor clashes with teachers are often misunderstood by parents. In such cases it is often helpful to arrange for the teachers concerned to participate in the discussions so that the parents can hear the teachers' viewpoint. Major conflicts are sometimes more difficult to deal with. However, again provided the teachers are properly prepared, discussions with the parents can often be very reassuring. Occasionally however, a change of class, house or tutor group may be indicated as part of the 'package deal' in returning the child to school.

Irrational fears

In many cases, in spite of measures to deal with the rational aspects of fears, many children still show pronounced avoidance reactions and distress symptoms to situations that no longer contain the component that they first complained about. For example, the child who complains about the English teacher asking him to read out loud in class may still be highly anxious about facing English lessons even though he has been told that this will not happen in the future. In behavioural terms it could be argued that the child's specific fears have generalised to other aspects of the English lesson. Thus many features of the English lesson may now evoke a conditioned anxiety response. Provided there is no longer any rational basis for anxiety, regular attendance at the English class should lead to the extinction of anxiety and avoidance responses.

In practice there may be several lessons that cause the child distress. Certain lessons lend themselves to a graded reintroduction process. For instance, the child with a fear of PE and games might first of all be involved in issuing and collecting equipment, refereeing or timing competitions and so on. Gradually, over an agreed period of time, the child could be expected to take part in a greater range of activities until eventually normal PE/games activities are being followed.

Many children are helped by monitoring their own subjective feelings of anxiety by keeping a simple diary recording self-assessed fear ratings on a ten point scale at various stages during the school day. Typically children rate themselves as feeling very high levels of anxiety in the first few days, particularly in the first few hours of each day or in particularly stressful lessons. Towards the end of each day or lesson self-assessed fear ratings tend to be lower and commonly fall off rapidly after the first few days. Self-monitoring and self-assessment give some children reassuring feelings of self-control. Diaries of this kind are also extremely helpful talking points at follow-up interviews.

Many school phobics find morning assemblies and large gatherings of children very stressful, often experiencing claustrophobic feelings. Simple, practical measures like ensuring the child is sitting at the end of a row near an exit can be enough to make these occasions tolerable. Some children may need to be given the freedom to leave the assembly without having to ask permission in the event of feeling faint. A few children may need to be excused morning assemblies for a specified period allowing them time to settle back into other aspects of school life before facing a specific aspect that they find especially threatening. It is important however, to make sure that the child is using the extra free time beneficially, e.g. catching up on previous work, etc.

With particularly resistant and anxious pupils, who express multiple worries about many lessons, a graded re-introduction to a normal timetable may be necessary. That is, whilst full-time attendance at school is insisted upon, the child may not necessarily be expected to attend every lesson from day one. For example, a pupil might be expected to choose two lessons to attend on the first day back; three the second day and so on, until the normal timetable has been resumed. This approach can be a little tedious and should be reserved for the most problematic of cases where it is felt that aspects of school life have made a very major contribution to the school phobia. Of course this approach will only be possible if the child can be constructively occupied during the free periods.

Practical measures

Perhaps the most important considerations here are the arrangements for receiving the child each morning. In the early stages of returning to school the majority of school phobics will feel extremely upset; quite a number will make very pronounced protests and a few will exhibit tyrannical temper tantrums. Parents and teachers will need to be well prepared for this. Both parties need to stay relaxed and calm and at the school end there need to be two teachers who can physically restrain the child if necessary when the parents leave. In addition, it is important to fix a time of arrival at school when there will be few children about in order to avoid secondary problems arising out of other children witnessing the child's distress. Occasionally, this may mean coming to school very early or more probably a little later than the normal time whilst morning assembly is in progress or after lessons have started.

A discreet, quiet area needs to be set aside where the child can be given time to calm down before starting the school day. This can also be an extremely good situation in which to: 1. remind the child about timetable arrangements for that day; 2. introduce a few teachers for reassuring chats; and 3. introduce a few carefully chosen and well-prepared friends. Apart from catching up on work missed and facing teachers, school phobics are frequently highly anxious about facing friends. A child who has been out of school for many months may have become socially isolated and the friendship issue may be very significant. In any case, trying to adjust to the school routine after a long absence will in itself, be heavy going for many pupils Accordingly, it can be helpful to break the ice by choosing one or two, sensitive, understanding pupils to make a point of shepherding the child around school for the first few weeks. Often other pupils can be remarkably understanding if they are approached in the right way. One way of gaining their involvement might be as follows:

I wonder if you can help me William? John Smith is coming back to school tomorrow after being away for seven months. He had an illness and there were some other personal worries at home with the result that he could not face school. He is now out of his routine and behind with his work. He is going to find it very difficult to settle back in and I know he has lost

151

contact with the few friends that he had. I believe that you used to be quite friendly with him. Do you think you could say a few reassuring things to him if I call you over to the quiet room tomorrow morning just after he has arrived? Perhaps you could make a point of ensuring that he arrives at lessons on time and stay with him during breaks and lunch-hours. I would also like you to bring him to me, just before lunch tomorrow so that I can have a few words with him about how the morning has gone.

The provision of an ally in school can greatly desensitise some children's worries in the early stages so long as the school phobic approves of the action and the pupil chosen to help is sufficiently responsible and sensitive.

Beyond these straightforward first-aid techniques it is important to find ways of building into the normal school day incentives and rewards for school attendance.

Negotiate areas of change required in the home

Once parents feel that school-related issues have been thoroughly investigated and appropriate steps planned to ameliorate any problems, they are often more willing to consider their own role in treatment. In parallel to the school problems, there are likely to be a series of additive home-related worries that will need systematic exploration. Each case is likely to be unique but once again it can be helpful to consider: 1. ways of minimising *realistic areas* of concern; 2. techniques for confronting *irrational fears*; 3. *practical measures* to ensure that the treatment approach works.

Reality issues

Inevitably, the ultimate confrontation over school attendance will be a painful experience for both child and parents. It is, therefore, worth reviewing worries and concerns that can be reasonably and quickly eliminated. Without wishing to duplicate many of the points made in the previous chapter, it is frequently necessary to discuss the child's faulty perceptions of home life. Parents are often surprised at the kind of worries and misunderstandings the child shows but on close analysis, can appreciate how the issues have developed. For instance, common fears over losing one or both parents are often set off by a death in the family or misinterpreted comments about a parental illness. Children can often witness a marital row but may not see the parents make up leading to insecurity. Discussion, explanation and reassurance often go a long way to desensitise or eliminate many concerns.

Naturally, there may be many worries that have to be lived with. The death of a close relative or pet, a friend leaving the area or the social upheaval associated with moving house are all everyday natural events that often cause stress. Sometimes there is no antidote although it can be helpful to frame such issues as developmental hurdles that prepare the child for some of the natural traumas of adulthood. Learning to cope with painful experiences is all part of growing up. An over-protective stance denies the child the opportunity of learning to cope. Sometimes discussions point to the need for specific kinds of support for various members of the family independent of treatment work with the child. Acknowledging these needs and making appropriate, separate treatment arrangements can remove significant obstacles to returning the child to school.

Irrational fears

Even though many worries will have been eliminated, reinterpreted or rationalised, residual anxieties will almost always remain. Often the child will seem quite rational and ready to plan a return to school but as soon as the plan is put into action the familiar anxieties and protests return. Ultimately having 'softened up' the school and addressed background concerns at home, the parents have to be helped to take a tough line.

An *immediate* and if necessary *forced* return to school is now presented as the most efficient, beneficial way forward. If the child has been brought to school for the diagnostic interview, the parents are told treatment should start straightaway by keeping the child in school whilst the parents leave. At this point, some parents may wish to postpone the start of treatment until the next day in which case a further round of discussion will be necessary making the following points: 1. an immediate return to school signals to the child that parents, teachers and therapist are working together; 2. there can be absolutely no compromise over school attendance — full-time attendance is to be resumed from now on; any other approach will just prolong the agony. The therapist must always be several jumps ahead. The parents can be mentally prepared for tantrums and protests and advised to ignore promises like: 'I'll come to school tomorrow if I can go home now.' Ready-made answers can be rehearsed for excuses like 'I can't stay in school now, I'm not in school uniform' or 'I don't have any sandwiches with me for lunch.' Parents and teachers need to be advised that planned ignoring of protests and tantrums typically leads to a short-term worsening in the behaviour almost as though the child is saying 'You won't ignore me, I'll see to that.' Giving in to the child at this stage can make the problem worse by reinforcing heightened protests or tantrums making treatment even more difficult in the future. In contrast, by remaining calm, firm and resolute the tantrums and protests will suddenly and dramatically subside providing a chance to reward more appropriate behaviours. If the child sees the *slightest* evidence of the parents or teachers losing their resolve, temper and protests will continue and the treatment programme will be unnecessarily lengthened. Parents and teachers should be prepared for a physical confrontation in the first instance and several weeks of disturbed behaviour. It is best to overestimate the kind of commitment required so that speedy results will be perceived as a bonus whereas long-term difficult cases will be regarded as perfectly natural. At the same time parents can be reassured that highly disturbed behaviour will quickly disappear once the child is in school. Although the child may still feel anxious there is rarely any evidence of it once the initial early morning trauma is over. Nevertheless, parents are likely to go home with painful memories of leaving a highly distressed child leading to guilt feelings, worry and unnecessary quizzing of the child on return from school Some of the anxiety can be taken out of the situation by encouraging the parents to telephone the school each day at a pre-arranged time to check on progress. Reassurance can be given without the child knowing about the parental level of concern.

Practical measures

Once the avoidance response has been blocked the child's school attendance success can be reinforced. Often praise is enough but sometimes there may be a good case for providing a small negotiated treat contingent upon one or two weeks full attendance. Care should be taken not to over-reward. Most children will be so relieved to feel relaxed and back into a normal routine that this will be sufficient reward in itself.

Sometimes children continue to complain of headaches and stomach aches particularly during the readjustment to school. Such complaints are best dealt with in a low key, matter of fact way with comments like: 'Headaches and stomach aches are only to be expected at the moment. The sooner you are back into your normal routine the sooner the aches and pains will disappear.' In the event of persistent physical symptoms, the child should be taken for a further medical check up *out of school hours*.

Parents should be discouraged from:

1. Communicating their anxiety to the child by:
   a. telling the child about any telephone conversations with school staff and other concerned professionals;
   b. asking the child if he has had a bad day on returning from school;
   c. being hesitant and inconsistent in the mornings;
   d. showing signs of distress through tone of voice, facial expression.
2. Focusing attention on the child's psychosomatic complaints by:
   a. frequently asking whether the child is feeling all right;
   b. giving the child pills for headaches, etc.;
   c. frequently taking the child to the doctor in school hours.

The precise details with regard to taking the child to school are left to the next section.

5. Find a suitable escort

If it is quite apparent that the parents alone will not be able to force their child to school, it may be necessary to think of other agencies who might escort the child if the need arises. Wherever possible responsibility for the escort procedure should remain with the family to avoid the possibility of setting up a dependency situation. Diagnostic details of the patterns of influence and control within the family will be invaluable here in considering who might be able to help.

In some cases, the grandparents (maternal or paternal) are so powerful within the family that they in effect function as parents of the grandchild. In these cases, it will be essential to enlist their full co-operation in the treatment plan. If they have not been included in the initial diagnostic school interview a follow-up home visit should be arranged that day to ensure their involvement.

Sometimes an elder brother or sister may be able to act as a suitable escort. In fact it is worth enlisting the help of any close relative who is held in high esteem by the child and is likely to be undisturbed by any tears, protests or tantrums that the child may display.

If family possibilities have been exhausted, the family should be encouraged to think of close friends who might assist. Again, a follow-up home visit might be required to ensure that the escort arrangements are clean and tidy.

In the event of family resources being inadequate, outside help may need to be enlisted. A social worker or educational psychologist may be able to help. In choosing the outside support it is worthwhile considering:

1. A person who will be minimally inconvenienced by the arrangements. Someone who passes the child's home and school each morning at the right time would be best.
2. Ideally the escort should be known to the family and school and well-respected by both.
3. The escort should be able to act as a co-therapist providing support and a calm, firm model to the parents whilst being able to ignore the child's distress and parents' anguish.
4. Finally, the person selected should be willing to escort the child to school for as long as necessary even if this means for weeks and weeks. In the majority of cases the escort procedure only needs to run for a few days. Nevertheless a long term commitment communicates determination and conviction to the child. If an outside agency is involved in taking the child to school, a member of the family should always assist for the following reasons:

a. often two people are required to deal with a protesting adolescent;
b. it safeguards the co-therapist against child or parental accusations of unprofessional conduct;
c. it means that some responsibility for the problem is still maintained by the family;
d. the confident, calm model of the co-therapist can strengthen and reinforce coping behaviours in the family members.

Typically, the fathers of the school phobics are either absent in the mornings or ineffectual, leaving all the handling of the children to the mother. In such cases, major attempts should be made to involve the father. The resulting shift in family dynamics increases both physical and symbolic control over the child and reduces the likelihood of one parent being played off against the other. At a more fundamental level, it can communicate a sense of security that both the mother and father are able to act together as a parental unit.

6. Discuss the treatment plans with the child

After all of the preparatory work with the parents and teachers, the child is brought into the room for a final résumé of the treatment plans. The child is told about the detailed arrangements for the escort procedure.

If the child is co-operative and asks to be allowed to come to school alone or with a friend, give the child the opportunity to do so by agreeing a definite time for leaving the house and then agree to implement the escort procedure if the child has not managed the task alone.

Every effort should be made to empathise with the child's plight. It can be helpful with some children to relate stories of heroes who have faced and overcome danger. Facing the challenges of returning to school can be presented in a similar light with accompanying emotive imagery. This can serve as a kind of mental rehearsal of the real event which can in turn desensitise the issues and strengthen the child's resolve to conquer the difficulties.

Pupils who protest violently and threaten to run away or refuse to get out of bed need treating more powerfully. These pupils need to be told unequivocally that no matter what they do they will return to full-time schooling. They should be warned that if they are still in their pyjamas when the escort arrives they will be taken to school in that state and given clothes to change into when they arrive.

Contingency plans need to be made to minimise the chance of the pupil running off. However, in the event of this happening, the child needs to know he/she will be found and *immediately* taken to school irrespective of the time of day or circumstances. No matter how long it takes, the child will be taken to school and monitored everyday until normal full-time schooling is resumed. Locks should be taken off bathroom and toilet doors and potential barricades removed from bedrooms in the case of particularly obstructive, strong-willed phobics.

Finally, any special arrangements in school need to be explained. Quiet room facilities, specialist tutoring, procedures for introduction to peers and any transition arrangements leading up to normal time-tabling need to be clearly understood.

At this point the parents are advised to leave and if necessary the child is physically restrained by the teachers to prevent violent protests or running off. Typically, extreme tantrums stop the moment the parents have left and the agreed school programme can go ahead.

7. Support and follow-up arrangements

The parents, child and teachers need to know that the psychologist will monitor the case closely until the problem is resolved. A formal follow-up interview should be arranged at school for one or two weeks after re-introduction and frequent telephone contact should be maintained with the school and family at all times during the confrontation stage. Even if the child settles quickly the case should be monitored for at least several months. Great care should be taken after an illness or a long holiday, especially if there has not been time for a thorough routine to be established before a normal break. Sometimes treatment does not go according to plan. In the event of unforeseen problems at home, the onus should be placed upon the parents to contact both the school and psychologist *immediately*. Likewise, if the child fails to arrive for school or else runs off from school, the psychologist and parents should be informed straightaway.

PROBLEMS AND SETBACKS IN TREATMENT

As Figure 7.1 shows a breakdown in the treatment programme signals the need for a fresh look at the problem and a revision to the treatment strategy rather than prematurely giving up or referring on to another treatment agency. In fact, with resistant, defensive families the analysis of initial treatment failure is often

Figure 7.1

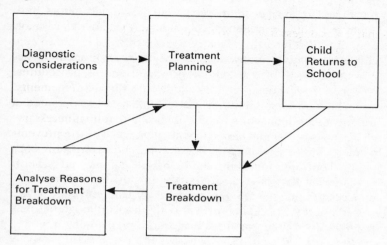

the only way that crucial information is revealed. Usually treatment breakdown is related to one of three areas: 1. breakdown in practical arrangements; and/or 2. problems in parental control or collusion; and/or 3. the influence of other parties.

Breakdown in practical arrangements

In spite of painstaking attention to detail, treatment can fail initially because of unforeseen circumstances. An illness in the family, an over-committed professional not managing the escort procedure, an important schoolteacher being absent or distracted by other problems are just a few of the possibilities. Normally, close scrutiny of the issues can lead to a speedy revision of the treatment plan and a successful treatment outcome.

Problems in parental control or collusion

In most other instances, treatment breaks down in families that have shunned help. They may have presented as so confident at the diagnostic and treatment planning stages that the resolution

159

of the problem has been left almost entirely to their own resources. It may be that the parents have just feigned co-operation and confidence all along. Perhaps they have temporarily denied their lack of control over their omnipotent child. Alternatively, they may have been unconvinced about the appropriateness of the school or important aspects of the treatment package and hence collude with the child. When the 'crunch' comes some parents just cannot face the prospect of forcing a screaming child to school fearing that it will make the child worse. Some parents will have a sufficiently low commitment to schooling that they will argue strongly against a painful confrontation. If the child is happy at home and school is not offering that much, why bother to put the child through unnecessary pressure? Some members of the family may have a vested interest in keeping the child off school although this may not have been apparent at the diagnostic and planning stages.

Often it is difficult to tell whether the parents are passively colluding or genuinely unable to exert authority and control over the child. In each case, further home visits are indicated to take a fresh look at the problem and devise a new treatment strategy.

In the case of co-operative parents unable to handle an omnipotent child a revised escort procedure needs to be arranged. In addition, a more authoritative interview needs to be organised with the child. Once again immediate return to school should be spelt out as the only palatable solution. The inability of the parents to protect the child from outside authority needs to be powerfully re-emphasised. The short-term discomfort associated with a return to school far outweighs the long-term anguish associated with the alternatives.

Collusive parents need to be confronted with their inconsistency and failure to carry through the agreed plan and, once again, the ultimate unpleasant consequences of treatment failure discussed. Often the resulting guilt and embarrassment causes the release of fresh information which can then be taken into a revised treatment approach. Very occasionally, legal intervention may be necessary before therapy can begin.

The influence of other parties

Sometimes treatment is misguidedly or unwittingly sabotaged by close friends or relatives who have not been involved in the treatment planning. Occasionally the dominating influence of grandparents or other family members has not been previously acknowledged. A follow-up family interview involving the additional parties enables the seriousness of the problem to be reiterated and the reasons for the treatment approach made explicit. In most cases, treatment can then proceed unobstructed.

Sociocultural influences are more difficult to deal with. In some cases, the school phobic will come from a neighbourhood where there is a high rate of truancy and where parental expectations of school are very poor. In these circumstances, the child may point to every other child in the street as a good reason for not returning to school. Here individual treatment needs to parallel appropriate intervention with all of the other problem families.

8

Case Studies

The following six cases have been selected from the series of 30 in Blagg and Yule (1984) in order to illustrate some of the processes, diagnostic and treatment issues outlined in the previous chapters. Fictitious names have been used throughout and minor changes have been made to the case histories to preserve the anonymity of the clients. A comment at the end of each case highlights important features.

CASE 1: 'SEBASTIAN'

Referral information

Sebastian, 14 years, was referred by his teachers because of school phobia with associated fear reactions and abdominal pain. The family doctor had been consulted. Paediatric investigations had revealed nothing physically abnormal and psychiatric referral was arranged. After two interviews the psychiatrist prescribed tranquillisers to reduce anxiety and suggested part-time schooling as a way of easing Sebastian back into school. The parents were given the support of a Psychiatric Social Worker (PSW) and, with a good deal of cajoling and upset, Sebastian started to attend school on a part-time basis after an absence of six weeks. Sebastian could not face normal lessons and spent the time working in his tutor's office. Each morning his fear reactions and protests became increasingly pronounced and after a further three weeks he relapsed into total school refusal. At the time of the referral he had been absent from school for a further three weeks and was reluctant to leave the home.

Preliminary school enquiries suggested that this was Sebastian's first major instance of school refusal. Attendance figures for the previous years were excellent and teachers reported that Sebastian was a conscientious boy without any significant learning difficulties. The current problems occurred in Sebastian's first term at his *new* upper school. There had been some reluctance to attend school in his infant days but Sebastian's middle school years (8–13 years) were uneventful.

The PSW was consulted and she agreed to advise the parents of the arrangements for the first interview in school, stressing the importance of bringing Sebastian along for the first session, even if it meant physically taking him. Flexible arrangements were organised in school to allow for a whole morning's interview if necessary. Key teachers were prepared to assist in diagnostic and treatment-planning work. The importance of modelling calm, relaxed, behaviour in spite of distressing reactions in the child and/or parents was particularly emphasised. The interview was timed to coincide with morning assembly so that there would be few pupils about to notice Sebastian's arrival.

Diagnosis and treatment

The parents were keen to receive help but unsure of their ability to bring Sebastian along for the initial interview. Nevertheless, they managed this with PSW support and the house tutor and deputy headmistress were available to meet the parents and make the necessary introductions.

Sebastian, a bespectacled, overweight boy, looked pale and shaky and clutched pathetically at his father. When I suggested that I should speak to his parents alone, he screamed, cried and hugged his father so that he had to be calmly but firmly pulled away by two teachers. He soon regained his composure in a nearby office and completed a personality questionnaire whilst I talked to his parents. I learned that Mrs W. had a history of agoraphobia, and was currently taking anti-depressants. She seemed tense and agitated. Mr W. seemed more relaxed but very puzzled by the boy's behaviour and uncertain how to deal with it. It became apparent that life at home revolved around Sebastian, who seemed to be quite a demanding, stubborn boy. He was a much wanted only child of elderly parents. I gathered that Sebastian had been generally anxious about separating from his parents ever since an incident that occurred 18 months previously. The parents had left him with relatives whilst they went out for the evening. Sebastian had been watching a thriller on TV. A car crash was involved. When they were late arriving back he was frightened they had been injured in a car crash. Discussions revealed that the parents had focused much attention on Sebastian's distress and had been reluctant to leave him with friends or relatives since. However, it was not until Sebastian changed schools that his separation anxiety resulted in school refusal. His previous two schools had been very close to home. In fact his middle school had been situated opposite his house. Both he and his father had always come home to lunch but the long journey to the new upper school now made this impossible for Sebastian.

I interviewed Sebastian alone, after more tears and protests. He impressed as being a very immature, dependent boy who seemed a good deal younger than his 14 years. He seemed primarily worried about something happening to his parents whilst he was at school. He also expressed anxiety about PE and games, which probably related to the fact that he was overweight and far from agile. Apart from this, he expressed concern about having to cope with the long journey each morning as well as the large size of the school. (He had grown accustomed to much smaller environments.) He was fearful of being teased and felt especially vulnerable on the school coach as his tears attracted interest. Eysenck and Eysenck (1975) Personality Questionnaire (EPQ) scores showed Sebastian to be more sensitive, introverted and emotional than most boys of his age (Z scores: Psychoticism (P) = -1.59 Standard Deviations (SDs); Extroversion (E) = -4.16 SDs; Neuroticism (N) = $+1.16$ SDs and Lie Scale (L) = $+2.79$ SDs). He seemed to be generally lacking in confidence and unsure of himself. Rutter and Yule (1968) Behaviour Scales completed by both parents and teachers suggested that Sebastian's behaviour at home and at school showed a neurotic pattern with an absence of antisocial features. Sebastian did not seem to have any anxieties about his school work. He was a very competent reader with a high average verbal scale IQ 107 (Wechsler Intelligence Scale for Children — Revised (WISC-R) 1974).

The parents and teachers were now brought together to achieve a common understanding of Sebastian's problems. A summative statement was made based on the information supplied by the various parties. Both parents and teachers were helped to understand how Sebastian's problems may have arisen and been maintained. The additive stress model was referred to. Sebastian's status as a much wanted only child was highlighted. Mrs W's. ill-health had resulted in the father taking a very active parenting role developing perhaps an over-close relationship with the boy. Separation experiences could be coped with in familiar, secure, controlled circumstances. However, separation worries were exaggerated by the TV/late night incident 18 months ago and probably maintained by the parents' subsequent behaviour. The additive anxieties of mother's ill-health and a change of school were pointed up. The transition from a small, familiar school close to home to a large, alien school a long journey away was threatening for Sebastian. He was unable to come home for lunch and found lunch hours very distressing. He felt sick in the mornings and the long coach journey was unpleasant. He was a good target for teasing. His worries about games and PE were understandable given his physique, condition and social sensitivity. Previous attempts to resolve the problem via part-time schooling did not result in Sebastian settling back into a normal schooling routine. His difficulties were painfully exposed but not resolved with the result that his tyrannical tantrums and protests had been unwittingly shaped up and reinforced. A new approach was required in which everybody worked together consistently and for long enough to overcome the mounting problems.

The parents and teachers agreed with this formulation adding supportive comments. It was accepted that Sebastian's current school placement was appropriate and that immediate treatment plans should be made. Mr W. left for work early and the mother admitted to being quite incapable of being firm with Sebastian. There were no other close friends or relatives living nearby. Eventually it was agreed that a teacher who passed the house each day and was known to the family would act as an escort. In order to make school more appealing, special privileges were arranged for Sebastian in the school. He was temporarily excused PE and games. The housemistress gave him special library responsibilities so that he was fully occupied during school break and lunch hours. It was agreed to start treatment immediately by insisting that he should remain in school despite protests. Parents and teachers were prepared for tyrannical tantrums and Sebastian was brought in. The plan was put to him calmly and firmly, emphasising the need to face frightening situations using a good deal of emotive imagery. He reacted fairly predictably so that it was necessary for two teachers to hold him once again while his parents left. Sebastian quickly calmed down and volunteered to help his housemistress. He even remarked that he realised the teachers were trying to help him. The parents rang the school half an hour later and were reassured.

Sebastian was escorted to school for a period of two weeks. His morning protests diminished each day so that by the second week he seemed quite relaxed. By the third week he was able to travel on the school coach. A more detailed follow up 15 months later showed that the initial therapeutic gains had been maintained and further developed. Rutter and Yule (1968) Behaviour Scales completed by both parents and teachers showed no evidence of a significant behavioural disorder. Sebastian seemed more confident and furthermore there were considerable changes on the Eysenck and Eysenck (1975) Personality Questionnaire scales (EPQ). His score on the P scale now fell within the average range, and his below average L score seemed to reflect his more mature and realistic outlook. His N score had also shown a significant fall suggesting that he was now a good deal more settled emotionally. However, the most dramatic change was noted on the E scale where there had been an upward movement of more than four standard deviations. (EPQ Z scores: P = -0.57 SDs; E = $+0.27$ SDs; N = -0.36 SDs; L = -1.14 SDs). In line with this, Sebastian's teachers had reported that he was enjoying good social relationships and, perhaps for the first time in his life, he had a number of genuine friends. School staff were also very pleased at Sebastian's academic progress.

Finally it was noted that Sebastian had shown an attendance in excess of 90 per cent over a 15 month period between treatment and follow up. The few days schooling that he had missed were attributed to genuine illness.

Comment

Although separation anxiety was a marked feature in this case, the additive stress model still applied with many school related issues causing concern. Separation worries were rather unusually related to the father rather than the mother. Both parents were anxious for advice and help.

The mother needed help in her own right and did continue to receive psychiatric and PSW support to ease her out of her agoraphobia. The father, who took the dominant role in child management, needed to feel totally confident in the treatment plan. The psychologist needed to take on the expert role in the summative feedback session with teachers and parents. Furthermore, the teachers needed to be convinced of their ability to see the plan through. Indeed a great deal of credit for the treatment success must go to the teachers who were able to present calm, firm models to the parents, assisted in bringing Sebastian to school in the mornings, increased incentives to Sebastian for being in school and were helpful and flexible in their timetabling arrangements.

It is worth noticing that what appeared to be uncontrollable hysteria in the presence of parents was dramatically switched off the moment they were out of sight. It is often difficult to decide whether protests and tantrum behaviour is a function of genuine anxiety learnt via respondent conditioning or 'brat' behaviour acquired through operant conditioning. Possibly Sebastian's dramatic behaviour change was caused by a removal of the contingencies maintaining the behaviour. On the other hand it may have been brought about by a rapid extinction process by blocking the avoidance behaviour and forcing immediate and continued confrontation with the anxiety provoking circumstances. Possibly both elements helped to bring about the improvement.

CASE 2: 'JOHN'

Referral information

John (CA 11 years 7 months) was referred for an assessment by the Chief Education Officer because of school phobia with accompanying anxiety symptoms. The family had moved into the county a few weeks prior to the referral. Preliminary notes from the county indicated that John had been refusing school for seven months, ever since transferring to the secondary school. A limited educational assessment suggested that he had serious educational difficulties. On the recommendation of an educational psychologist, home tuition had been arranged with a view to boosting the boy's self-esteem and educational attainments

167

before planning a return to school. Apparently John and his family were extremely happy with the home tuition arrangements and were expecting the same facilities in the new county.

Diagnosis and treatment

In view of the previous history and the uncertainty about which would be the appropriate school for John to attend, an initial home visit was made. The family lived in isolated circumstances. The father had just taken over the management of a farm and the mother helped with some of the farm duties. The family impressed as being a warm cohesive unit, and up until 18 months ago both parents had lived very near to their own parents. I gathered that the mother had found it quite a wrench when the family moved away from their home town because of the father's work. The mother gave the impression of being a caring, affectionate woman, although somewhat over-protective. The father seemed an easy-going, amiable character, who left matters of schooling and discipline problems to his wife.

John was the younger of two boys: the elder boy seemed altogether more mature, competent and capable. Apparently he had very little time for John. Schooling did not present any difficulties to the elder boy. Apparently John had always been a sensitive, emotional child from his early years. He had to cope with only one separation from his mother, and that was when he was 18 months old and for a period of only three days. The mother remembered this quite clearly because John was so distressed at being away from her that she felt that she had to return home immediately. Ever since then John had never liked leaving his mother, even when the maternal grandparents were close at hand. In turn, the mother had felt very distressed by John's anxiety and worried unduly about leaving him alone even for brief periods.

Perhaps not surprisingly, John was a very reluctant school attender. Even in his early infant school days his mother had to escort him to school every day, frequently under protest. Each change of class and change of school resulted in mounting stress and anxiety in both John and his mother. From the age of seven years onwards, the mother reported, John was taken to his doctor regularly because of anxiety over school attendance. Tranquillisers were frequently prescribed. The school attendance difficulties finally reached a climax at secondary transfer age when he became exceptionally anxious and refused to attend. The educational welfare officer tried to intervene but without success. Home tuition seemed to be the answer to all of their problems. John was happy at home with his mother, sleeping better, no longer exhibiting signs of anxiety and the mother did not have to cope with the stressful experience of taking a protesting and distressed adolescent to school. Furthermore, to some extent, the parents felt that John could receive an adequate education at home and they pointed out that the farm provided many useful and interesting experiences for him. Finally, the mother may have derived some comfort in having John around during the day, having only recently moved away from her own parents.

A psychometric assessment showed John to be effectively functioning with a below average intelligence range (WISC-R 1974 Verbal Scale IQ 78). John's reading attainments were well below average. He experienced particular problems with basic arithmetic, coping only with very simple addition and subtraction. In general personality, this slightly overweight boy presented as being extremely immature and dependent. He had a high pitched, whiney voice, which in normal school would probably attract considerable amusement. He interacted with his mother like a much younger child, often asking to be kissed and the mother seemed to reinforce this dependency. He seemed to lack confidence especially in his peer relationships. His pattern of scoring on the Eysenck and Eysenck (1975) Personality Questionnaire showed him to be significantly more introverted, more sensitive and more socially naïve than most boys of his age (Z scores: $P = -1.14$ SDs; $E = -2.29$ SDs; $N = +0.27$ SDs; $L = +1.04$ SDs).

The mention of a return to full-time school attendance resulted in tears, tantrums and protests from John and distressed, protective reactions from the mother. She claimed that she could not cope with a recurrence of John's nightmares and the anxiety and upheaval that would be associated with full-time schooling. John left the room and I spent some time reassuring the mother that the school I had in mind for John would be a very sensitive and caring environment. I pointed out firmly that home tuition would not be in his interests in that it would reinforce his dependency and make an eventual return to school more difficult. Furthermore, the secondary gains associated with the consid-

169

erable freedom afforded by being at home were emphasised as probably maintaining his pattern of school refusal. It was left that I would check on possible suitable schools and then call back for a further discussion. At this stage it was quite clear that neither John nor his parents would willingly co-operate in a planned return to full-time schooling. Nevertheless, it was important to emphasise at the outset that return to full-time schooling would be the clear expectation of the education department.

Bearing in mind John's marked immaturity and limited attainments, it was felt unrealistic to suggest integration at a normal comprehensive school. It was thought that one of the county's special schools catering for children with mild learning difficulties would probably be the best placement. Within this small, sheltered environment, John could receive more personal attention and intensive remedial help. Beyond this, a special school environment would afford greater timetable flexibility and more chance to offer significant positive reinforcements for being in school. The special school was eight miles away from home, although special school transport would be possible. Unfortunately, it was over-subscribed and the headmaster was initially unwilling to accept another pupil for at least half a term. In the absence of a suitable local school for the boy to attend, I was very reluctantly forced into *temporarily* recommending an individual teacher for John. However, it was *insisted* upon that John should visit the teacher's house rather than vice versa.

In the meantime, the headmaster of the special school agreed to interview John and his parents and also agreed that the boy could be taken to the school for several visits by his home tutor. The home tutor was advised not to become too involved with the case for fear of setting up a dependent relationship.

A second home visit was made. John and his mother were advised of the provisional arrangements. They were delighted about the home tutor and accepted visits to the tutor's house. Both John and his parents visited the special school and all were impressed. John was, however, very clinging and his parents doubted that he would ever manage to attend school regularly. Nevertheless, John separated from his mother quite easily to attend the special tuition classes at the teacher's house. On the second morning, unbeknown to the mother, John agreed quite happily to visit the special school to collect some books. However, he was not expected to go into classes or stay in the school long. When the mother came to collect John and learnt of the school visit she was very angry and refused to send him to the home tutor thereafter. Fortunately, John had made a favourable impression at the school and in view of the breakdown in the home tutoring arrangements, the headmaster agreed to admit him straightaway.

A third house visit was made to review the situation and explore possibilities for admission to the special school. The mother was far from happy with this prospect and in view of this it was felt appropriate to explore other ways of dealing with the problem. It was suggested that if John was too ill to be helped back to a day school, residential special schooling could be looked into. Alternatively, psychiatric referral could be arranged with the possibility of psychiatric in-patient treatment and attendance at the hospital school. On the other hand it was argued that if John was just being difficult and did not need psychological or psychiatric help, the matter would go out of my hands. If John continued to refuse school thereafter, the education department would probably take legal action. This might result in the parents being fined and/or John being taken into care. It was emphasised that none of these options were particularly pleasant or necessary. If we all worked together, John would quickly adapt to his new school. Short-term distress would soon give way to long-term relief. However, if firm action was not taken now, mounting discomfort would be the likely outcome. The parents reluctantly agreed to the principle of special schooling. The method of implementing this was now discussed with John in the company of his parents.

John became very anxious and felt that he would be laughed at because he could not read very well. He talked about not wanting to do games and mentioned feeling anxious about attending morning assemblies. He was reassured about his work and told that he would temporarily be excused PE and morning assemblies. John said he would not travel on the school taxi. The mother seemed incapable of being firm and the father refused to take time off farming duties to help. In the absence of close friends, relatives and neighbours to help, I agreed to take John each morning as long as would be necessary.

During the weekend John sprained his ankle badly. When I arrived on Monday morning, the mother was just about to take the boy to the family doctor. The GP excused him from school for three weeks. At the end of this time I called at the home yet again to take John to school. On this occasion, the mother, father and maternal grandparents (who were visiting) were sitting in the kitchen. As I approached John cried and protested and grabbed the leg of the kitchen table. His mother broke down into tears and ran out of the kitchen. Fortunately the father remained calm and with a little bit of verbal backing from the grandparents, assisted me in removing him from the table leg and carrying him into the car. I drove off quickly. As soon as we were out of the farm gate John almost magically changed. He stopped crying, wiped his eyes and engaged in interesting, spontaneous conversation relating to his pets and farm activities. We had a thoroughly amiable chat on the way to school and apart from a slight apprehension on arrival, he went into school quite normally.

Apparently he had a very good day. The teachers made a special point of giving him a lot of attention and occupied him with interesting, practical pursuits. The parents were telephoned from the school to reassure them. The following day I called again at the home. On this occasion there was only a slight protest and once again John accompanied me quite happily to school. On the third day John was encouraged to bring one of his pets to school. By now there were no protests and the parents were showing signs of beginning to relax.

I continued taking John to school without any problems for the rest of the week. His mother called to collect him in the evenings. The following week I agreed to take John to school but suggested that he could travel home on the school transport. In view of the inconvenience to the mother in transporting the boy, she readily agreed to this. There were no problems on the way home. After taking the boy to school for a total of two weeks, it was suggested that he could now travel on the school transport. However, it was arranged that in the event of his not making it, the mother would telephone me so that I could call and take him to school.

There were no problems in attendance thereafter. John grew to like school more and more and after attending some special afternoon assemblies asked if he could go into the normal morning assemblies. He was excused games for several months but after gaining confidence he asked if he could take part in normal games lessons.

The follow up one year later revealed that all therapeutic gains had been maintained. He was attending school regularly and taking a full part in school activities. His pattern of scoring on the Eysenck and Eysenck (1975) Personality Questionnaire showed that he was still more sensitive, more introverted and more socially naïve than most boys of his age. However, there had been a significant drop in his neuroticism score suggesting that he was now generally a far less worried individual (EPQ Z scores: P = -1.14 SDs; E = -2.29 SDs; N = -1.01 SDs; L = $+3.25$ SDs). Rutter and Yule (1968) Behaviour Scales completed by both parents and teachers showed that there was no longer any evidence of a significant behavioural disorder either at home or at school. John gave the impression of being altogether more confident. On the academic front he had made significant advances with his reading and maths. There was no evidence of symptom substitution and no evidence of separation anxiety. During the year following treatment he was absent on a number of occasions because of genuine illness and his grandfather died.

However, in spite of these problems there had been no recurrence of school phobia and his total attendance figures for the year were in excess of 86 per cent.

Comment

This case was unusually problematic and took considerably more treatment time than the other 29 cases in the treatment studies. The limited background information and consequent uncertainty about appropriate schooling arrangements meant a departure from the preferred approach of an initial diagnostic session at the appropriate school. The boy's school phobia had shown an incipient onset over many years with transfer to secondary education being 'the final straw to break the camel's back'. Consequently anxieties about school and separation fears had become firmly entrenched. The domestic upheaval associated with moving house and job with loss of friends and separation from maternal and paternal grandparents brought the mother and son even closer together with each turning to the other for continual reassurance and affection. Administrative delays, the boy's learning difficulties and problems in finding a suitable school placement made the early negotiations with the family even more lengthy. Unfortunately, the severely sprained ankle delayed the return to school by a further three weeks. The escort procedure was problematic because of the isolated home situation and the long journey to school. The protest behaviour on the first morning was so intense and so disturbing that it was tempting to abandon the treatment in favour of a graded return using systematic desensitisation. However, the dramatic and instant change in the boy's behaviour the moment we drove off from the house coupled with the need to block the powerful operants maintaining the behaviour suggested that immediate forced return to school was the most efficient and appropriate intervention.

CASE 3: 'ELVIE'

Referral information

Elvie (CA 13.1) had been refusing school for 16 weeks when she was referred by her family doctor and a consultant psychiatrist. Her problems started towards the end of the first term in her third year at the local comprehensive school. Apparently she had a slight disagreement with some friends which coincided with a bout of 'flu and some anxiety about her mother being ill. When she recovered from her illness she refused to attend school claiming that she was worried about being teased by other children in her class.

The social worker arranged for Elvie to transfer to an alternative class. However, she was still unwilling to return to school and so the maternal grandparents decided to pay for her to receive private education at a nearby convent school from the start of the new term. Elvie managed to attend the new school on only one day and refused thereafter. She was extremely tearful, not sleeping very well and showing signs of appetite loss. The parents became increasingly anxious about her problems and consulted their family doctor. Physical investigations revealed nothing abnormal. Anti-depressants were prescribed and there was a marked improvement in the child's appetite and sleep pattern. The doctor also arranged for Elvie to see a consultant psychiatrist. By this time she had been refusing school for ten weeks, excluding the holiday period.

On the eleventh week the consultant psychiatrist recommended that the drug therapy should continue and suggested that Elvie should remain off school for a further month during which time the parents should decide on which school they would like her to attend. By the fifteenth week the parents decided that she should return to the local comprehensive school. However, whenever the subject was brought up Elvie displayed tears, tantrums and protests. She pleaded with her parents not to send her back to school saying things like 'If you really love me you'll not make me go.' At this stage I was asked to see Elvie.

Diagnosis and treatment

Background enquiries at the school revealed that the family was well known to one of the teachers. Apparently Elvie had always been reluctant to attend school. She had been very distressed at the infant stage. She was extremely reluctant to separate from her mother in the mornings and for 18 months it was necessary to take her to school every day crying. Eventually she settled into a reasonably normal school routine. However, each change of class and change of year was greeted with fuss and anxiety. Somewhat surprisingly, her attendance at the local comprehensive school during the first year was quite reasonable and during the second year she hardly missed a day. She seemed to have quite a number of friends and did not appear to have any major worries about school work.

It was arranged for Elvie to be brought to school by her parents for the first interview. The appropriate school staff were prepared to participate in discussions where necessary. Unfortunately the parents did not manage to bring Elvie for the appointment so I made a home visit. The mother (Mrs D.) said that Elvie had run off from home the previous night and stayed out until very late. She was over-tired in the morning and refused to dress herself. Mrs D. felt unable to take a strong line with her daughter.

I learned that Elvie was the middle one of three girls, all of whom were living at home. The eldest girl had left school and was in regular employment. She had never experienced any attendance problems. There was a considerable age-gap between Elvie and the youngest child who was only three years old. The mother presented as an overweight, over-anxious, over-protective woman who had never become independent of her own parents. The father was rather inarticulate and ineffectual. He left the talking to the mother and the grandparents. I gathered that he was poorly educated and did not lay great store by regular schooling. The dominating influence of the grandparents was maintained by the fact that they owned the house the family lived in and also the farm that the father worked on. It was clear they made all the financial decisions and in effect, acted as parents to the grandchildren as well as parents of the mother.

The parents allowed me to interview Elvie alone. I found her to be a pleasant looking but somewhat sullen child. She was reluctant to co-operate in the interview. However, she did complete a number of test items. Her overall performance on the WISC-R (1974) Verbal Scale showed her to be effectively functioning within the average intelligence range (WISC-R Verbal Scale IQ 94). Her reading attainments were slightly below average although not poor enough to cause major difficulties. Her pattern of scoring on the Junior Eysenck (1965) Personality Inventory fell within normal limits on the extroversion-introversion dimension, neuroticism and lie scales. Elvie confirmed that she had been worried about her mother's illness but said that that was no longer of concern. She did, however, seem particularly jealous of the attention the younger child received from both the grandparents and the mother. Apparently this had been very noticeable during the weeks she had been off school. There was also some anxiety about facing friends and she expressed dislike of certain teachers. It was clear that Elvie was highly manipulative with her mother and grandparents and rather too powerful in the family context. Mr and Mrs D. seemed unable to take a firm line with her. In view of this the legal requirements and alternatives with regard to school attendance were made very clear to Elvie. It was pointed out that she was legally obliged to return to school immediately. The family doctor had pronounced her physically fit and the psychiatrist had felt she was not in need of in-patient treatment, further drug therapy or other forms of psychiatric help. If she did not return to school the education department would be likely to take her and/or her parents to court. It would be a waste of time pleading with her parents. They had no choice but to send her to school. At the same time I agreed it would be very difficult for her to go back to school and we would need to think of ways of making life a little easier, at least in the early stages.

At this point Elvie reluctantly considered going back to school. She was asked 'If your life depended on it so that you had to return to school what would worry you the most?' Her priority worries were facing friends and facing teachers, especially the ones she disliked. In view of this we spent some time rehearsing reasonable responses to question from friends like 'Where have

176

you been all this time?' She was reassured that teachers would not quiz her about her absences. Furthermore, in order to make her first day tolerable it was suggested that she could be attached to one of her favourite teachers and given special jobs to do. The next day she could choose to take part in one lesson of her choice. On each subsequent day she would need to choose one more lesson to join until she was back to a full timetable. Elvie agreed to the plan. She said she would go to school the following day with her parents' assistance.

It was emphasised that the parents and grandparents should forcibly escort Elvie to school if she felt unable to make it alone. The grandfather protested at this and made comments like: 'What if she runs off and gets run over?' Remarks like this were dealt with by pointing out that facing problems and unpleasant emotions were all part of growing up. Shielding a child from reality for fear of something untoward happening would only lead to more serious difficulties in the future. The grandfather was asked 'Would you stop a baby from learning to walk in case it fell over and hurt itself?' It was stressed that once Elvie was in school her behaviour would be quite normal. Furthermore, it was underlined that provided her parents could be consistent and firm in their resolve, serious protest behaviour would disappear very quickly and any worries would subside. On the other hand forcing Elvie to school, but eventually giving up because of increasingly severe protests, could only serve to teach Elvie that tantrums pay off. The parents accepted the advice but were not fully convinced. Unfortunately, that night Elvie ran off from home again and stayed in the cow-sheds all night. She returned early in the morning whereupon she was fussed, fed, bathed and put to bed. Her mother did not take her to school.

I made a second home visit at lunch-time. In view of the parental collusion the legal aspects were once again stressed. I pointed out to the parents that Elvie was rapidly going beyond their control and suggested that if we could not resolve the situation the matter might go out of my hands with the education department taking legal action leading to Elvie being placed in a residential setting. Somewhat surprisingly the father lost his temper and insisted that Elvie should attend school the following morning. Advice was given on contingency management. It was emphasised that any special treats, attention and fuss should be reserved and organised for the evenings and weekends after Elvie had managed to attend school.

The following day Elvie was taken to school by her grandfather without protest. She had a good day in school and found that she could manage to face friends. I made a point of seeing her towards the end of the school day and complimented her on her achievements. Elvie went through an unsettled patch for about one week and it was necessary for her grandfather to take her to school on 15 occasions before she managed to attend on her own. Thereafter there were no further problems.

A follow up two years three months later showed that there had been no recurrence of attendance difficulties and no evidence of symptom substitution: her attendance over the past year had been greater than 95 per cent. She remarked that she was now very keen on school and anxious to do well in her CSE and 'O' level examinations. Rutter and Yule (1968) Behaviour Scales completed by both parents and teachers showed no evidence of a significant behavioural disorder. She impressed as confident and outgoing. Her replies to the Eysenck and Eysenck (1975) Personality Questionnaire showed her to be more extroverted and somewhat more stable than most girls of her age. Like many other school phobics she did however show continued evidence of social naïvety. (EPQ Z scores: P = -0.44 SDs; E = $+1.49$SDs; N = -1.94 SDs; L = $+1.75$ SDs).

Comment

Once again a series of additive factors seemed to trigger the school refusal episode. The education welfare officer's simplistic approach (a change of class) did not address the depth and range of issues necessary for effective management. The grandparents' attempt to resolve matters by organising private education delayed facing the real issues. Medical investigations followed up by tranquillisers and legitimised time off school further delayed the main problem of how to confront a rather wilful, omnipotent child. By the time Elvie was referred she had been absent for 16 weeks. The original trigger factors were no longer a major source of anxiety. Secondary maintaining factors were now the main issue. In particular she was anxious about facing friends and teachers after such a long absence. Her tantrums, tempers and school avoidance had been shaped up through inconsistent management. Finally she derived much pleasure from being the centre of attention in the family in preference to her much younger sister.

Although medical investigations and psychiatric advice did initially delay treatment, the eventual removal of medical and psychiatric alibis afforded considerable therapeutic leverage over the child and family. In a sense the family was running out of options. However uncomfortable, some system of returning Elvie to her local school was perhaps the best way ahead. The main treatment problem involved convincing the parents and grandparents that a forced return to school was appropriate given Elvie's tyrannical behaviour. The therapist's ultimate option of withdrawing from treatment and leaving matters to the legal department needed to be made explicit to both Elvie, her parents and grandparents. The turning point came when the father finally lost his temper and took an active role in the family. I suspect that his anger also coincided with the grandparents realising that an immediate return to school had to be engineered. Forced attendance effectively severed the contingencies maintaining the school phobic pattern. Elvie's self-esteem was preserved by allowing her some control over school events in the first couple of weeks. Regular school attendance meant that this more acceptable behaviour pattern could be rewarded both in school and at home.

CASE 4: 'KELVIN'

Referral information

Kelvin was referred for assessment and treatment by a colleague in the Psychological Service. When first interviewed, he had been refusing school for eleven and a half weeks with accompanying fear reactions, crying and temper tantrums. Kelvin who was eleven and a half years old, had not shown school attendance problems until the first term of his third year in the middle school. His school phobia showed a sudden and dramatic onset. His parents were very distressed by his behaviour and took him to their family doctor. Valium was prescribed and it was suggested Kelvin should remain off school for a few weeks. Once the pressure was removed he became quite calm. However, when it came to attending school again, his difficulties and protests reappeared with a vengeance.

One of the teachers at the middle school made several home

visits in order to discover the source of Kelvin's anxiety. The boy would not say anything and so it was suggested that he should return to school on a part-time basis until the anxieties were overcome. He managed to cope with his fear for three and a half weeks until the Christmas holidays. Nevertheless, he still exhibited anxiety on attending school and when the new term started he could not face school even on a part-time basis. Both parents were concerned that undue pressure on the boy might make him emotionally more disturbed.

During the third week of the new term, Kelvin and his parents were seen by a consultant psychiatrist. He felt that it was going to be exceedingly difficult to ensure Kelvin's return to full-time schooling in the near future and suggested that boarding school education might have to be considered eventually. However, in the first instance home tuition should be supplied, backed up by psychotherapy sessions at the child-guidance clinic. It was hoped that the home tutor might be able to assist in the programme of gradually reintroducing Kelvin to school at a later date. However, before these arrangements were finalised, the case was referred for a direct behavioural approach with the emphasis on an immediate return to school.

Diagnosis and treatment

Background information from the school revealed that Kelvin was a shy, quiet boy with well below average reading attainments. He was receiving a certain amount of remedial help. He was good at sport and had plenty of friends. I wrote to the parents inviting them to bring Kelvin into school for an initial interview. On the day, the mother arrived at school on her own looking somewhat sheepish. The father was apparently working and she claimed that she had been unable to persuade Kelvin to come along to the interview. I took down a history of the problems and then followed her home where I was able to interview the boy. I later met the father on his return from work. I noted that Kelvin was the second of three boys, the eldest of whom was living and working away from home. Apparently, he had a very successful school career and was now in a responsible job. The youngest boy gave the impression of being considerably more alert and outgoing than Kelvin. He was reading better than Kelvin even though he was only seven years old. The father seemed a sensible character, but left the major decisions to his wife. He worked long hours as a railway technician so that he was never at home in the mornings to deal with Kelvin's tantrums. The mother impressed as an emotionally flat, weak character. She seemed to find it very difficult to be assertive and leaned heavily on her own elderly mother who lived only a few houses away.

Both parents were aware of Kelvin's limitations in relation to the other boys and had tended to over-compensate for this by continually giving in to the boy's demands. He was therefore, somewhat manipulative at home, although up until the time of his school refusal, his behaviour in school had been very good.

I gathered that Kelvin's school refusal had been precipitated by a change from class-based to subject-based teaching. This meant that instead of having just one teacher for most of the time, he now had to cope with being taken by more than ten different teachers. Apart from the withdrawal of more personal attention, this also meant a good deal more upheaval and mounting anxiety about being able to cope academically. In addition to these problems, Kelvin had also quarrelled with his best friend. By the time Kelvin was interviewed, a number of secondary factors had developed: he was worried about missed school-work and anxious about facing friends. I reassured him that he could receive extra individual help in school and we rehearsed responses to possible questions from friends. He no longer seemed worried about meeting his best friend, feeling that the quarrel would be forgotten.

An intellectual assessment on the WISC-R (1974) Verbal Scale showed Kelvin to be effectively functioning within the below average intelligence range (WISC-R 1974 Verbal Scale IQ 84). The boy's reading attainments were well below average (Burt Rearranged Word Reading Test 1974 Revision, reading age 6 years 10 months). It was felt that Kelvin's current school placement was the correct one provided he could receive more remedial help.

Rutter and Yule (1968) Behaviour Scales completed by Kelvin's teachers showed evidence of a significant neurotic disorder. A similar behaviour scale completed by the parents, however, showed no evidence of a significant disorder. As far as the parents were concerned, Kelvin's only problem was in relation to going to school. Kelvin's profile on the Eysenck and Eysenck (1975) Personality Questionnaire showed him to be significantly more sensitive, more introverted and more socially naïve than most boys of his age (EPQ Z scores: P = -1.15 SDs; E = -1.75 SDs; N = $+0.10$ SDs; L = $+2.04$ SDs).

Factors precipitating and maintaining Kelvin's problems were discussed with both parents. It was suggested that whilst their reluctance to put pressure on the boy was understandable, it would also delay and worsen the inevitable confrontation. It was pointed out that there was no easy, painless solution. However, a swift and immediate return to school under escort if necessary, would produce quick and dramatic results that would far outweigh the initial discomfort. At the same time, it was indicated that if Kelvin did not manage to return to school in the near future, residential schooling would be highly probable. Home tuition was ruled out as an option. The parents reluctantly agreed to my proposals, but the father said he would not be at home in the mornings to help in an escort procedure. He claimed he had already taken quite a lot of time off work and was worried about the security of his job. It seemed unlikely that the mother would manage to bring Kelvin to school on her own and in view of this, I agreed to call at the house to help the mother on the first day.

The following day I found Kelvin dressed and ready for school but sobbing in his bedroom. He had to be carried out of the house screaming and kicking furniture *en route*. He settled down as soon as he was put in the car, but ran off upon arrival at school. Fortunately I was able to catch him and he came sulkily back to school. He reluctantly joined his class, but very quickly settled down and seemed to enjoy the rest of the day.

Kelvin lived a long way from my office base and, in view of this, it was agreed that on future mornings a social worker, known to both the child and the parents, would continue with the escort procedure. Unfortunately, the social worker did not have much success. Kelvin barricaded himself in his bedroom every morning. The mother stood by helplessly and said she could do nothing. After three unsuccessful calls half-term arrived. Immediately after half-term, I called at the house with a view to taking over the escort procedure again. Kelvin was fully dressed in his bedroom, but a trunk was wedged up against his bedroom door to stop anyone going in. He sobbed and cried and refused to come downstairs. I suggested that his mother should remove the trunk from the room later that day so the behaviour could not be repeated the following day.

When I called at the house the next morning there was no

reply. I visited the school and found that Kelvin was absent. In view of this I called at the grandmother's house. She expressed surprise and said that she was sure Kelvin was at home. I followed her to the house. She quietly opened the door and beckoned me in. Much to my surprise I found the mother working in the kitchen doing her washing and Kelvin wedged in his bedroom as on previous occasions. The mother was obviously highly embarrassed and distressed that I had discovered that she was at home after all. She 'ranted and raved' and said that she would end up in a mental hospital. She said she had done what she could, but Kelvin was too difficult for her to handle. I quietly reassured her and paradoxically agreed that she had done all she could; Kelvin was clearly beyond her control and possibly in need of care and supervision. The psychiatrist was right, boarding education would be needed after all.

With support from the grandmother, I spoke to Kelvin through the bedroom door and informed him that unless he opened the door and came down immediately, the case would go out of my hands and would become a legal matter. His grandmother reinforced my points and pleaded with him to come out. Eventually, Kelvin unlocked the door and came downstairs without any protests. I took him to school and complimented him on his efforts. Later I called back at the house and reassured the mother that everything would be alright.

Kelvin settled down into the normal school routine remarkably quickly and easily. I arranged for him to have extra remedial help on an individual basis three times a week. A follow-up six months later revealed that he was happily attending school and making good progress. He had not missed a day's schooling in over six months. His reading attainments had shown a marked improvement. I noticed a significant change in the extroversion score on the Eysenck and Eysenck (1975) Personality Questionnaire. Before treatment Kelvin appeared significantly more introverted than most boys of his age. However, following treatment his E scale score fell within the normal range (EPQ Z scores at follow-up: $P = -0.51$ SDs; $E = +0.13$ SDs; $N = -0.90$ SDs; $L = +2.54$ SDs). Rutter and Yule (1968) Behaviour Scales completed by both parents and teachers showed no evidence of a behavioural disorder. Furthermore, there were no signs of symptom substitution.

Comment

Although the school phobia had shown a sudden onset, the case was still quite difficult to handle. The eleven and a half week absence had created secondary problems. Furthermore, the unsuccessful treatment attempts by the family doctor and the schoolteacher combined with the pessimistic psychiatric prognosis probably reinforced the parents' reluctance to confront the issues. Neither parent was convinced that pressure was a good thing. Although they readily agreed to co-operate, the father was not available in the mornings and the mother's willingness to allow Kelvin to barricade himself in his bedroom each day meant that she was obviously colluding with his school refusal. Whether the collusion was active in the sense that she wanted him at home or passive in the sense that she was frightened to be firm with him is difficult to say.

The absence of the father in the mornings meant that the therapist needed to temporarily exert authority and control. The social worker unfortunately accepted the boy's barricaded position and simply called back at the house each morning without insisting that the obstacle should be removed. The long distance from my office made escorting inconvenient but justified in view of the relatively few occasions on which it was necessary. The elimination of home tuition as a treatment option, involvement of the maternal grandmother, the exposure of the mother's collusion and the final threat from the therapist to withdraw treatment brought about the necessary shift in the mother and boy's positions. Once it was demonstrated that Kelvin could attend school without anxiety and protest the mother relaxed and became considerably more co-operative. Once Kelvin had attended school for several days he quickly settled into his normal routine. His anxieties over school work were realistic. He desperately needed extra remedial help and he responded to it well.

CASE 5: 'AMBROSE'

Referral information

Ambrose aged 14 years 10 months, was referred by his family doctor who felt that the boy was suffering from a generalised anxiety state. He had been refusing school for three and a half weeks and complaining of feeling ill without any apparent physical cause. He had been reluctant to leave the house and meet people and had even given up football on a Saturday morning, which was always a favourite occupation.

Detailed medical notes suggested that Ambrose had always been a temperamentally anxious boy. He had suffered from intermittent diarrhoea and abdominal pain since he was four years old and even now still suffered from headaches and occasional stomach problems. Recent paediatric investigations for frequent loose stools and persistent bowel pain revealed nothing abnormal. In his early years he had genuine kidney trouble with associated enuresis. However, the problem had been successfully treated before he reached secondary school age. The family doctor felt that Ambrose was physically fit for school.

Diagnosis and treatment

At the time of the referral, heavy commitments meant that I could not manage a flexible morning session in school that week. Knowing that speed of intervention was as important as the interview setting, I departed from tradition and called at the boy's house having previously obtained background details from the school. His teachers reported that he was a popular boy, good at sport and average at his work. A Rutter and Yule (1968) behaviour scale completed by the teachers suggested that Ambrose showed evidence of a neurotic disorder. I called at the home out of school hours in order to avoid the possibility of secondarily reinforcing his non-attendance. Furthermore, I called on a Friday night with a view to arranging a return to school for the Monday morning. I learned that Ambrose was the second of three boys. The elder boy was a soldier currently posted in Northern Ireland. The boy's younger brother was mildly spastic and epileptic. He had serious learning difficulties but was managing to attend a local primary school. Unlike many of the mothers of school phobics, this particular mother gave the impression of being a realistic and amazingly resilient woman who tended to take everything in her stride. In contrast, the father seemed ineffectual and rather a worrier.

I gathered that this was Ambrose's first period of outright school refusal although he had been a reluctant attender from time to time. The parents confirmed that from their knowledge there were no major problems at school. A Rutter and Yule (1968) Behaviour Scale completed by the parents produced a pattern suggestive of a neurotic disorder. Apparently Ambrose had led a sheltered existence, having lived in a small village community where he attended one local primary school before transferring to secondary education. He had been separated from his parents on three occasions because of hospitalisations at 6 years, 11 years and 12 years.

Ambrose co-operated willingly in the interview situation and tried to be cheerful but nevertheless his jerky movements and nervous laugh suggested that he was tense and anxious. Intelligence testing showed him to be functioning within the average intelligence range (WISC-R 1974 Verbal Scale IQ 92). Reading attainments were slightly below average but not serious enough to cause any major problems. Ambrose's pattern of scoring on the Eysenck and Eysenck (1975) Personality Questionnaire fell within normal limits on each of the four personality dimensions (EPQ Z scores: P = +0.04 SDs; E = −0.81 SDs; N = +0.05 SDs; L = −0.84 SDs). I was unable to discover any school-related anxieties that could have caused or precipitated the school refusal problem. However, Ambrose did seem concerned about the secondary issue of facing his friends after being absent for a long time. There were , however, a series of physical/health related events that had caused him much distress over the past few months. Ambrose started to refuse school during the first term of his fourth year. Over the previous summer months his maternal grandmother had died and, just before starting school, he was involved in an unfortunate incident in which he nearly drowned. To add to all this, the family lost two puppies from weed-killer poisoning during the summer period and a third dog was killed only five weeks before the school refusal started. In addition, there had been recent family concern about his younger brother who had been fitting more frequently in recent months. As if all this was not enough, there had also been mounting concern about the safety of the elder brother who had recently written home saying that his friend had been shot.

In summary it was felt that Ambrose was a temporarily anxious boy who had suffered from a variety of psychosomatic symptoms over the years. His recent difficulties related to a series of health-related circumstances. His consequent school phobia had been secondarily reinforced by the extra freedom associated with staying at home and watching TV. In addition, the secondary problem had arisen of facing friends. This interpretation was related to both Ambrose and his parents who were clearly anxious for advice and guidance and puzzled by their son's physical symptoms and reluctance to leave home. We joked about his bowel problems and wondered whether they might be partly associated with a high roughage diet. The family ate large quantities of home-grown vegetables and the mother baked her own wholewheat bread. It was suggested that Ambrose would only overcome his problems if he could re-establish his normal school routine. This would not be easy and it might be necessary for his parents to escort him to school for the first few days. On the other hand, if Ambrose could not manage to return to school, his future looked grim. Although highly anxious, Ambrose basically wanted to overcome his difficulties. In view of this he was encouraged to think of a return to school as rather like the frightening challenges that mountaineers or explorers pit themselves against. It would be very difficult but once the problem was conquered he would feel proud of himself. It was pointed out that in school, arrangements could be made to gradually sensitise him back into a full time-table and that if he felt unable to face certain lessons he could spend the time working in the library for the first few days. Possible conversations with friends were rehearsed so that Ambrose would have satisfactory answers to the expected inquisition about where he had been for the past three and a half weeks. Everyone was reassured that once Ambrose faced the initial stage of going back to school, his anxiety symptoms would gradually subside.

The school was well known to me and the staff familiar with this sort of problem. I telephoned the school early on the Monday morning to confirm that Ambrose would be arriving with his parents and called later on that day to check that he was in school. The senior mistress, who had been very helpful, arranged for one of Ambrose's friends to talk to him in a quiet room to break the ice over meeting friends before going into a normal class. When I spoke to Ambrose briefly, he was feeling a little apprehensive and nervous, but was nevertheless proud of the fact that he had managed to attend school. He subsequently attended an increasing number of lessons each day and was on a normal time-table by the end of the week.

I followed up his progress several times by telephone over the next few weeks. I learned that he was attending regularly and was not showing any problems at home. It was left that his parents should feel free to contact me at any stage in the event of further problems. They were advised that an illness, a long holiday or a series of unfortunate incidents could spark off a similar problem. Two months later, after the Christmas holidays, Ambrose's mother telephoned me to say that he was reluctant to attend school again. It was pointed out that Ambrose had only attended school for a month before the Christmas holidays started and that this had probably not given him long enough time to settle back into his normal routine. Under the circumstances, it was suggested that the mother should be firm and adopt the previous strategy agreed upon when he first showed attendance problems.

The treatment was highly successful. The mother took Ambrose to school on only two occasions. Once when he started back at school before Christmas and once when he experienced the slight relapse after Christmas. Therafter there were no further problems. Ambrose integrated into the normal school routine practically straight away.

A follow-up one year, seven months later revealed that he was still attending school regularly without showing anxiety. Over the previous 19 months there had been no evidence of school phobia or symptom substitution. Rutter and Yule (1968) Behaviour Scales completed by both teachers and parents did not show any evidence of a behavioural disorder. Ambrose's pattern of scoring on the EPQ adult scale showed him to be significantly more tough-minded than other youths of his age (Z scores: P = +2.25 SDs; E = +0.83 SDs; N = +0.65 SDs; L = −0.80 SDs). Ambrose had made excellent academic progress. He told me that he was following in his brother's footsteps by joining the Army. I gathered that he led a very active social life and often went away for weekends.

Comment

This case was more straightforward than most. The relevant information surrounding school and home issues was readily accessible. The teachers were well known to me and key members of staff had already built up an expertise and confidence in dealing with this sort of problem. The family doctor had been thorough and efficient in eliminating physical problems and supplied very detailed information. Ambrose had only been out of school for three and a half weeks at the time of referral. The parents were anxious for help and advice. They quickly achieved an understanding of the dynamics of the problem and were able to handle the escort procedure themselves. Although Ambrose did not want to face school, he did at least admit to having a problem. He was co-operative from the outset, in spite of being highly anxious.

The case vividly illustrates how a host of home-related anxieties centering around physical/health-related issues can precipitate school phobia in certain individuals. The crucial role of the teachers was again highlighted. In this case it was very helpful to gain the assistance of some of Ambrose's friends in helping him readjust to school life. This kind of intervention can be very powerful but needs careful handling. This study also shows the importance of close monitoring and follow-up work until the routine of regular schooling is firmly established. This applies in all cases but school phobics who are helped back to school a few weeks before the end of term are particularly at risk of relapsing after the holiday period and should be followed up at the very beginning of the new term.

CASE 6: 'MELODY'

Referral information

Melody (12 years 8 months) had been refusing school for two weeks. I gathered from school that she had experienced a bout of school refusal at the primary school stage, coinciding with friendship problems. Apparently the headmistress intervened very quickly and Melody soon resumed normal school attendance. When she started at the middle school she was initially rather apprehensive and nervous, but settled after about a month. At the beginning of her second year she refused school again, but with firm handling by the senior mistress, she managed to resume normal school attendance after several days absence. However, she soon relapsed and started refusing again with associated stomach aches and suicide threats. At this stage she was referred for an assessment. Before making an appointment, I discussed the case with Melody's family doctor. He felt that physical problems were not an issue and the suicide threats were manipulative gestures that should be ignored.

Diagnosis and treatment

Melody and her parents were invited to attend school for an interview but when they failed to arrive I made a home visit. The father was at work and the mother claimed she was not able to persuade Melody to come to school. I was able to interview Melody alone. I found her to be an immature, strong-willed girl who found it difficult to cope when things went against her. She seemed particularly possessive in her friendships.

Her pattern of scoring on the Eysenck and Eysenck (1975) Personality Questionnaire showed her to be somewhat more sensitive and more socially naïve than most girls of her age (Z scores: $P = -108$ SDs; $E = +0.23$ SDs; $N = +0.72$ SDs; $L = +1.71$ SDs). Parents and teachers completed Rutter and Yule (1968) Behaviour Scales which showed that both at home and at school, Melody showed evidence of a neurotic disorder. This child's pattern of scoring on the WISC-R (1974) Verbal Scale showed her to be effectively functioning towards the lower end of the average intelligence range (IQ 91). Melody's reading attainments were found to be well below average.

In spite of her academic limitations, she did not seem particularly concerned about her school work. The main factor precipitating her school phobia seemed to be the recent break-up of her friendship group. Apparently this was brought about at the beginning of the second year in the middle school when she changed from class-based to subject-based teaching. The girls she was particularly friendly with were placed in higher sets.

Melody's mother seemed pleasant, co-operative and anxious for advice. I did not manage to see the father, but gathered he was somewhat ineffectual and had a drink problem. Melody was the elder of two children. For the first nine years of her life, the family lived with the paternal grandparents. The paternal grandmother was always a very domineering character who overindulged the children. However, when the paternal grandfather died, the grandmother became even more difficult to live with and in view of this, Melody and her parents moved into a nearby house, leaving the grandmother to live alone. Apparently since that time (three years ago), the only person to keep regular contact with the paternal grandmother had been Melody. Unfortunately, whenever Melody had been reprimanded at home she had always been able to run to her grandmother where she would receive sympathy and affection. The family feud between the grandmother and the parents had generated a good deal of tension over the years.

During the period that Melody had been refusing school her parents had tried to coax her to go back by giving her treats. On one occasion they took her shopping and bought her a new pair of shoes and on another day they took her to the hairdressers during school hours. However, not surprisingly, the rewards at home did not help to resolve the problems. Furthermore, when Melody's mother went out to work the child used to visit the paternal grandmother who was quite lonely and always willing to give her shelter during the daytime.

It seemed that Melody was an emotionally vulnerable, immature girl who had been over-indulged and handled inconsistently over the years by both her parents and paternal grandparents. She seemed to find it difficult to cope with change and upheaval and particularly a loss of friends. Rather than face her difficulties, she immediately retreated to the safety of home where her problems were maintained by the considerable attention and fuss lavished upon her by her mother. If the attention was not forthcoming at home, she turned to her paternal grandmother.

Factors precipitating the problems were discussed with the mother and much time was spent explaining operant principles, demonstrating how Melody's difficulties could be maintained by the freedom and special attention she received when off school. It was stressed that treats should only be given when Melody had managed to return to full-time schooling. In view of her omnipotence and emotional blackmail, the legal requirements for full-time school attendance were clearly spelt out to her in front of the mother. The need to resume regular schooling immediately was strongly emphasised.

The school staff were very helpful in agreeing to be flexible regarding time-tabling arrangements and in particular, it was agreed that Melody would be able to transfer back into a tutor group where she would be with her old friends. At the same time, extra remedial provision was arranged. In spite of these special arrangements, however, it was suggested that Melody might still find it difficult to attend school without some physical support in the mornings in the first instance. Accordingly, it was agreed that if Melody did not manage to catch the school bus, she would be taken to school by a close friend of the family. Apparently, the father had to leave for work early in the morning and the mother was not able to drive. The suicide threats were not mentioned to Melody. However, it was privately agreed with the mother that if the threats continued, psychiatric referral and hospital in-patient treatment might be indicated. Melody was not in school the next day. Her mother had left for work after Melody had run off from home straight after breakfast. I located Melody at her paternal grandmother's house. I had a long discussion with the grandmother emphasising the seriousness of Melody's problems. It was indicated that unless normal school attendance was quickly resumed some form of residential provision might need to be considered. I explained that providing shelter for Melody during the daytime was helping to maintain her problems. We discussed operant principles and the dangers of unwittingly rewarding Melody for being away from school. After providing a detailed and bitter account of the family feuds, the grandmother agreed to co-operate. Melody was encouraged to return to school that day; thereafter she did not experience any more problems.

A follow-up nine months later revealed that Melody was still attending school regularly with an attendance rate in excess of 95 per cent. Rutter and Yule (1968) Behaviour Scales completed by both parents and teachers no longer showed evidence of a neurotic disorder. Melody's reading attainments had shown a great improvement. Her pattern of scoring on the Eysenck and Eysenck (1975) Personality Questionnaire showed that she was still more sensitive and socially naïve than most girls of her age. However, there had been a significant drop in her score on the neuroticism scale (Z scores: P = −1.08 SDs; E = +0.96 SDs; N = −1.73 SDs; L = +2.23 SDs). I found no evidence of symptom substitution.

Comment

Melody's vulnerability seemed to stem from the inconsistent and inappropriate handling by both parents and grandparents. The trigger factor in this case was a switch from class-based to subject-based teaching. This meant that Melody was put into different subject sets according to her ability. As a result, she was separated from her friends and had to cope with a series of new teachers rather than the one familiar teacher. As in the past she refused school and stayed at home where she felt in control and able to manipulate the adults around her. Therapeutic leverage over the child, mother and grandmother was gained by implying that if a return to school was unsuccessful, residential education might have to be considered.

The case demonstrates the importance of understanding the family relationships and patterns of influence and control. In this family the paternal grandmother played a key role in maintaining the problem and needed to be actively involved in treatment. A strong emphasis was placed on teaching the mother and grand-mother operant reinforcement principles.

Nevertheless, it is doubtful whether the immediate return to school would have worked without flexible time-table arrangements being made in school. It was important to find a way of Melody having contact with her old friends without indulging her by unfairly bending the system. This was made possible by placing Melody in the same mixed ability tutor group as her friends whilst maintaining her appropriate subject groupings (without her friends). This was perfectly acceptable to the school and allowed Melody to save face.

Appendix

SCHOOL PHOBIA RECORD FORM

Name:
Date of Birth: Date of interview:
Age:
Address:

School:

Professionals currently involved with the child and family:

GP: Social Worker:

Psychiatrist: Education Welfare Officer:

Paediatrician: Educational Psychologist:

Other Professionals: Clinical Psychologist:

DESCRIPTION OF PROBLEM AND RELATED DIFFICULTIES

History and Pattern of School Phobia

1. How long has the child been refusing school?
                                        Number of weeks ....
2. Is this the first period of refusal?   YES/NO
3. Has there been a history of poor attendance without outright school refusal?   YES/NO
    and/or
4. Have there been previous episodes of school phobia?   YES/NO
5. At what age was attendance first a problem?   ....
6. How many bouts of school phobia has the child experienced in the past?   ....

7. Detailed attendance record for the current year and previous year.

Mon.	Tues.	Wed.	Thurs.	Fri.	Week Ending	
					September	Autumn
					October	
					November	
					December	
					January	Spring
					February	
					March	
					April	Summer
					May	
					June	
					July	

Mon.	Tues.	Wed.	Thurs.	Fri.	Week Ending	
					September	Autumn
					October	
					November	
					December	
					January	Spring
					February	
					March	
					April	Summer
					May	
					June	
					July	

N.B. Are there any regular features in the attendance pattern relating to home and/or school issues.

8. How severe were previous difficulties and how were they resolved?

9. Has the child stayed away from school with the knowledge and consent of the parents at some stage in the course of the problem?   YES/NO

Further details .....

10. When off school does the child remain at home?   YES/NO

If no: who does the child spend time with? What does the child do?

Associated symptoms

1. Do attempts to encourage school attendance result in:
   (a) Complaints of feeling ill without apparent organic cause?
   (b) Crying and protests?
   (c) Physical signs of anxiety, e.g. pallor, trembling, vomiting and running off in panic?
   (d) Severe temper tantrums?
   (e) General lethargy and depression?
   (f) No obvious anxiety?

2. Is the child eating normally?

3. Is the child sleeping normally?

4. Are the child's bowel habits normal?

5. Is the child bed-wetting or having urinary frequency problems?

6. If the child complains of feeling ill, note the symptoms in detail ...

7. Does the child show any evidence of a conduct disorder — (persistent lying, wandering off from home, stealing, destructiveness, inappropriate sexual activities, etc.)   YES/NO

     If YES — explore in detail ...

8. Has the child shown any evidence of suicide threats?   YES/NO

     If YES — explore the details and circumstances ...

Medical issues

Have the child's physical symptoms been thoroughly investigated?　　　　　　　　　　　　　　　　　　　　　YES/NO

    If YES —
        (a)　Is the child medically fit for school?　　　　YES/NO

        (b)　How long has the child been fit for school?
           or
        (c)　When will the child be fit for school?

    If NO —

        (a)　Are the results of medical tests completed?
           or
        (b)　The results of medical tests pending?

Child's behaviour outside school

1. At home, is the child usually:

    (a) wilful/stubborn/demanding,
        or
    (b) obedient and passive,
        or
    (c) depressed/lethargic/uncommunicative.

2. Are there any separation worries with respect to —

    (a)　The father,

    (b) The mother,

    (c) Other family members.

3. If the pressure to attend school is removed does the child's behaviour at home appear normal?　　　　　　YES/NO

4. Can the child walk past the school gates in the evenings or at the weekends without feeling or showing signs of distress?
　　　　　　　　　　　　　　　　　　　　　　　　　YES/NO

5. Does the child have normal contact with peers in the evenings and at weekends?　　　　　　　　　　　　　　YES/NO

6. Exactly what happens each morning prior to school?

Details of home-related anxieties

Physical/health-related issues	Expressed by child	Expressed by parent	Comments by psychologist /teacher
Illness (physical or mental) in a parent, close relative, friend or pet.			
Death of a parent, relative, close friend or pet.			
Health concerns with respect to the child.			
Other (please specify)			

Social anxiety issues

Physical/health-related issues	Expressed by child	Expressed by parent	Comments by psychologist /teacher
Sudden separation from mother			
Sudden separation from father			
Sudden separation from close friends and/or relatives (as involved in moving school or house)			
Marital disharmony			
Birth of a new child			
Young child at home demanding enormous attention			
Other (please specify)			

Miscellaneous issues

Physical/health-related issues	Expressed by child	Expressed by parent	Comments by psychologist /teacher
Accidents (e.g. home catching fire)			
Financial worries			
Other (please specify)			

Details of school-related anxieties

	Expressed by child	Expressed by parent	Comments by psychologist /teacher
Being bullied			
PE/games activities — being injured			
Travel sickness			
Other (please specify)			

Social anxiety issues

	Expressed by child	Expressed by parent	Comments by psychologist /teacher
Change of school			
Exams/tests			
Reciting in class			
Being criticised by teachers			
Making mistakes			
Dislike of certain teachers			
Upsetting a teacher			
Teasing on school bus			
Feeling lonely in lunch hours/breaks			
Sudden separation from a friend (e.g. change of class, set, school etc.)			
Being in too high or low a set			
Other (please specify)			
Miscellaneous issues Noise			
Other (please specify)			

Home-related maintaining issues

1. Do the parents over-attend to:
    (a) psychosomatic complaints?
    (b) minor school-related worries?

2. Does the child enjoy:
    greater personal freedom at home?
    special treats when *off* school?

3. Are the parents unable or unwilling to take the child to school? Explore fully:

4. Other issues

School-related maintaining issues

1. Is the child's school placement inappropriate because of:
    (a) Staff rejection?
    (b) Excessive and insurmountable peer group difficulties?
    (c) Major curriculum difficulties?
    (d) Unreasonable travelling distance to school?
    (e) Other issues

THE FAMILY

Structure and relationships

(a) Who does the child live with?

Mother		Comments:
Father		
Step-mother		
Step-father		
Cohabitee		
Other		

(b) Number of brothers and sisters:

1	2	3	4	5	6	7	8	9
M	M	M	M	M	M	M	M	M
F	F	F	F	F	F	F	F	F

(c) Position in family

(d) Age of youngest child . . . years

(e) Do the family have close contact with:

Maternal grandmother		Comments:
Maternal grandfather		
Paternal gramdmother		
Paternal grandfather		

(f) Parental relationships:

Good relationship		Comments:
Marital disharmony		
Divorced		
Separated		
Single parent through death of wife or husband		

(g) Does the separated or divorced parent live nearby?   YES/NO

(h) Does the child see the separated or divorced parent —

	Mother	Father
Frequently?		
Occasionally?		
Never?		

Comments:

(i) Other important features

Factors relating to the mother and father

(a) Parental characteristics:

	Mother	Father
Domineering		
Over-protective		
Ineffectual		
Neurotic		
History of mental illness		
Guilt-ridden		
Generally well adjusted		

Comments:

(b) Are there any significant events in the mother's history to account for over-protection and/or over-indulgence?

1. Much wanted child of elderly parents
2. History of life-threatening illness in the child
3. Difficult pregnancy
4. Previous loss of a child
5. Previous sterilityi problems
6. History of post-natal depression or other psychiatric problems
7. Inadequate experiences in the mother's own childhood
8. Inadequate marital relationship
9. Unresolved separation issues with respect to the mother's own parents
10. Painful memories of schooldays
11. Painful separation experiences
12. Other

205

(c) Are there any significant events in the father's history that have a bearing on the child's difficulties and family relationships other than those already covered in (b)?
e.g.s.

1. Painful memories of schooldays
2. History of inadequate parenting
3. Heavy work demands (long irregular hours; much time away from home etc.)
4. Marital problems
5. History of psychiatric problems
6. Other

Parental motivation to resolve the school phobia problem

(a) Parental attitude towards child's school refusal:

	Mother	Father
Unconcerned		
Colludes with child		
Very anxious		
Inconsistent		
Other		

Comments:

(b) Are the parents keen to receive help?

Father: YES/NO
Mother: YES/NO
If NO — why not?

(c) Do the parents have the confidence in the original school and staff?

Father: YES / NO
Mother: YES / NO
If NO — why not?

(d) Do the parents have confidence in the child's new school and staff (in the event of a change of school being part of the treatment)?

    Father: YES / NO
    Mother: YES / NO
    If NO — why not?

(e) Are any of the other children in the family poor school attenders?

              YES / NO

    Further details

(f) What are the costs and benefits of the school phobia to individual family members and the whole family unit?

(g) What steps have the parents taken to resolve the problem? What has been the outcome so far?

Are there any additional family pressures?

e.g.s

(a) An illness in the mother or father

(b) Financial worries

(c) Work pressures

(d) Problems with other children or dependent relatives

(e) Other

207

THE SCHOOL

Staff motivation to overcome the pupil's difficulties

(a) Attitude of significant staff towards child's problem:

Sympathetic/realistic

Anxious/inconsistent

Uncooperative/rejecting

Other

(b) Which members of staff are most concerned to resolve the child's problems?

(c) What steps have the child's teachers taken to resolve the problem?

School organisation and flexibility

(a) Who are the key school personnel responsible for pastoral care?

(b) Is there flexibility to change the child's house or tutor group?

(c) Can the child change sets or groups for specific subjects?

(d) Is extra remedial help available?

(e) Can the child use a quiet room, library or tutor's office to catch up on work missed during the settling-in period?

(f) Is there a member of staff who would be willing and able to take on a key role escorting the child to school if necessary?

School system issues

1. Is there a widespread attendance problem at the school?

2. Are there attendance problems in the child's year group or tutor group?

3. Are there widespread behavioural problems at the school?

4. Is there high teacher turnover at the school?

5. Are there any other school issues likely to undermine treatment?

THE CHILD

Intellectual and personality characteristics

(Attach test questionnaire information and teacher comments)

1. Note behaviour in school and at home

2. Note details of intellectual characteristics

3. Details of attainments (areas of strength and weakness)

4. Personality characteristics

Attitude towards school phobia

(a) Does the child accept there is a problem?

(b) How does the child view the school avoidance? Is it felt to be a reasonable response to unreasonable demands and pressures?

(c) How does the child feel the situation should be resolved?

Schooling history

Schools attended	Dates	Problems

Significant events in the child's life

(a) Birth problems?

(b) Maternal/paternal separation?

(c) Serious illnesses?

(d) History of fears and phobias?

(e) History of allergic/psychosomatic problems — e.g. migraine, asthma, eczema, etc.

PREVIOUS TREATMENTS

Professionals consulted	Dates	Treatment/advice/ outcomes
1.		
2.		
3.		
4.		
5.		

ADDITIONAL NOTES

Bibliography

Arieti, S. (1961) 'A re-examination of the phobic symptom and of symbolism in psychopathology.' *American Journal of Psychiatry*, *118*, 106–10.

Ayllon, T., Smith D. and Rogers, M. (1970) 'Behavioural management of school phobia.' *Journal of Behaviour Therapy and Experimental Psychiatry*, *1*. 125–38.

Azrin, N. H. and Nunn, R. G. (1973) 'Habit-reversal: a method of eliminating nervous habits and tics.' *Behaviour Research and Therapy*, *11*, 619–28.

Baker, H. and Wills, U. (1978) 'School phobia: classification and treatment.' *British Journal of Psychiatry*, *132*, 492–9.

—— and —— (1979) 'School phobic children at work.' *British Journal of Psychiatry*, *135*, 561–4.

Bakwin, H. (1965) 'Learning problems and school phobia.' *Pediatric Clinics of North America*, *12*, 995–1014.

Bandura, A. (1969) *The principles of behaviour modification*. Holt, Rinehart and Winston, New York.

Barker, P. (1968) 'The inpatient treatment of school refusal.' *British Journal of Medical Psychology*, *41*, 381–7.

Beck, A. T. (1976) *Cognitive therapy and the emotional disorders*. International Universities Press, New York.

Berecz, J. M. (1968) 'Phobias of childhood: etiology and treatment.' *Psychological Bulletin*, *70*, 694–720.

Berg, I. (1970) 'A follow-up study of school phobic adolescents admitted to an inpatient unit.' *Journal of Child Psychology and Psychiatry*, *11*, 37–47.

—— Butler, A. and Hall, G. (1976) 'The outcome of adolescent school phobia.' *British Journal of Psychiatry*, *128*, 80–5.

—— Marks, I., McGuire, R. and Lipsedge, M. (1974) 'School phobia and agoraphobia.' *Psychological Medicine*, *4*, 428–34.

—— and McGuire, R. (1971) 'Are school phobic adolescents overdependent?' *British Journal of Psychiatry*, *124*, 10–13.

—— Nichols, K. and Pritchard, C. (1969) 'School phobia — its classification and relationship to dependency.' *Journal of Child Psychology and Psychiatry*, *10*, 23–41.

Blagg, N. R. (1977) 'A detailed strategy for the rapid treatment of school phobics.' *Bulletin of the British Association for Behavioural Psychotherapy*, *5*, 70–5.

—— (1979) 'The behavioural treatment of school refusal,' unpublished PhD thesis, Institute of Psychiatry, University of London.

—— (1981) 'A behavioural approach to school refusal. Behaviour modification in education.' *Perspectives*, *5*, School of Education, University of Exeter.

—— and Yule, W. (1984) 'The behavioural treatment of school refusal: a comparative study.' *Behaviour, Research and Therapy*, *22*, 119–27.

—— and Yule, W. (1987) 'A replication of Hersov's Study.' In preparation.

Berryman, E. (1959) 'School phobia: management problems in private practice.' *Psychological Reports*, 5, 19–24.

Bornstein, B. (1949) 'The analysis of a phobic child.' *Psychoanalytic Study of the Child*, 3 and 4, 181–226.

Bransby, E. R. (1951) 'A study of absence from school.' *Medical Offprints*, 86, 223–30, 237–40.

Broadwin, I. T. (1932) 'A contribution to the study of truancy.' *Orthopsychiatry*, 2, 253–9.

Bryce, G. and Baird, D. (1986) 'Precipitating a crisis: family therapy and adolescent school refusers.' *Journal of Adolescence*, 9, 199–213.

Burt, C. (1925) *American Journal of the Young Delinquent*, University of London Press, London.

—— (1974) *The Burt (rearranged) word reading test*. (Revised edn), University of London Press, London.

Cameron, K. (1955) 'Diagnostic categories in child psychiatry.' *British Journal of Medical Psychology*, 28, 67–71.

Cantrell, R. P., Cantrell, M. L., Huddleston, C. M. and Woolridge, R. L. (1969) 'Application of contingency contracts to four school attendance problems.' *Journal of Applied Behavioural Analysis*, 2, 215–20.

Cautela, J. R. (1968) 'Behaviour therapy and the need for behavioural assessment.' *Psychotherapy: Theory, Research and Practice*, 5, 3, 175–9.

Chapel, J. L. (1967) 'Treatment of a case of school phobia by reciprocal inhibition.' *Canadian Psychiatric Association Journal*, 12, 25–8.

Chazan, M. (1962) 'School phobia.' *British Journal of Educational Psychology*, 32, 209–17.

Coolidge, J. C., Brodie, R. D. and Feeney, B. (1964) 'A ten-year follow-up of sixty-six school phobic children.' *American Journal of Orthopsychiatry*, 34, 675–84.

—— Hahn P. B. and Peck A. L. (1957) 'School phobia: neurotic crisis or way of life.' *American Journal of Orthopsychiatry*, 27, 296–306.

—— Willer, M. L., Tessman, E. and Waldfogel, L. (1960) 'School phobia in adolescence, a manifestation of severe character disturbance.' *American Journal of Orthopsychiatry*, 30, 599–607.

Cooper, M. G. (1966a) 'School refusal.' *Educational Research*, 8, 2, 115–27.

—— (1966b) 'School refusal: an inquiry into the part played by school and home.' *Educational Research*, 8, 3, 223–9.

Croghan, L. M. (1981) 'Conceptualising the critical elements in a rapid desensitisation to school anxiety: a case study.' *Journal of Pediatric Psychology*, 6, 165–9.

Davidson, S. (1960–61) 'School phobia as a manifestation of family disturbance: its structure and treatment.' *Journal of Child Psychology and Psychiatry*, 1, 4, 270–87.

DES (1974) Press notice: 'Results of school absence survey', DES, London.

Doleys, D. M. and Williams, S. C. (1977) 'The use of natural consequences and a make-up period to eliminate school phobic behaviour: a case study.' *Journal of School Psychology*, *45*, 44–9.

Eisenberg, L. (1958) 'School phobia — a study in the communication of anxiety.' *American Journal of Psychotherapy*, *10*, 682–95.

Estes, H. R., Haylett, C. H. and Johnson, A. L. (1956) 'Separation anxiety.' *American Journal of Psychotherapy*, *10*, 682–95.

Esveldt-Dawson, K., Wisner, K. L., Unis, A. S., Matson, J. L., Kazdin, A. E. (1982) 'Treatment of phobias in a hospitalised child.' *Journal of Behaviour Therapy and Experimental Psychiatry*, *13*, 1, 77–83.

Eysenck, H. J. and Eysenck, S. B. G. (1964) *Manual of the Eysenck Personality Inventory*, University of London Press, London.

—— and Eysenck, S. B. G. (1975) *Manual of the Eysenck Personality Questionnaire (Junior and Adult)*, Hodder and Stoughton, London.

—— and Rachman, S. (1965) *The causes and cure of neurosis*, Routledge and Kegan Paul, London.

Eysenck, S. B. G. (1965) *Manual of the Junior Eysenck Personality Inventory*, University of London Press, London.

Fogelman, K. and Richardson, K. (1974) 'School attendance: some results from the National Child Development Study.' In B. Turner (ed.) *Truancy*, Ward Lock International, London.

Forehand, R. (1979) 'Parent behavioural training to modify child noncompliance: treatment generalisation across time and from home to school.' *Behaviour Modification*, *3*, 1, 3–25.

Framrose, R. (1977) 'A framework for adolescent disorder: some clinical presentations.' *British Journal of Psychiatry*, *131*, 281–8.

—— (1978) 'Outpatient treatment of severe school phobia.' *Journal of Adolescence*, *1*, 353–61.

Frick, W. B. (1964) 'School phobia: a critical review of the literature.' *Merrill-Palmer Quarterly*, *10*, 361–73.

Galloway, D. (1976a) 'Size of school, socioeconomic hardship, suspension rates and persistent unjustified absence from school.' *British Journal of Educational Psychology*, *46*, 1, 40–7.

—— (1976b) 'Persistent unjustified absence from school.' *Trends in Education*, *303*, 22–7.

—— (1978) Personal communication.

—— (1980) 'Problems in the assessment and management of persistent absenteeism from school.' In L. Hersov and I. Berg (eds) *Out of School*, Wiley, Chichester.

—— (1985) *Schools and persistent absentees*, Pergamon, Oxford and New York.

—— and Miller, A. (1978) 'The use of graded in vivo flooding in the extinction of children's phobias.' *Behavioural Psychotherapy*, *6*, 7–10.

Garvey, W. P. and Hegrenes, J. R. (1966) 'Desensitisation techniques in the treatment of school phobia.' *American Journal of Orthopsychiatry*, *36*, 147–52.

Glaser, K. (1959) 'Problems in school-attendance: school phobia and related conditions.' *Paediatrics*, *23*, 371–83.

Goldberg, T. B. (1953) 'Factors in the development of school phobia.' *Smith College Studies in Social Work*, *23*, 227–48.

215

Gray, J. (1971) *The psychology of fear and stress*, Weidenfeld and Nicholson, London.

Graziano, A. M., DeGiovanni, I. S. and Garcia, K. A. (1979) 'Behavioural treatment of children's fears: a review.' *Psychology Bulletin*, *86*, 4, 804–30.

Greenbaum, R. S. (1964) 'Treatment of school phobias: theory and practice.' *American Journal of Psychotherapy*, *18*, 616–33.

Hallam, R. S. (1976) 'The Eysenck Personality Scales: stability and change after therapy.' *Behaviour Research and Therapy*, *14*, 369–72.

Hampe, E., Noble, H. H., Miller, L. C. and Barrett, C. L. (1973) 'Phobic children one and two years post-treatment.' *Journal of Abnormal Psychology*, *82*, 446–53.

Healy, W. (1915) *The individual delinquent*, Heinemann, London.

Hersen, M. (1968) 'Treatment of a compulsive and phobic disorder through a total behaviour therapy program: A case study.' *Psychotherapy*, *5*, 220–5.

—— (1970a) 'Behaviour modification approach to a school-phobia case.' *Journal of Clinical Psychology*, *26*, 128–32.

—— (1970b) 'The complementary use of behaviour therapy and psychotherapy, some comments.' *Psychological Record*, *20*, 395–402.

—— (1971a) 'Resistance to direction in behaviour therapy: some comments.' *Journal of Genetic Psychology*, *118*, 121–7.

—— (1971b) 'The behavioural treatment of school phobia.' *Journal of Nervous and Mental Disease*, *153*, 99–107.

Herrnstein, R. J. (1969) 'Method and theory in the study of avoidance.' *Psychological Review*, 76, 46–9.

Hersov, L. A. (1960–61a) 'Persistent non-attendance at school.' *Journal of Psychology and Psychiatry*, *1*, 2, 130–6.

—— (1960–61b) 'Refusal to go to school.' *Journal of Child Psychology and Psychiatry, 1*, 2, 137–45.

—— (1977) 'School Refusal.' In M. Rutter and L. A. Hersov (eds) *Child psychiatry: modern approaches*, Blackwell, Oxford.

—— (1980) 'Hospital inpatient and day-patient treatment of school refusal.' In L. Hersov and I. Berg (eds) *Out of School*, Wiley, Chichester.

Hodges, V. (1968) 'Non-attendance at school.' *Educational Research*, *11*, 1, 58–61.

Hsia, H. (1984) 'Structural and strategic approach to school phobia/school refusal.' *Psychology in the Schools*, *21*, 360–7.

Johnson, A. M. (1957) 'School phobia.' *American Journal of Ortho-psychiatry*, *27*, 307–9.

—— Falstein, E. L., Szurek, S. and Svendsen, M. (1941) 'School phobia.' *American Journal of Orthopsychiatry*, *11*, 702–11.

Jones, M. C. (1924) 'The elimination of children's fears.' *Journal of Experimental Psychology*, *7*, 383–90.

Jung, C. G. (1911) 'A case of neurosis in a child.' In *The collected works of C. J. Jung*, Bollington Foundation, New York.

Khan, J. H. and Nursten, J. P. (1962) 'School refusal.' *American Journal of Orthopsychiatry*, *32*, 707–18.

——, —— and Carroll, H. C. (1981) *Unwillingly to school*, 3rd edn, Pergamon Press, Oxford.

Kavanagh, A. and Carroll, H. C. (1977) 'The pupil attendance in three comprehensive schools. A study of the pupils and their families.' In Carroll, H. C. (ed.) *Absenteeism in South Wales. Studies of pupils, their homes and their secondary schools*, The Faculty of Education, University College of Swansea, 40–50.

Kennedy, W. A. (1965) 'School phobia: rapid treatment of fifty cases.' *Journal of Abnormal Psychology*, *70*, 4, 285–9.

King, N. (1987) *Children's phobias* (in press), Wiley, Chichester.

Klein, E. (1945) 'The reluctance to go to school.' *The Psychoanalytic Study of the Child*, *1*, 263–79.

Kline, L. W. (1897) 'Truancy as related to the migratory instinct.' *Pediatric Seminars*, *5*, 381–42.

Lang, P. (1970) 'Stimulus control, response control and desensitisation of fear.' In D. Levis (ed.) *Learning approaches to therapeutic behaviour change*, Aldine Press, Chicago.

Lawrence, D. (1979) 'Self-esteem inventory forms A and B,' unpublished — personal communication.

—— (1981) 'The development of a self-esteem questionnaire' *British Journal of Educational Psychology*, *54*, 245–51.

——(1987) *Enhancing self-esteem in the classroom*, Harper and Row, London.

Lazarus, A. A. (1960) 'The elimination of children's phobias by deconditioning.' In H. J. Eysenck (ed.) *Behaviour therapy and the neuroses*, Pergamon Press, Oxford.

—— and Abramovitz, A. (1962) 'The use of "emotive imagery" in the treatment of children's phobias.' *Journal of Mental Science*, *108*, 191–5.

——, Davidson, G. C. and Polefka, D. A. (1964) 'Classical and operant factors in the treatment of a school phobia.' *Journal of Abnormal Psychology*, *70*, 225–9.

Leventhal, T. and Sills, M. (1964) 'Self-image in school phobia.' *American Journal of Orthopsychiatry*, *34*, 4, 685–95.

—— Weinberger, G., Stander, R. J. and Stearns, R. P. (1967) 'Therapeutic strategies with school phobics.' *American Journal of Orthopsychiatry*, *37*, 64–70.

Levis, D. J. (1967) 'Implosive therapy: the subhuman analogue, the strategy and the technique.' In S. G. Armitage (ed.), *Behaviour modification techniques in the treatment of emotional disorders*, Veterans Admin., Battle Creek, Mich.

Macmillan, K. (1977) *Education welfare: strategy and structure*, Longman, London.

Malmquist, C. P. (1965) 'School phobia: a problem of family neurosis.' *Journal of the American Academy of Child Psychiatry*, *4*, 293–319.

Marks, I. (1970) *Fears and phobias*, Academic Press, New York.

—— (1972) 'Flooding (implosion) and allied treatments.' In W. S. Agras (ed.), *Learning theory, application of principles and procedures to psychiatry*, Little, Brown and Co.

Mateson, J. L. (1981) 'A controlled outcome study of phobias in

217

mentally retarded adults.' *Behaviour Research and Therapy*, *19*, 101–7.

McAdam, E. and Gilbert, P. (1985) 'Cognitive behavioural therapy as a psychotherapy for mood disturbance in child, adolescent and family psychotherapy,' *Journal of Child Psychology and Psychiatry*, 7, 1, 19–27.

Miller, L. C., Barrett, C. L. and Hampe, E. (1974) 'Phobias of childhood in a prescientific era.' In A. Davies (ed.) *Child personality and psychopathology: current topics,* Vol. 1, Wiley, New York, pp. 89–134.

—— Barrett, C. L., Hampe, E. and Noble, H. (1972) 'Comparison of reciprocal inhibition, psychotherapy and waiting list control for phobic children.' *Journal of Abnormal Psychology*, *79*, 3, 269–79.

Miller, N. (1951), 'Learnable drives and rewards.' In S. Stevens (ed.) *Handbook of experimental psychology*, Wiley, New York.

Miller, P. M. (1972) 'The use of visual imagery and muscle relaxation in the counter-conditioning of a phobic child: a case study.' *Journal of Nervous and Mental Diseases*, *154*, 457–9.

Minuchin, S. (1970) 'The use of an ecological framework in the treatment of a child.' In E. J. Anthony and C. Koupernik, (eds) *The child in his family*, Wiley Interscience, New York.

Model, A. N. and Shepherd, E. (1958) 'The child who refuses to go to school.' *Medical Offprints*, *100*, 39–41.

Mohr, I. (1948) 'Fears in relation to school attendance, a study of truancy.' *Bulletin of the National Association of School Social Workers, 24,* 1.

Montenegro, H. (1968) 'Severe separation anxiety in two pre-school children: successfully treated by reciprocal inhibition.' *Journal of Child Psychology and Psychiatry*, *9*, 93–108.

Morgan, G. A. V. (1959) 'Children who refuse to go to school.' *Medical Offprints*, *102*, 221–4.

Mowrer, O. H. (1939) 'Stimulus response theory of anxiety.' *Psychological Review*, *46*, 553–65.

Murgatroyd, S. J. (1974) 'Ethical issues in secondary school counselling.' *Journal of Moral Education*, *4*, 27–37.

Murphy, W. C. (1938) 'A comparative study of 50 truants and non-truants.' *Journal of Juvenile Research*, *22*.

NACEWO (1975) *These we serve: the report of a working party set up to enquire into the causes of absence from school*. National Association of Chief Education Welfare Officers, Bedford.

Nichols, K. A. and Berg, I. (1970) 'School phobia and self-evaluation.' *British Journal of Psychiatry*, *11*, 133–141.

Olsen, I. A. and Coleman, H. S. (1967) 'Treatment of school phobia as a case of separation anxiety.' *Psychology in the Schools*, *4*, 151–4.

Pacella, B. L. (1948) 'Behaviour problems of children.' *Medical Clinics of North America*, May, 655–87.

Partridge, J. M. (1939) 'Truancy.' *Journal of Mental Science*, *85*, 45–81.

Patterson, C. H. (1968) 'Relationship therapy and/or behaviour therapy.' *Psychotherapy: Theory, Research and Practice*, *5*, 226–33.

Patterson, G. R. (1965) 'A learning theory approach to the treatment of the school phobic child.' In L. P. Ullman and L. Krasner (eds) *Case studies in behaviour modification*, pp. 279–85, Holt, Rinehart Winston, New York.

Phillips, D. and Wolpe, S. (1981) 'Multiple behavioural techniques in severe separation anxiety of a twelve-year-old.' *Journal of Behaviour Therapy and Experimental Psychiatry*, *12*, 4, 329–32.

Rachman, S. (1972) 'Clinical applications of observational learning, imitation and modelling.' *Behaviour Therapy*, *3*, 379–97.

—— (1976) 'The passing of the two-stage theory of fear avoidance: fresh possibilities.' *Behaviour Research and Therapy*, *14*, 125–34.

—— (1977) 'The conditioning theory of fear-acquisition: a critical examination.' *Behaviour Research and Therapy*, *15*, 375–87.

—— and Hodgson, R. (1974) 'Synchrony and desynchrony in fear and avoidance.' *Behaviour, Research and Therapy*, *12*, 311–18.

Radin, S. (1967) 'Psychodynamic aspects of school phobia.' *Comprehensive Psychiatry*, *8*, 2, 119–28.

Registrar General (1970) *Classification of occupants*. HMSO, London.

Renik, O. (1972) 'Cognitive ego function in the phobic symptom.' *Psychoanalytic Quarterly*, *41*, 537–55.

Reynolds, D. (1976) 'When pupils and teachers refuse a truce: the secondary school and the creation of delinquency.' In G. Mungham and G. Pearson (eds) *Working class youth culture*, Routledge and Kegan Paul, London.

—— (1978) 'Truants under suspended sentence.' *Community Care*, 31 May, 20–2.

—— and Murgatroyd, S. (1974) 'Being absent from school.' *British Journal of Law and Society*, *1*, 78–80.

—— and Murgatroyd, S. (1977) 'The sociology of schooling and the absent pupil. The school as a factor in the generation of truancy.' In H. C. Carroll (ed.) *Absenteeism in South Wales. Studies of pupils, their homes and their secondary schools*, The Faculty of Education, University College of Swansea, 51–67.

Rines, W. B. (1973) 'Behaviour therapy before institutionalisation.' *Psychotherapy: Theory, Research and Practice*, *10*, 281–3.

Robinson, D. B., Duncan, G. and Johnson, A. M. (1955) 'Psychotherapy of a mother and daughter with a problem of separation anxiety.' *Proceedings of Staff Meetings, Mayo Clinic*, *30*, 141–8.

Rodriguez, A., Rodriguez, M. and Eisenberg, L. (1959) 'The outcome of school phobia: a follow-up study based on 41 cases.' *American Journal of Psychiatry*, *116*, 540–4.

Rosenberg, M. (1965) *Society and the adolescent self-image*, Princeton University Press, Princeton.

Rutter, M., Tizard, S. and Whitmore, K. (eds) (1970) *Education, health and behaviour*, Longman, London.

—— and Yule, W. (1968) *Scale A (2) A parents rating scale*, Institute of Psychiatry, London.

—— and —— (1968) *Scale B (2) A teachers rating scale*, Institute of Psychiatry, London.

Schermann, A. and Grover, V. M. (1962) 'Treatment of children's behaviour disorders: a method of re-education.' *Medical Procedures*, *8*, 151–4.

Seligman, M. E. P. (1970) 'On the generality of the laws of learning.' *Psychological Review*, *77*, 406–18.

—— (1971) 'Phobias and preparedness.' *Behaviour Therapy*, *2*, 307–20.

—— and Johnston, J. (1973) 'A cognitive theory of avoidance learning.' In J. McGuigan and B. Lumsden (eds) *Contemporary approaches to conditioning and learning*, Wiley, Washington.

Shapiro, T. and Jegede, R. O. (1973) 'School phobia — a babel of tongues.' *Journal of Autism and Child Schizophrenia*, *3*, 168–86.

Skinner, B. (1953) *Science and human behaviour*, Macmillan, New York.

Skynner, A. C. R. (1974) 'School phobia: a reappraisal.' *British Journal of Medical Psychology*, *47*, 1–16.

Smith, R. E. and Sharpe, T. M. (1970) 'Treatment of a school phobia with implosive therapy.' *Journal of Consulting Clinical Psychology*, *35*, 239–43.

Smith, S. L. (1970) 'School refusal with anxiety: a review of sixty-three cases.' *Canadian Psychiatric Association Journal*, *15*, 257–64.

Snaith, R. P., Bridge, W. K. and Hamilton, M. (1976) 'The Leeds Scale for the self-assessment of anxiety and depression.' *British Journal of Psychiatry*, *128*, 156–65.

Spedling, M. (1951) 'The neurotic child and his mother.' *American Journal of Orthopsychiatry*, *21*, 368–80.

Sperling, M. (1961) 'Analytic first aid in school phobias.' *Psychoanalytic Quarterly*, *30*, 504–18.

Stampfl, T. G. (1967) 'Implosive therapy: I. The theory.' In S. G. Armitage (ed.) *Behaviour modification techniques in the treatment of emotional disorders*, Veterans Admin., Battle Creek, Mich.

—— (1968) 'Implosive therapy: a behavioural therapy?' *Behaviour Research and Therapy*, *6*, 31–6.

—— and Levis, D. J. (1967) 'Essentials of implosive therapy: a learning-theory-based psychodynamic behavioural therapy.' *Journal of Abnormal Psychology*, *72*, 496–503.

Suttenfield, V. (1954) 'School phobia: a study of five cases.' *American Journal of Orthopsychiatry*, *24*, 308–80.

Tahmisian, J. A. and McReynolds, W. T. (1971) 'Use of parents as behavioural engineers in the treatment of a school phobic girl.' *Journal of Counselling Psychology*, *18*, 225–8.

Talbot, M. (1957) 'School phobia: panic in school phobia.' *American Journal of Orthopsychiatry*, *27*, 286–95.

Tennent, T. G. (1970) 'The use of Section 40 of the Education Act by the London Juvenile Court.' *British Journal of Criminology*, *9*, 175–80.

—— (1971) 'School non-attendance and delinquency.' *Educational Research*, *13*, 3, 185–90.

Thompson, J. (1948) 'Children's fears in relation to school attendance.' *Bulletin of the National Association of Social Workers*, *24*, 1.

Tyerman, M. J. (1958) 'A research into truancy.' *British Journal of Educational Psychology*, *28*, 217–25.

—— (1968) *Truancy*, University of London Press, London.

—— (1972) 'Absent from school.' *Trends in Education*, 26, 14–20.

Tyrer, P. and Tyrer, S. (1974) 'School refusal, truancy and neurotic illness.' *Psychological Medicine*, 4, 416–21.

Vaal, J. J., (1973) 'Applying contingency contracting to a school phobic: a case study.' *Journal of Behaviour Therapy and Experimental Psychiatry*, 4, 371-3.

Valles, E. and Oddy, M. (1984) 'The influence of a return to school on the long-term adjustment of school refusers.' *Journal of Adolescence*, 7, 35–44.

Van Der Ploeg, H. M. (1975) 'Treatment of frequency of urination by stories competing with anxiety.' *Journal of Behaviour Therapy and Experimental Psychiatry*, 6, 165–6.

Van Houten (1948) 'Mother-child relationships in twelve cases of school phobia.' *Smith College Studies in Social Work*, 18, 161–80.

Van Ophuijsen, J. (1946) *Primary conduct disturbances in modern trends in child psychiatry*, International Universities Press, New York.

Waldfogel, L., Coolidge, J. C. and Hahn, P. B. (1957) 'The development, meaning and management of school phobia.' *American Journal of Orthopsychiatry*, 27, 754–80.

—— Tessman, E. and Hahn, P. B. (1959) 'A program for early intervention in school phobia.' *American Journal of Orthopsychiatry*, 29, 324–32.

Warnecke, R. (1964) 'School phobia and its treatment.' *British Journal of Medical Psychology*, 37, 71–9.

Warren, W. (1948) 'Acute neurotic breakdown in children with refusal to go to school.' *Archives of the Disturbed Child*, 266–72.

—— (1965) 'A study of adolescent psychiatric in-patients and the outcome six or more years later. II: The follow-up study.' *Journal of Child Psychology and Psychiatry*, 6, 141–60.

Watson, J. and Rayner, R. (1920) 'Conditioned emotional reactions.' *Journal of Experimental Psychology*, 3, 1–14.

Waugh, M. (1967) 'Psychoanalytic thought on phobia: its evolution and its relevance for therapy.' *123*, 1075–80.

Wechsler, D. (1974) *Wechsler Intelligence Scale for Children — Revised*, National Foundation for Educational Research Publishing Co. Ltd., Slough.

Weiss, M. and Burke, G. B. (1967) 'A five-ten year follow-up of hospitalised school phobic children and adolescents.' *American Journal of Orthopsychiatry*, 37.

—— and Cain, B. (1964) 'The residential treatment of children and adults with school phobia.' *American Journal of Psychiatry*, 34, 103–14.

Weissman, M. M. and Paykel, E. S. (1974) *The depressed woman*, University of Chicago Press, Chicago.

Welch, M. W. and Carpenter, C. (1970) 'Solution of a school phobia by contingency contracting.' *School Applications of learning theory*, 2, 11–17.

Will, D. and Baird, D. (1984) 'An integrated approach to dysfunction in interprofessional systems.' *Journal of Family Therapy*, 6, 275–90.

221

—— and Wrate, R. (1985) *Integrated family therapy: a problem centred psychodynamic approach*, Tavistock Publications, London.

Williams, P. (1974) 'Collecting the figures.' In B. Turner (ed.) *Truancy*, Ward Lock Educational and the National Children's Bureau, London.

Wolpe, J. (1954) 'Reciprocal inhibition as the main basis of psychotherapeutic effects.' *Archives of Neurological Psychiatry*, 72, 205–26.

—— (1958) *Psychotherapy by reciprocal inhibition*, Stanford University Press, Stanford.

Yates, A. J. (1970) *Behaviour therapy*, Wiley, New York.

Young, A. J. (1947) 'Truancy: a study of mental, scholastic and social conditions in the problem of non-attendance at school.' *British Journal of Educational Psychology*, 17, 50–1.

Yule, W. (1977) 'Behavioural approaches to treatment.' In M. Rutter and L. Hersov (eds) *Child psychiatry: modern approaches*, Blackwell Scientific Publications, London.

—— Hersov, L. and Treseder, J. (1980) 'Behavioural treatments of school refusal.' In L. Hersov and I. Berg (eds) *Out of school*, Wiley, Chichester.

Index

additive stress model 20, 118, 127, 144–5
Arieti, S. 27
asthma 8

Baker, H. 45, 49, 51, 89
Bakwin, H. 6
Bandura, A. 32, 77
Barker, P. 28, 36, 47, 50, 60, 109, 112
Beck, A.T. 88
Berecz, J.M. 61
Berg, I. 4, 6–8, 10, 18, 36–7, 45, 48–50, 85, 89, 104, 109
Blagg, N.R. 6, 10, 13–20, 26, 35, 54, 56, 58, 60–1, 69, 71, 76, 81, 87–8, 90, 92, 98, 106, 109, 110–212 passim
Bornstein, B. 36, 39
Bransby, E.R. 12
Broadwin, I.T. 5, 9
Bryce, G. 28, 37–8, 58
bullying, teasing 20, 131, 134, 138

Cameron, K. 15
Cantrell, R.P. 75
Cautela, J.R. 106
Chapel, J.L. 63
Chazan M. 6, 8, 12, 14–17, 19–20, 28, 36, 38, 41
classical conditioning 62–71
emotive imagery 68–9, 78
flooding 31, 71, 138
implosive therapy 31, 69–70
reciprocal inhibition 30–1, 62–85 passim
systematic desensitisation 24, 30–1, 62–85 passim
clinical psychologists 118–21
cognitive behaviour therapy 64, 88
cognitive perspectives 56, 64, 88, 124–7
common issues in treatment 24,

36–8, 43, 58–60, 81–2, 90–2, 106–13
see also rapid treatment approach to school phobia
comparative treatment studies 93–105
control groups 93–4
psychodynamic therapy 94–6
reciprocal inhibition therapy 94–6
conduct disorder 15
contingency contracting 24
Coolidge, J.C. 6, 21–2, 28, 36, 41
Cooper, M.G. 6, 9–10, 15–16, 18
Croghan, L. M. 64

Davidson, S. 6, 8, 13, 15–16, 20, 28, 36–8, 40
death-related issues 16–17, 65, 132
Department of Education and Science (DES) 13
dependency 18
depression 15, 24, 46, 129–30, 132
DES see Department of Education and Science
discriminant functions analysis 17, 21
disturbed home background 16
domestic material standards 16
drug therapy see medication

eating disturbance 15
education welfare officers 7, 10–12, 44, 54, 113–14, 118–21, 123, 125, 178
educational psychologists 118–21, 156, 162–93 passim
Eisenberg, L. 6, 20–1, 37–8, 42
employment 15, 97
enuresis 14, 65, 68
escort systems 54, 88, 110–11, 123, 155–7
Estes, H.R. 16, 27

223

Esveldt-Dawson, K. 77
examinations 20, 41
Eysenck, H.J. 6, 64–5, 90, 98, 131

family 15–17, 46, 132–8, 144–8, 152–93, 201–7
  child 144–7, 149–52, 154–8
  costs and benefits 136–7
  grandparents 135–8, 155–6, 159–61, 204–7
  home factors 15–17, 46, 132–4, 144–5, 199–201, 203–7
  patterns of influence and control 137, 204–7
  size 15
  stresses 136, 204–7
  structure and relationships 135–8, 204–7
  treatment work 144–5, 147–8, 152–7, 158–93
family doctors 7, 118–21, 162, 171, 174, 176, 178–9, 184, 185, 190
family therapy 52–8
  concurrent family psychotherapy 52–4
  strategic family therapy 57–8
  structural family therapy 54–8
fears and phobias 4, 20, 34–5, 56, 148–54
  assemblies 150
  irrational fears 149–50, 153–4
  reality issues 148–9, 152–3
  self-monitoring 150
Fogelman, K. 13
Forehand, R. 76
Framrose, R. 28, 36, 37, 38, 54–6, 111
Frick, W.B. 5, 9, 14

Galloway, D. 4, 10–11, 13, 69
Garvey, W.P. 66–7
general practitioners see family doctors
Glaser, K. 36–7, 42–3, 109
Goldberg, T.B. 6, 8, 15–17, 19
Gray, J. 33
Graziano, A.M. 4
Greenbaum, R.S. 28, 37

Hampe, E. 19
Healey, W. 5
Hersen, M. 74–5, 106
Herrnstein, R.J. 33
Hersov L.A. 5–7, 10, 13–20, 22–3, 28, 35–7, 46, 50, 61, 104, 109
Hodges, V. 16
home-based motivational system 73
home discipline 16
home tuition 40, 96–105, 110, 112–13, 167–74, 179–84
hospitalisation 28, 37, 41, 45–51, 60, 65, 77, 96–105, 110, 112, 145–6
hospital out-patient 38–45 passim
Hsia, H. 28, 36–45, 56–7
hypnosis 63

immediate return to school 28, 36–7, 42–5, 52–8, 59, 83–92 passim, 117–93 passim
incipient school phobia 38
intelligence 18–19
inter- and intra-professional factors 57–9, 118–21
  communication 118–21
  conflict 57–8

Johnson, A.M. 6, 16–17, 21, 28, 36, 39
Jones, M.C. 30
journey to school 134
Jung, C.G. 39
juvenile court appearance 14

Khan, J.H. 6, 24
Kavanagh, A. 5, 11–12
Kennedy, W.A. 12, 21–4, 35, 47, 54, 58, 61, 71, 83, 87, 89, 92, 104–5, 110–11
King, N. 76, 77
Klein, E. 27–8, 36, 37
Kline, L.W. 5

Lang, P. 8, 80
Lawrence, D. 29, 97
Lazarus, A.A. 61, 63, 66, 68, 79, 83

learning theory 30–5
  information transmission 32
  operant conditioning 32–3
  respondent conditioning 30
  safety signals 33
  synchrony and desynchrony
    in fear and avoidance 34–5
  theoretical weaknesses 31
  two stage theory of fear and
    avoidance 33
  vicarious learning 32
legal issues 4, 9, 14, 53, 56, 118,
  126, 144, 146, 160
level of aspiration 67, 135
level of expectation 133

Macmillan, K. 3
Malmquist, C.P. 36
Marks, I. 31
Mateson, J.L. 77
McAdam, E. 85
medical issues 120, 130, 132,
  171, 174, 178, 184–5, 198
medication, drug therapy 41, 54,
  79, 97, 162, 168, 174, 179
metacognition 56
Miller, L.C. 4, 93, 94, 106,
  108–10, 117
Miller, N. 33
Miller, P.M. 64, 65
Minuchin, S. 55
Model, A.N. 17
Mohr, I. 9
Montenegro, H. 24
Morgan, G.A.V. 17
Mowrer, O.H. 33
Murgatroyd, S.J. 12, 19
Murphy, W.C. 14, 18

National Association of Chief
  Education Welfare Officers
  (NACEWO) 3, 12
neurotic disorder 8, 9, 15
Nicholas, K.A. 8, 18

occupational therapy 48
Olsen, I.A. 66–7
operant conditioning 71–6, 78
  antecedent stimulus control 76
  contingency contracting 75–6
  instruction training 76
  rationale 71–2
  single case studies 72–6

Pacella, B.L. 15
parents 5–7, 9–10, 15–17, 21–6
  passim, 27–8, 29, 32–3,
  117–212 passim
participant modelling 77
Partridge, J.M. 5
Patterson, G.R. 78, 82, 106
paediatricians 118–21
persistent absenteeism 3–4,
  8–11, 19
  definition of 10
  national surveys 3
  reasons for 10
  school factors 11, 19
  survey inadequacies 4
  typologies of 8
persistent lying 14
Phillips, D. 35, 61, 82–3
physical factors 56–7, 64, 67,
  155, 184–9
preventative approaches 113,
  135
problem-solving approaches 35,
  58, 61, 113, 117–212 passim
psychoanalytic theory 27–8
psychiatric disorders 13
psychiatrists 118–21, 162–3, 174,
  178–80, 183–4
psychodynamic treatment of
  school phobia 36–60
  child-focused 39
  community and patient 38–45
  family system 52–8
    see also family therapy
  historical perspective 36–8
  hospital treatments 45–51
  mother–child relationship
    39–51

Rachman S. 31–2, 34
Radin, S. 37, 41–2
rapid-treatment approach to
  school phobia 117–212
  case studies 162–90
    comments 163–6, 168–73,
    175–8, 180–3, 185–8

diagnosis and treatment
163–6, 168–73, 175–8,
180–3, 185–8
reasons for referral 162–3,
167–8, 174–5, 179–80,
184–5, 189–90
diagnostic content issues
127–40
attendance pattern of
siblings 128
background information
127–8
child's attendance pattern
128–9, 194–5
development history 132
family costs and benefits
136–7
family patterns of influence
and control 137, 204–7
family stresses 136, 204–7
home- and school-related
anxieties 132–5, 199–209
intellectual functioning and
attainments 131
out-of-school activities 130,
198
peer relationships 131
personality characteristics
131
school factors 137–40
symptomatology 129–30,
162–3, 167–8, 174–5,
179–80, 184–5, 189–90,
197
diagnostic process issues
121–7
client motivation 121, 123
interview setting 122–4
interviewing style and client
expectation 124–5
speed of intervention 121–2
techniques to reduce anxiety
126–7, 155
timing and pacing 122
prerequisites and pragmatics
118–21
interprofessional communications 118–20
medical issues 120
school placement 120–1

rationale 117–18
treatment 142–58
child 145–7
choosing an escort 145–7
confirming the mandate
147–8
negotiating home change
152–5
negotiating school change
148–52
negotiating treatment with
the child 157–8
parents 144–5
teachers 142–4
treatment setbacks 158–93
passim
parental control and col-
lusion 159–60
practical arrangements 159
treatment issues 163–6,
168–73, 175–8, 180–3,
185–8, 192–3
Registrar General 97
Renik, O. 27
residential placement 53, 57, 145
resistance to treatment 72–5,
124–7, 136–7, 142
Reynolds, D. 5, 12, 19
Rines, W.B. 69, 71, 87, 110
Robinson, D.B. 40
Rodriguez, A. 6, 13, 19, 36–7,
42–3, 53, 109
role rehearsal 146–7, 154
Rosenberg, M. 49
Rutter, M. 13, 15

Schermann, A. 64
Schizophrenia 6, 24, 43, 54
school factors 11, 19–21, 38,
40–1, 134–5, 142–4, 148–52,
201–3, 208–9
school phobia, nature of 4–212
passim
aetiology 27–35
learning theory 30–5
psychoanalytic theory 27–8,
41–2
self-concept theory 29
age of onset 13
anxiety assessment 8, 80

birth order 14
clinical description 5–8
definition of 7–8, 10, 21–6
depression 15, 24, 46
historical perspective 5, 36–8
home and family factors
    15–17, 128, 132–7, 199–209
intelligence and attainments
    18–19, 131, 164, 166, 169,
    172–3, 176, 178, 181–3,
    186–8, 190–2
legal issues 4
maternal characteristics 17
paternal characteristics 17
pattern of associated
    symptoms 14–15, 129–30,
    162–3, 167–8, 174–5,
    179–80, 184–5, 189–90,
    197–8
personality characteristics 18,
    131, 164, 166, 169, 172–3,
    176, 178, 181–3, 186–8,
    190–2
prevalence 12–13
research issues 4, 8
school factors 20–1, 38, 40–1,
    56, 64–92 passim, 131,
    137–40
sex distribution 13–14
social class 4–5, 15
systems analysis 24–6
terminology 5, 6
typologies of 21–6
    neurotic and character-
    ological 21, 93
    pattern of family relation-
    ships 22–3
    type 1 and type 2, 22–3, 83,
    87, 105
    treatment implications 24, 113
school phobia record form 128,
    194–212
school placement 120–1
Seligman, M.E.P. 31–3
self-concept theory 29, 41
separation anxiety 6, 16, 24,
    27–8, 32–3, 40, 42, 46–7, 57,
    62–7, 78–9, 81–2, 100, 104,
    123, 130, 133, 162–74
'shaping and prompting' 67,

72–3, 78, 132–3
Shapiro, T. 25–6
Skinner, B. 78
Skynner, A.C.R. 28, 36–7,
    52–6, 58, 110–11
Smith, R.E. 69, 92
Smith, S.L. 6, 8, 13–14, 16, 20,
    23–4
social isolation 130, 151
social services 53, 113–14
social workers 118–21, 123, 156,
    162–3, 179–84
social-skills training 76–7
Sperling, M. 27, 36–7
spontaneous remission 93–4, 104
Stampfl, T.G. 69
Suttenfield, V. 6, 17, 36
systems analysis 24–6

Tahmisian, J.A. 66, 81
Talbot, M. 6, 14, 28, 36, 37, 40
teachers 6–7, 14–15, 19, 29,
    32–3, 38, 40–1, 56–7, 62–92
    passim, 113, 117–212 passim
teasing see bullying
Tennent, T.G. 9, 12, 14
terminology (school phobia) 5–6
Thompson, J. 9, 13, 16–17, 36–7
token economy 79
treatment issues 81–2, 90–2,
    134, 166–7, 173–4, 178–9,
    184–5, 188–9, 192–3
    see also common issues in
    treatment; resistance to
    treatment
treatment outcome 39–45,
    50–60, 84–146 passim
    age factors 40, 41, 43, 45, 54,
    59, 60, 84–6, 109–11
    attendance rates 39, 43, 50,
    59, 99
    behavioural treatment studies
    84–6
    comparative treatment
    studies 93–105
    emotional adjustment 45, 59
    enforced school attendance
    with comprehensive
    behavioural management
    96–105, 110–11, 113

see also rapid treatment of school phobia

Eysenck Personality Questionnaire, changes 101

home tuition 96, 105, 110, 112–13

hospitalisation 50, 60, 96–105, 110, 112, 145, 146

number and duration of treatment sessions 39, 43, 50, 59, 60

performance in school 45, 59

performance in work and further education 45

self-esteem 100

separation anxiety 100

social adjustment 51, 53, 57

traditional psychodynamic studies involving immediate return to school 43

treatment, time and cost 103–4

truancy
age of onset 13
birth order 14
comparative studies 9–10
court appearance 9, 14
definition of 9, 10
distinguished from school phobia 8
historical perspective 5, 6
home and family factors 15–17
intelligence and attainments 18–19
maternal characteristics 17
paternal characteristics 17
pattern of associated symptoms 14–15

personality characteristics 18

prevalence 12–13

research issues 4, 8–9

school environment factors 19–21

sex distribution 13–14

social class 4–5, 15

systems analysis 24–6

terminology 5, 6

Tyerman, M.J. 9, 12, 16, 18

Tyrer, P. 4

unemployment 15

Vaal, J.J. 75, 82

Valles, E. 24, 49, 51

Van Der Ploeg, H.M. 68

Van Houten 36, 40

Van Ophuijsen, J. 15

Waldfogel, L. 8, 13, 16, 37–8, 93

Warnecke, R. 14, 17–18, 28, 36–7, 42–5, 52–4, 109, 110

Warren, W. 9, 14, 16, 19, 28, 36–7, 45–6, 50

Watson, J. 30

Weiss, M. 22–3, 28, 36–7, 46–7, 50

Weissman, M.M. 49

Welch, M.W. 75

Will, D. 37, 57–8

Williams, P. 3

Wolpe, J. 30, 36, 61, 62

Yates, A.J. 32

Young, A.J. 14

Yule, W. 16, 20, 24, 35, 58, 61, 66, 81, 106, 118